Embodied Kabbalah

"An evolutionary text that heralds the dawn of a true age—one where transcendence and immanence are indistinguishable from each other. This is the path that will save us—the path of the wholly holy. It's all God, even the dust that falls from our awakening hearts. Highly recommended!"

— Jeff Brown, author of *Grounded Spirituality* and *Soulshaping*

"Matthew Ponak's *Embodied Kabbalah: Jewish Mysticism for All People* is a treasure-trove of wisdom and insight. This beautifully formatted book surrounds carefully selected and explicated texts, which speak to integrated concerns of body, heart and spirit, with a sensitive modern commentary that brings these teachings to life for contemporary seekers. Readers of all stripes will enjoy this collection of spiritual practices and reflections from Jewish teachers across nearly a millennium!"

— Ariel Evan Mayse, Professor of Religious Studies, Stanford University, author of *Speaking Infinities: God and Language in the Teachings of Rabbi Dov Ber of Mezritsh*, and Rabbi-in-Residence at Atiq: Jewish Maker Institute

"This is a work that I would be happy to give to spiritual seekers, confident that they will find inspiration and illumination that is yet grounded and balanced."

— Nehemia Polen, Professor of Jewish Thought at Hebrew College and author of *Stop, Look, Listen: Celebrating Shabbos through a Spiritual Lens*

Embodied Kabbalah

Jewish Mysticism for All People

Matthew Ponak

Foreword by Arthur Green

Albion Andalus
Boulder, Colorado
2022

"The old shall be renewed,
and the new shall be made holy."
— Rabbi Avraham Yitzhak Kook

Albion-Andalus, Inc.
P.O. Box 19852
Boulder, CO 80308
www.albionandalus.com

Design by Montana Spetifore in collaboration with Albion-Andalus Books
Cover image by Pinchas Segal
ISBN: 978-1-953220-23-3

Manufactured in the United States of America

For my wife, Melina.

"Love does not consist of gazing at each other,
but in looking outward together in the same direction."
–**Antoine de Saint-Exupéry**

Table of Contents

Foreword IX
Preface XI
Acknowledgements XV
Introduction 1
Page Guide: How to Read the Commentary 5

Kalonymus Kalman Epstein
Maor VeShemesh, Sukkot 1:11 6

Isaiah ben Avraham HaLevi Horowitz
Shnei Luḥot HaBrit, Toldot Adam, Beit Yisrael 35 7

Abraham Abulafia
Sefer HaYashar 8

Baḥya ben Asher ben Ḥlava
Midrash Rabeinu Baḥya, Shemot 3 9

Naḥman of Bratslav
Likutei Moharan, 24:1 11
Likutei Moharan, 22:5 12
Likutei Moharan, 65:4 13
Likutei Moharan, 2:24:1–2 14

Kalonymos Kalmish Shapira
Esh Kodesh, pp. 178–179 15

Israel ben Eliezer, the Ba'al Shem Tov
Keter Shem Tov, 1:24:2 16
Keter Shem Tov, 1:27:1 17
Keter Shem Tov, 1:39:3 18
Keter Shem Tov, 1:61:1 19
Keter Shem Tov, 2:13 20
Sefer Ba'al Shem Tov, Kedoshim 21 21
Tzava'at HaRivash, 64 22

Zvi Elimelekh of Dinov
Bnei Yisaskhar, Adar, 6:8 23

Levi Yitzḥak of Berdichev
Kedushat Levi, Yitro 8 24

David Solomon Eibeschitz
Arvei Naḥal, Lekh Lekha 3 26

Elimelekh of Lizhensk
Noam Elimelekh, Shemot 2 28

The Zohar
Zohar, 1:83a 29
Zohar, 1:180b 30

Sholom Noaḥ Berezovsky
Netivot Shalom, 2:281 31

Zvi Hirsh of Nadvorna
Tzemaḥ HaShem LeZvi, Ekev 2 32

Mordekhai Yoseph Leiner of Izbica
Mei HaShiloaḥ, Koraḥ 3 33

Ze'ev Wolf of Zhitomir
Or HaMeir, Lekh Lekha 1 34
Or HaMeir, Shavuot 35

Moshe Cordovero
Pardes Rimonim, 22:2 36
Pardes Rimonim, 3:1 38

Tikkunei Zohar
Tikkunei Zohar, 17a 39

Schneur Zalman of Lyady
Tanya, Sha'ar HaYiḥud, 9 40

Menaḥem Naḥum of Chernobyl
Meor Einayim, Ki Tisa 1 41
Meor Einayim, Shemot 3:2 43
Meor Einayim, Ve'Etḥanan 4 44

Abraham Joshua Heschel of Apt
Ohev Yisrael, BeShalaḥ 7:8 46

Yehudah Aryeh Leib Alter
Sefat Emet, 2:91 48

Isaac ben Samuel of Acco
Meirat Einayim, pp. 281-282 49

Dov Baer (The Maggid) of Mezeritch
Maggid D'varav L'Ya'akov, 68:6 50

Ḥayim ben Moshe ibn Attar
Or HaḤayim, Leviticus 16:1 51

Abraham Isaac Kook
Shmoneh Kevatzim, 4:6 52
Naphshi Takshiv Shiro, MeOlam Raḥok 53
Shmoneh Kevatzim, 7:112, Shir Meruba 55

Appendix 1:
Names and Associations of the Ten Sephirot 57
Appendix 2:
Timeline of Jewish Mysticism 58
Appendix 3:
Hebrew Versions of the Texts 61
Glossary 73
Endnotes 77
Works Cited 79
Index 83
About the Author 86

Foreword

Of the several hats I have worn during my long and blessed life, I write here from beneath that of **translator**, something I have been doing with Jewish mystical texts for about sixty years. While I have lots of thoughts that stand outside the act of translation, as a *ba'al mel'akhah* or craftsman, I see this as my primary skill. I have translated whole books and short selections, have used prose format and poetic line, have followed the Torah reading cycle as well as the sacred seasons. Still, the work of proper translation of these sources for our own time stands as a challenge to me.

Translation, of course, means much more than moving the words from one language to another. It is a cultural task, making words spoken (as is often the case in the Hasidic sources) or written in one cultural context accessible and meaningful to readers who live in another. How do you do it without overburdening the text with endless explanatory footnotes? May you edit the often long and repetitious sermons from which you are translating? How perfectly consistent do you need to be in the choice of terms, when the English vocabulary is vastly wider than the limited Hebrew of the authors? What do you do about passages that will deeply offend the contemporary reader? Dare you skip them? Is that fair to the sources? But then, to whom do you owe greater loyalty? To the author, who passed from this earth centuries ago, or the reader, whose soul and mind you are trying to open?

All of these questions and more stand before us as we take on this sacred labor, a form of *'avodat hashem*, worship of the ever-present *YHWH*. As I stand in the last phase of my work in this field, I warmly greet a new generation of translators, among them my dear student Rabbi Matthew Ponak. In *Embodied Kabbalah*, he offers you his own readings of selected mystical sources from a wide range of kabbalistic and Hasidic works. Choosing to set them up like a Talmudic page, he offers a proper translation in the center, surrounded by a series of comments. Pay special attention to his "Reflection" and "Practice" comments. That is where he "lets himself go" and offers you something of his personal attempt to apply these text to our own lives. There you will see his Torah of Embodied Kabbalah most fully manifest. Ponak represents a new generation of translators that also reminds me of an older one, in what perhaps turns out to be a bit of dialectical history. This work is making a self-conscious choice to offer these sources not only to the Jewish seeker, who wants to relate to them as part of her/his own tradition, but to the broader world of seekers. The comparative insights offered here are of great importance to him, and he writes them honestly and without apologetics, never seeking to find Judaism "better." That honesty is a great blessing. But I am also taken back in history by this effort. When I began studying Jewish mysticism around 1960, the only things I could find of Kabbalah in English (after reading Scholem's *Major Trends*) were translated by occultists, often not Jewish and with limited language skills, and intended for the Theosophical Society audience.

Our situation today is vastly different. Thanks to the efforts of many (largely within the Ultra-Orthodox community), there are many translations of Jewish mystical sources, done with a variety of skill levels. But these often do not have a contemporary look that will open them to seekers, non-Jewish as well as Jewish, but located far from the tradition. Now perhaps we are ready to come full circle, as it were. Here is a work of careful selection and translation, offered in a format made to appeal to the widest circle of readers.

Blessings to you, Matthew, on these *bikkurim*, first fruits, in your translator's workshop. May they be followed by many more!

Avraham Yitshak (Arthur) Green
Jerusalem
23 Iyyar 5782/May 24, 2022

Preface

Amidst the wreckage of a spiritual journey gone horribly wrong, I could not understand: how had I been betrayed? Traveling to Israel as a teenager, I had joined a *yeshiva*—a seminary for the deep study of Jewish wisdom. Within this highly ecstatic community, I had followed the guidance of my teachers and religious tradition to a fault. I had prayed for several hours a day, immersed myself in sacred texts, sought Divine light in every waking hour, and slept very little. But, in the aftermath of the ruptured mind that became my reward for mystical striving, I had far more questions than answers.

Five years later, recovered but shaken, I was in the final days of my undergraduate degree when I walked into an appointment that changed my life forever. I wanted to know what had happened to me as a teenager and to find help for afflictive thought patterns. I got what I was seeking and abundantly more! My mentor was a transpersonal psychologist with a particular brilliance for grounded spirituality and healing through intuition. She introduced me to the art of embodiment: living a spiritual life while also being an everyday reasonable, responsible, and relatable person.[1]

My mentor taught me that powerful, blissful, and illuminated experiences are gifts. They should not be coveted. They come and they go, leaving behind their traces and imprints as blessings. While some strive to repeat them, we can never own them or control them. The best approach for mystically sensitive people is to focus on bodily health and body awareness—to let the expansive states of consciousness come as they may. The process of inner change happens largely on its own from the afterglow of these moments as long as we maintain balance.

She also taught me that turning towards my own inner turmoil, as opposed to distracting myself from it, would allow for gradual self-growth. Bit by bit, my inner world began to shift. The anxiety, sadness, anger, and other difficult emotions transformed, whispering their wisdom as they cycled in and out.

I was so taken with this new way of living that I began to view grounded spirituality as my true path. After studying academic religious studies in university, much of the magic of Judaism was gone. The profound teachings of embodiment put the final nail in the coffin of the religion I had inherited.

"Judaism is dead," I would say to myself, at least as far as any practical spiritual guidance was concerned. I decided to study world religions at Naropa, a Buddhist-inspired university in Boulder, Colorado, to continue my quest for universal truth and personal realization. But, as I came to realize, sometimes you have to leave home in order to find it.

Two weeks after I moved to Colorado, I went back to my home in Calgary, Canada for a wedding. Someone at my reception table used a word I had never heard before, "*communitas*." She told me that it meant "the feeling of community." A couple of days later, I found that same word in my text book. The next day, I saw it again in another book from Naropa.

At that point I had some skepticism about looking for signs in everyday life, but I also believed deeply in synchronicity: when life seems to have unlikely repeating patterns there is often meaning lying beneath. I had the feeling that the repetition of the word *communitas* was significant, but at that point I did not know why.

Despite my declarations that I had moved past Judaism, a part of me hoped that I would find what I was seeking in the more universal and mystical Jewish life in Boulder. After I returned to Colorado, I sat in a guided meditation led by the compassionate and fiery Rabbi Tirzah Firestone. It was *Rosh Hashanah*, the Jewish New Year, and she asked us to listen inwardly for what we should work on in the next year. What arose inside of me loud and clear was that I should work on my relationship with the Jewish community. This was surprising at the time, but also struck me as important.

I was reflecting at home with my roommate a week later. I told her how the word *communitas* had appeared to me from multiple angles. She responded wisely, "It sounds like the Universe is trying to send you a message!" It was then that I realized that the message I had gotten from the word *communitas* was very related to the one I had received in meditation.

---

1 In this book I use the terms "embodiment," "grounded spirituality," and "spiritual groundedness" interchangeably.

I began to tear up. For a moment, a whole world opened before me. I thought, "Wow, God is watching over me!" It felt real! I continued talking with my roommate for another minute and then, as if from beyond, I experienced the loudest thought I have ever had,"I'm going to be a rabbi!"

It was a huge insight, a revelation!!! It took me by surprise but I also knew something significant in my life was changing. I began receiving dreams about helping community members make peace and about being ordained as a rabbi.

I went to see Reb Zalman Schachter-Shalomi, a great Jewish spiritual teacher and local sage. I told him my story. Then in his late eighties, with a hefty white beard, his exact words were, "So God wants you to be a rabbi, what can I do for you?"

Internally I cried, "To tell me THAT and to verify that this was actually a calling!" But externally, we talked about practical actions that I could take to see if this path was really for me.

And so I started to act on my insight. I talked to rabbis. I looked into rabbinical schools. I contemplated what it would be like for a spiritual-but-not-religious universalist like me to train to become a Jewish lineage holder.

In my final semester of Naropa I was blessed to meet the love of my life, Melina. Our first few months were emotionally euphoric and transcendently powerful. During that time I also formed a bond with an incredible professor and teacher of Jewish mystical embodiment. This was a potent time in my life, filled with the ecstatic states I had trained so hard to balance. At my final examination—a public, oral "Warrior's Exam," in front of my teachers, peers, and many guests—I was asked to describe the types of Kabbalah which I had been researching. In this style of testing, we were encouraged to be present with what was arising in the moment, besides the intellectual content the questions prompted.

I began to reflect on the nature of my own kabbalistic journey, which had felt very cosmic and other-worldly. The pursuit of expanded consciousness had brought me great joy but also great suffering. Even when I was able to integrate big states of illumination there was usually a more painful period of after-effects. As I had travelled farther on that road, the moments of bliss had intermixed with the knowledge that there would be another difficult process to come. I realized out loud that the happiest I had ever been was surrounded by good friends, good family, and good food—a simple, stable, yet profoundly satisfying state.

"I guess the cosmic journey is not so cosmic after all," I pondered.

My professor paused for a moment, looked at me, and said, "So you had to explore the cosmos in order to be grounded in everyday, ordinary, reality."

In one instant, I became aware that my entire spiritual journey had been ordinary, equal in all ways. The ups and the downs, the growth, and the catastrophes were all totally neutral. Within me was an almost imperceptible place, always present, that could witness the world from a state of total nonchalance and equanimity. I could feel this aspect tangibly in the very center of my head. It was an empty void without substance or essence, yet infinitely holy. My moment of realizing the value of everyday life had almost instantaneously led me to a point of reality more subtle, fundamental, and truly indescribable than anything else I had ever experienced.

"It took me a while to get here," I proclaimed to the group, "But I finally made it."

Amidst the erupting laughter that surrounded, I added, "I just want to be normal again..."

But, the next several months were anything but normal. My training in grounded spirituality became indispensable in the aftermath of this event. The new light, though almost imperceptible, was far more powerful than anything I had ever encountered. It shook me to the core.

With the tools I had learned, along with guidance from my professor and a few cherished teachers, I gradually regained my center. My foothold in everyday reality was reestablished, accompanied now with an awareness of the profound Ordinary which was slowly integrating into my being. This Emptiness or Nothingness caused, among other things, a noticeable decrease in sensations of physical pain, along with a growing calmness, and newfound access to my most basic instinctual drives. It opened me to a new and distinct reality—one with which I am still working to comprehend and integrate. The ups and downs of householder life have never ceased. Another layer of perception now accompanies them, whispering of equanimity. If it had not been for my initiation into embodied living I surely would have been shattered for a second time by the overwhelming revelation of the Ordinary within me.

At that point on my path I had received a call towards the rabbinate and had found great harmony with my personal journey, but I still could not understand how the two worked in collaboration. Five years after receiving the call, I decided to take the plunge even if I could not see the big picture. Perhaps I would only last one year in rabbinical school, but I needed to know what this guidance was pointing towards. At Hebrew College, in Newton Massachusetts, it all came together.

The greatest single gift I received in rabbinical school was the ability to decode Jewish texts. Knowledge of the original languages of Hebrew and Aramaic gave me the foundation to be a life-long learner. As a neo-Hasidic rabbinical school, Hebrew College had faculty, including the unbelievably learned Rabbi Arthur Green, who could transmit the esoteric (though increasingly proliferated) skills to translate and understand kabbalistic and Hasidic sources.

In the last half of my five year program, I began finding Jewish mystical sources that spoke to the essence of spiritual groundedness. These were not the teachings of my Jewish youth nor were they the exuberant approaches of the outreach arm of Israeli Orthodoxy. These were an articulation of the path of the sacred bridge—a person who can be present in the physical world while being intimately connected to the spiritual: a Jewish language of embodiment, integration, spiritual freedom, emotional depth, and rooted transcendence.

These are the texts of Embodied Kabbalah.

Acknowledgements

There are so many amazing people who have helped me along the journey of writing this book. First and foremost, I would like to thank my wife, Melina Ponak, to whom this book is dedicated. You are a wonderful thought partner and a transformational listener. You have been incredibly motivational and supportive of me following my path, including when that meant late nights of writing. In that vein, I want to extend my gratitude to my children Orion and Sephira for tolerating my absence while finalizing my first draft. I hope you enjoy this when you are older!

Many thanks to my teacher and mentor Rabbi Arthur Green for your guidance and feedback in translations, your ability to point me in the right direction through your immense knowledge of mystical texts, and your powerful encouragement for my universal path as a rabbi. Rabbi Zvi Ish-Shalom, thank you for providing so much illumination in the path of embodied Jewish transformation—experientially and intellectually—and for your robust endnotes section in *The Kedumah Experience* from which many of these texts are drawn. Thank you also to Beth Hedva for first helping me realign to the path of groundedness and balance. Without your help this book would not exist.

Thank you Albion-Andalus Books for giving me this opportunity as a first-time author. Netanel Miles-Yepez, your excitement for this project has been very inspiring. Montana Spetifore, I was blessed to find such a creative graphic designer with such a love for this unique project, thank you! Pinchas Segal, I looked long and hard for the right artist, and you were it! Much gratitude for your beautiful cover art.

Thank you so much Shirlee Hoffman, my mother-in-law, for the many hours you spent helping me edit and format the rough draft. Your work effort was surpassed only by your glowing praise for this project—your help has been truly phenomenal! Thank you to my father Allen Ponak for being so supportive throughout my educational journey. Your help has allowed me to gain the knowledge and skills for this book and my life path. Thank you to my mother Margaret Ponak for being my original, enthusiastic cheer-leader—you have had my back from the beginning for leading a non-conventional life. Thank you also for being a great collaborator when I bounced ideas off of you for this book.

Thank you to my teacher Rabbi Itzchak Marmorstein for introducing me to the treasure trove of Rav Kook's writings. Thank you to Cesilia Harel, Dr. Melila Hellner Eshed, Rabbi Ebn Leader, and Rabbi Nehemiah Polen for helping me to locate sources for this project and to Rabbi Alan Lehman for your guidance in reading Hasidic texts. Moshe Leiser, I appreciate your thorough work on adding the vowels to the Hebrew and Aramaic texts. Rabbi Joel Goldstein, thanks for reading over those texts and catching the scribal errors. I am also grateful to Batya Ellinoy and Genevieve Greinitz for printing and scanning pages for my capstone project from across the Atlantic and for being generally awesome spiritual collaborators! Thanks as well to Susannah Slocum for spending time listening to me articulate commentaries out loud so they could be transcribed.

Thank you to Eric Hoffman for relaying teachings about enlightenment that I have used in my commentary. Much appreciation for Dr. Judith Simmer Brown, Dr. Galen Ferguson, and David Frenette for teaching me the World Wisdom from Naropa that is included in this book. Professor Eliezer Siegal, you introduced me to the academic study of Jewish mysticism and Gershom Scholem in particular. It was a very challenging undertaking at the beginning but the effort has certainly come full circle—thank you! Rabbi Ayalon Eliach, thanks for being an amazing thought partner. Your philosophical engagement and insightful feedback have helped fuel and inspire my work. Andrea Silverstone, I have great appreciation for the Jewish classes I took from you when I was a teenager. They had a big enough impact that some of those first lessons are found in these very pages. Dr. Joan Klagsbrun, I am grateful for the training I received from you to be a Certified Focusing Professional which, among its many gifts, has helped me articulate the language of body-based insight much more fully.

Lastly, I send enormous gratitude and love to the departed Dr. David Lertzman for being my friend and spiritual mentor, for introducing me to the wisdom of eco-psychology and to the ancient practice of extended solo time in nature. The lasting imprints you left on me have found their way into many of these pages. May your memory be for a tremendous blessing and may your joy, compassion, and wise heart live on through all of your students.

Introduction

Embodied Kabbalah is a collection of 42 mystical texts with commentary that articulates a Jewish language for embodied and grounded spirituality.

What is Kabbalah?

The term Kabbalah has two main meanings. First of all, it commonly refers to all of Jewish mysticism.

Mysticism is a mode of spiritual practice that aims to encounter the Divine directly. True reality, in mysticism, is more about experience than belief. Kabbalah is often used to refer to the entire history of mysticism within Judaism. Dating back thousands of years, this is a collection teachings, practices, and personal accounts from individuals or groups who encountered deeper layers of existence.

Kabbalah's second meaning, used most commonly by academics, is a specific era of mysticism that arose in Western Europe in the 13th century. It centered around the ten gradations between our world and God, known as the *Sephirot*[1], and was profoundly impactful on all Jewish mysticism that followed.

The Jewish mystical path has changed over time but has maintained its emphasis on the balance between the inner life and outer actions. The Jewish people have not had a monastic community for thousands of years and have been led, almost exclusively, by individuals with families and worldly duties to fulfill. Being a householder tradition, Judaism and its mystical components emphasizes a balance between the earthly and the spiritual. It describes a path of inner change that happens while engaging with important non-religious duties and being beholden to act ethically in each area of life. As such, Jewish mysticism is intensely relevant to spiritual seekers today, most of whom are not choosing the life of monks or nuns. They are working, studying, caring for dependents, or otherwise engaging in everyday modern life.

What is Embodiment?

Also known as grounded spirituality, embodiment is a form of practice that cultivates an intimate relationship with the body as opposed to transcending it. Embodied spiritual practice emphasizes conscious action and right living as integral parts of the path. Balance between inner cultivation and external responsibilities is essential to this approach. The terms "disembodied" or "ungrounded" refer to a state of being disconnected from one's own physicality. Everyone experiences disembodiment at least some of the time.

Kabbalah, as a vast and varied lineage, contains elements which are aligned with embodiment to a greater or lesser degree. This book brings perspectives which emphasize the harmony between the physical and the spiritual. Embodiment has seen an enormous resurgence in our culture in the last sixty years through movements such as Focusing, Somatic Experiencing, and the Diamond Approach. What all of these schools have in common is the understanding that the body's sensations are a gateway to the inner world. By tuning into the body (in contrast with more head-centered practices such as visualization, for example), inner shifts that lead to personal growth have a greater chance to be accessed while staying grounded and responsive to our outer lives.[2]

Our body communicates more clearly when we treat it well. Adequate sleep, healthy food, and regular exercise lay the foundation for embodied spirituality. When the body is at peace and we turn our gaze to it with curiosity and compassion, it becomes a source of inner guidance that has no end. With this in mind, embodiment is not an ascetic path that commonly withholds pleasure. Quite the opposite, the embodied practitioner meets the Divine by investing more in physicality with the understanding that Spirit is found in all places. Embodied Kabbalah is where Jewish mysticism and body-centered spirituality meet.

---

1 See Appendix One: Names and Associations of the Ten Sephirot.

2 As a student and teacher, I have found that especially mystically sensitive people benefit from an embodied approach which allows them to maintain balance. However, there are many contexts and types of practitioners for whom head-centered practices will be appropriate.

Who or What is the Divine?

This book does not prescribe any particular theological views. The texts and commentaries are an invitation to explore for yourself what lies beyond your ordinary perceptions. In mystical circles there are limitless names for what some call "God": Spirit, Creator, Deep Reality, Ultimate Reality, the Infinite, the Divine and many more. In this book, these names are used interchangeably. But what do they mean? Each of them points to an understanding that there is something more subtle and profound to this world than meets our physical senses. Different eras of Jewish mysticism understood God differently. Amidst this great plurality, we find that there are no "right" answers on the inner journey—but there are authentic understandings that come to people as they delve deeper. The insights and theologies of others can be useful up to a point but, ultimately, the seeker's question is not, "Do I believe in someone's else's notion of the Divine?" but, "What is the nature of reality?" The best guide you can possibly have is your own experience.

What is Meant by "Jewish Mysticism for All People?"

This book's subtitle means that everyone is welcome to read it and benefit from its teachings. If you resonate with the understandings contained within, then you are the right person to be reading it, regardless of what personal or societal categories you fall into. In the same way that cultures in many parts of the world have benefited from mindfulness (originating in Buddhism) and yoga (originating in Hinduism), people can benefit from the universal insights found in Judaism. Our planet, our people, and our societies need help from as many sources as they can access. Embodied Kabbalah is a peek into the rich and diverse world of Jewish mysticism, open and accessible to all who seek transformation and wisdom.

Some of the teachings in this book were chosen to be part of the larger conversation being had in the world of global spirituality—also known as New Age. Topics such as Shabbat, the Jewish day of rest, are presented to open the gates towards teachings that are incredibly valuable for anyone seeking balance in their life. These offer supplements and alternatives to mindfulness for those seeking calm and awareness. My hope is to enrich the global dialogue about the best ways that we can live.

What is Transpersonal Psychology?

This branch of psychology is referenced many times in this book. Transpersonal means "beyond the personal" and this branch of psychology explores human experiences in which the self identifies with something beyond the individual. Sometimes called the psychology of mysticism, this school was originally founded by a small group in the 1970s who included Abraham Maslow, Anthony Sutich, and Stanislov Grof. Importantly for this book, transpersonal literature provides very practical guidance on how to be balanced within an ecstatic mystical journey.

HOW TO USE THIS BOOK

Commentary

Commentary is ongoing in the Jewish tradition. This book is structured to emulate classic rabbinic writing: the main text is in the center of the page and different remarks surround it. Each type of commentary has its own purpose, such as explaining the text or comparing it to another tradition.

While each section has specific ideas to express, they are by definition not the final word. As any teaching makes its way through the generations and through different communities, it is understood and reflected upon in different ways. You, the reader, also have a voice in this. If you feel inspired, please write your own notes in the margins. Judaism and Jewish mysticism have always been developed through discussion and new voices are needed as our ever-changing tradition meets an ever-changing world.

At the end of the introduction is a sample page that shows how the different types of commentary are laid out on the page. The most linear way through a teaching is to read the central text first, followed by the explanation section found on the inside margin of each page. After that, you could read the other commentaries in whichever order you choose. With this being said, these pages nor this book need to be read in any particular order. You can access each type of commentary, text, or author in whichever way speaks to you or you can choose a page at random to see what synchronicity reveals to you in the moment.

The Different Types of Commentary

Explanation of Text: The inside margin on any page is devoted to explicating the message of the central teaching. Even when translated into English, these texts use many symbols and phrases which are not familiar to most people who have never studied Kabbalah. As such, this section "translates" the teaching's symbols to make it more comprehensible. Each time another text is referenced, such as a biblical verse, the full verse is provided along with its original context and meaning, as much as that is discernible. Next, I show how the mystical text is making use of the reference, often by interpreting it to articulate a spiritual lesson.

About the Author: The teachings are organized by author. The first page at the beginning of each section includes a description of the origins of the text. Traditionally, the name of the author and the name of their book could be used synonymously. This custom appears in many instances in this book (for example, on page 6 Rebbe Kalonymus Kalman Epstein is called by the name "The Maor VeShemesh"). Not every mystical book has a known author, but the background and context of its emergence are always discussed. In some cases, the original teaching was recorded by students and compiled after the rabbi's death. In those cases, the text is ascribed to its progenitor.

A Comparative Look: These sections highlight similarities or differences between other religious traditions or fields of study.

Reflection: Questions to prompt deeper insights or philosophical ideas are found here.

Practice: Spiritual tools to engage with the material experientially are included in these sections.

Related Jewish Sources: In this type of commentary, Jewish teachings which relate to the main text itself are brought in.

Comments: These are my own interpretations of the text. Sometimes my commentary appears within the Explanation of Text section, usually to discuss a difficult ethical or theological statement of the author. Commentary which stands as its own block on a page is offered to draw out meaning for our lives today.

A few other sections appear only once and are specific to the text they surround. In those instances, the purpose of the commentary is clear from context.

Translations

Unless otherwise indicated, I translated all of the texts even when other English translations were available. For the texts which I translated, under the guidance of Rabbi Arthur Green, I endeavored to write in a way that was true to the original Hebrew or Aramaic but with a style familiar to English readers. Practically, this meant that (1) I often shortened and broke apart sentences and (2) I varied word choices because English tends to offer more options than the originals.

Accessibility and readability for certain texts also meant changing the pronouns to be more gender-neutral. For texts where I have changed the pronouns I indicate it with an endnote. As well, in sections of texts that diverged sharply from my own values, rather than using interpretive language I favored literal word choices and supplemented them with commentary to elaborate on their complexity. Where I have chosen to use the translations of others, I have done so either out of admiration for the original or, in the case of the text by Abraham Abulafia, the original manuscript in Hebrew was very hard to track down and the English version was done very well.

This book makes the following texts available in English for the first time: Ohev Yisra'el, BeShalaḥ 7:8; Rav Abraham Isaac Kook, Shmoneh Kevatzim 4:6; Bnei Yisaskhar Adar 6:8; Arvei Naḥal, Lekh Lekha 3; Or HaMeir, Lekh Lekha; and Maggid D'varav L'Ya'akok, 68:6.

Rav, Rebbe, and Rabbi

Most of the central teachings in this book were spoken or written by somebody bearing one of these titles. Today these titles are more or less interchangeable and all mean "teacher" or "master." Going back two thousand years, the term "rabbi" originated in *Eretz Yisrael* amongst Hebrew speaking teachers. The term "rav" emerged from Babylon amidst a group that spoke Aramaic. Rebbe is a Yiddish term that emerged in Eastern Europe as the title given to Hasidic teachers. It often denotes a mystical teacher and, specifically, one who has greater access to Divine flow than the average human. In today's spiritual vernacular, rebbe could be translated as "guru" because of the power dynamic between Hasidic master and disciple.

How Did I Choose the Texts in Embodied Kabbalah?

Out of the 42 main texts, many were drawn from the endnotes of *The Kedumah Experience* by Rabbi Zvi Ish-Shalom. Kedumah is a new form of embodied Jewish mysticism first taught in Boulder, Colorado in 2014. Its principles are expressed in universal language while referencing a number of primary Jewish sources. Amongst these teachings, I picked the ones I loved the most, which all have to do with transformation, embodiment, equanimity, and Nothingness. The other texts in this book were selected from my studies over the last fifteen years. They were chosen because they relate to questions that seekers of wisdom are asking today. They all push the status quo of either Judaism or universal spirituality in some way. Besides Kabbalah and embodiment, their themes include nature, enlightenment, non-dualism, self-actualization, death, kindness, karma, music, joy and sorrow, Shabbat, and spiritual leadership.

Why Forty-Two Texts?

In actuality, 42 was the result of my negotiation with Rabbi Arthur Green, my advisor at Hebrew College's Rabbinical School. He said 50. I said 36, a kabbalistically important number that has to do with hidden light. He then said 42, another kabbalistic number that has to do with the 42 letter Divine name. That is where we settled.

The Missing Voices in these Sources

As you read through the 42 texts, you will notice that they are either from men or from anonymous sources that were most likely men. With few exceptions in the last three thousand years, the vast majority of recorded Jewish mystical voices have been male. With the emergence of the latest phase of Jewish mysticism, echoed in broader culture and global spirituality, the gates are now thankfully wide open for women and people of any gender to learn, interpret, and teach. As a scholar of past mystical sources, choosing male voices has been unavoidable, but the evolution of our spirituality is up to all of us. It is my hope that these pages will inspire and challenge diverse sets of readers so that this ancient lineage can be renewed, refreshed, and reimagined.

Proceed with Caution

Some of these texts contain very powerful messages. Reading about topics like mystical union and ineffability can be enticing and even blissful. However, as you will find with many of the other topics, big insights need to be kept in balance with patience and levelheadedness. Ancient and contemporary teachers alike warn of the dangers of moving too quickly on a mystical journey. It is important to take a break if you are feeling overwhelmed, light-headed, or elated. Truly, the journey never ends so there is no rush. Also, remember that a foundation of healthy foods, exercise, and adequate sleep are essential for integrating the teachings of Embodied Kabbalah.

Intuitive Mind

Intuitive or Sacred Mind is an orientation towards the world which allows insights to arise. It is a posture of openness and curiosity. With regards to the teachings in this book, no matter the original cultural and historical context of sacred writings, the mystical Jewish mentality of Torah study is to meet the text directly with a receptivity to whatever messages may come through.[3] Though knowledge of the origins of the texts can help us build a framework through which to approach them, the essence of mystical study involves trusting the words themselves to reveal to us what we need (this same sense of trust is beyond valuable for learning from our inner worlds as well). Regardless of any commentary in the book or any sense of the "proper" way to learn from it, the lessons and messages that arise in your mind are the ones that are truly meant for you.

The very first letter of the very first book of the Torah is *beit*. It looks like this: ב. This letter is part of the word *bereishit*, which means "in the beginning." It is the first spark in this entire lineage of sacred study. A *beit* is open on one side and closed on the other. This is a hint to the nature of spiritual learning. If a person is open to Torah, then Torah will be open to them. But, if a person is closed to what may be revealed, then the text will be closed to revealing. Regardless of where you believe these teachings come from—whether they are historical documents or revelations from a Divine Source—having a posture of receptivity will allow you to enter into the shared communal wisdom that has been cultivated by Jewish mystics for millennia.

I hope you enjoy the journey.

3 Often the word Torah refers to the first five books of the Hebrew Bible. In this case, Torah study refers to studying any text from the collection of Jewish wisdom. Torah can be used in the same way that Buddhists use the term "Dharma," pointing to the treasure-house of guidance and insight which the tradition offers.

Page Guide: How to Read the Commentary

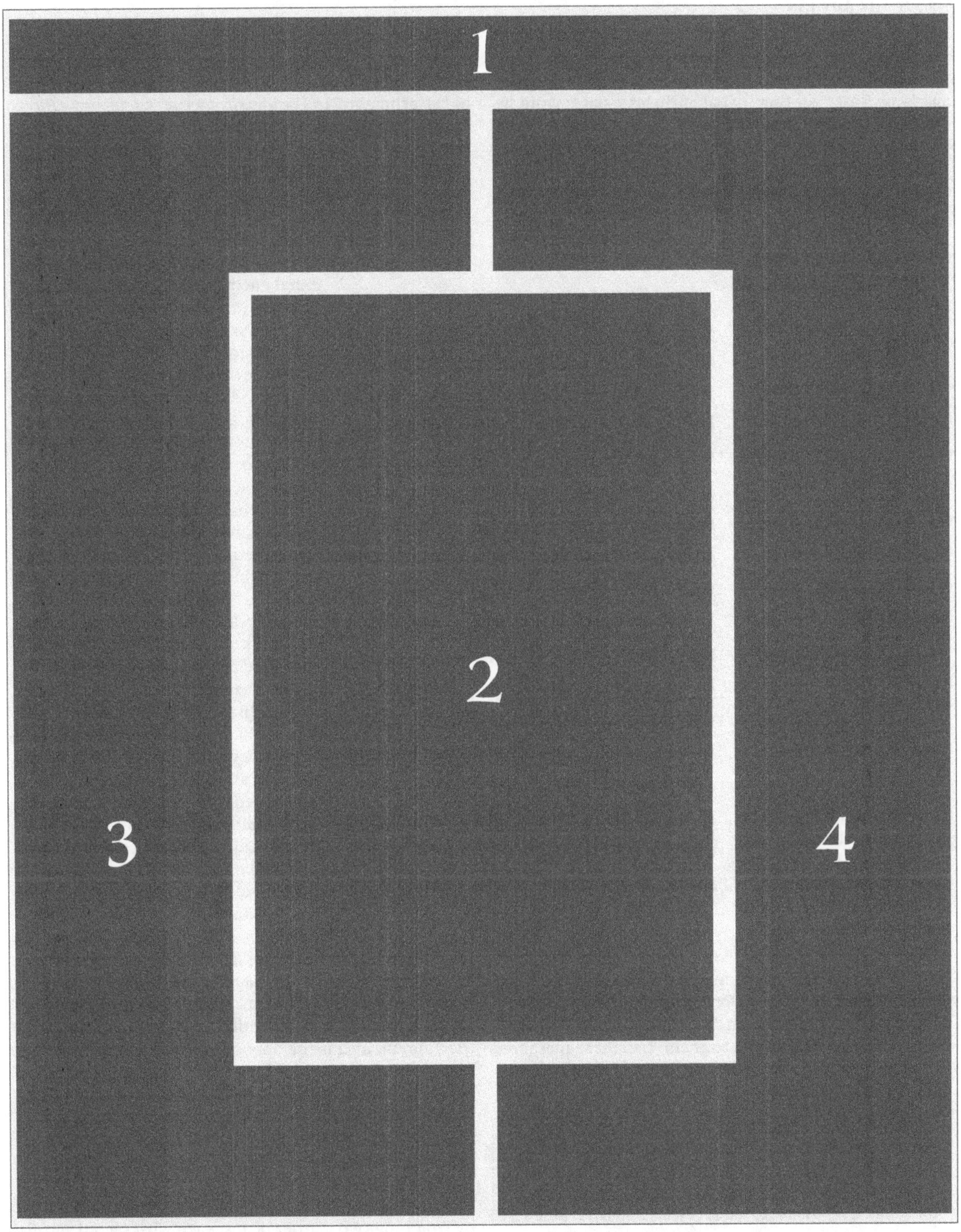

1. **Book name and section:** The name of the book and section from which the "text that will be studied" belongs.
2. **Text that will be studied:** Each page contains a section of a mystical text that all the surrounding commentary is relating to. The text contains footnotes corresponding to those in the "explanation of text".
3. **Explanation of text (inside column):** Each footnote from the "Text that will be studied" is listed and examined.
4. **Commentary (outside column):** Additional comments, reflections, practices and more.

About the Author

Rebbe Kalonymus Kalman Epstein (c. 1753–1823) was a child prodigy and one of the great teachers of early Hasidism. He learned under the renowned masters Elimelekh of Lizhensk and Jacob Isaac "The Seer" of Lublin. In his younger years, he organized prayer groups [*minyanim*] in Cracow in which he and his disciples used ecstatic body movements in their worship. Being so out of the ordinary, their prayer upset the local rabbinic authorities and the *Hasidim* were excommunicated in 1786 and 1787. Despite this, Epstein was very successful in spreading his teachings to Galicia, which straddles modern day Ukraine and Poland. Epstein's main text, the Maor VeShemesh, is a mystical commentary on the Torah and is considered a classic of Hasidic spirituality.

The *tzadik*[A] who has reached the level of *devekut*[B] with the Infinite, he is connected [to God] in his mind at each moment. Contemplation is his main spiritual practice.[C] As [our sages] of blessed memory said, "Abraham our Father fulfilled the whole Torah,[D]" though it had not yet been given. Although we find nowhere that Abraham actively performed such commandments as wearing *tefilin* or making a *sukkah*,[E] he nonetheless connected with the inner holiness that is pointed to by those deeds. [He did this] by way of his sacred contemplation which was attached to the Infinite.

A Comparative Look

There is a Buddhist parable found in the Allagadupama Sutta that relates to this teaching. The Buddha said that there was a man who was traveling and came across a large body of water. He saw that its farther shore was safer than the shore he was currently on. Seeing no other way across, he gathered grasses, twigs, leaves and branches. He built a raft and, with some effort, it carried him across the water. "Once he made it across," the Buddha asked, "should he carry the raft with him for the rest of his journey?" The Buddha advised his students that the man should leave the raft behind, just as they should leave the Buddha's teachings behind when it is time.

In a similar vein, the American spiritual teacher Ram Dass says in *Polishing the Mirror*: "Don't get trapped in your expectations. Spiritual practices can themselves become obstacles if you become too attached to them. Use these methods as consciously as you can, knowing that, if they are truly working, eventually they will self-destruct."

Reflection

1. Have you ever found a spiritual practice useful and later found that you no longer need it? If so, what changed in you or in your life that led you to feel that way? If not, do you think that it is possible to move beyond a spiritual practice?
2. Do you believe it is possible for people to reach a spiritual stage in which they do not need contemplative practices? What about a stage of consciousness in which outward ritual expressions are not needed, like in this text? How do your answers to these questions affect how you orient your own spiritual life?

A. **The word *tzadik*** literally translates as "righteous person." In the Hasidic world, it often means "mystic leader."

B. **The term *devekut*** is literally translated as "cleaving" or "attachment." In Hasidic mysticism it refers to various kinds of direct contact with the Divine. It can be translated more loosely as "mystical connection" or "mystical experience." In the context of this teaching, it refers to someone who is in a constant spiritual bond with God.

C. **In the time** period in which the Maor VeShemesh lived, this was an incredibly radical statement. Such was the nature of early Hasidism. These Jewish mystics were having profound encounters with the Divine that shook them to their very core, along with their views of tradition. If their moments of *devekut* told them that the Infinite was present everywhere and at all times, then why did they need specific ritual practices, at certain appointed times, to connect to God? This idea, however, was very controversial, especially in the eyes of the dominant rabbinic authorities. So what did these early Hasids do? They followed the ancient tradition of reinterpreting the text. They used Abraham, a righteous biblical figure who lived before the Torah but still had an incredibly close relationship to God, as a means to communicate their message. It was safer to reimagine Abraham than it was to state their challenging new thoughts outright. In the Maor VeShemesh's teaching, Abraham was a Jewish mystic who was so connected with God that he did not need any of the ritual practices. In other words, when a person reaches a certain spiritual state, they can live like Abraham did, without prescribed ritual acts, and be in constant connection with the Divine. In this way, the challenges that deep insights of *devekut* surfaced in the minds of the Hasidic mystics could be expressed (See *Devotion and Commandment: The Faith of Abraham in the Hasidic Imagination* by Arthur Green for a deep exploration of this phenomenon).

D. **b. Yoma 28b.** This quotation, in its original context in the Talmud, means the opposite of how it is used in this text. This statement means that even though Abraham lived before the Torah was given, he still lived according to its laws and was able to derive them from other means. The Maor VeShemesh reinterprets its meaning, however, saying that Abraham fulfilled the inner purpose of the commandments by being intimately connected with God at all times.

E. **The wearing of** tefilin is performed during the daytime by wrapping two leather boxes, each with sacred scrolls inside, around the arm and the head. A sukkah is a temporary dwelling place that is constructed in the fall for the joyful holiday of Sukkot, linked with the last harvest in Israel.

A. This text is taken from a section in which the Shelah is teaching about ways in which God is found in the body. Like many kabbalistic teachings, his interpretation is based on playing with Hebrew letters. He is working with the ineffable Divine name *YHWH*, which is also known as the Tetragrammaton and is considered the central name of God. He is showing how *YHWH*, when split into two parts—YH and WH—can be found in the human hand. YH and VH are each Divine names on their own as well. **B. The Shelah shows** how the letters YH, *yud heh* in Hebrew, can be found in the right hand. He does this by using the interpretive method of *milui*, which means "filling out." This involves writing each letter out as though it were a word. In English, this would be like spelling the letter "d" as "dee" and the letter "m" as "em" (see Figure 1, which shows two rounds of milui). In Hebrew, the letter *yud* is spelled out as *yud-vav-dalet* and the letter *heh* is spelled out as *heh-aleph*. Now the two letters have been transformed into five letters (See figure 2). **C. The Shelah then** does another filling out, another *milui*, of the five letters that were created from the first round. This results in fourteen letters that stem from five letters (see Figure 2). **D. The fourteen letters** generated from the two *miluis* form four groups of three and one group of two. This is because some letters take more letters to spell out in full. This is similar to English where "d" is spelled "dee" and "m" is spelled "em". These sections line up with the human hand, which has four fingers with three sections and one finger, the thumb, with two (see Figure 3). **E. In Hebrew, each** letter has a numeric value. This would be like assigning "a" as 1, "b" as 2, and so on. Jewish practitioners make use of these values in a practice called *gematria*. The Hebrew word for "hand" is *yad*, which is composed of the letter *yud* (with a value of 10) and the letter *dalet* (with a value of 4). The word *yad* thus has a numerical value of 14, equal to the number of sections in the fingers and the number of letters in the Shelah's filling out of letters. **F. The rest of** the text (not shown here) goes on to show how WH, the second half of *YHWH*, fits onto the left hand's fingers using the same approach of double *milui* as above.

You will find another hint of *YHWH* in the ten fingers... How? See, in each finger there are three sections, except for the thumb that has two sections. And the One who formed the human being with wisdom formed it with wondrous meaning. The right hand hints to the letters *yud heh*, and the left hand hints the letters *vav heh*.[A] He took the letters *yud heh* in full form like this, "*yud-vav-dalet, heh-aleph*.[B]" Now they are five letters, and they are the five fingers. And he took these letters and filled them out a second time like this, "*yud-vav-dalet, vav-aleph-vav, dalet-lamed-tav, heh-aleph, aleph-lamed-feh sofit*.[C]" In four of the letters there are three sections and in the letter heh there are only two sections. So too in four fingers. In each finger there are three sections, and in the thumb there are two sections.[D] There, the hand [*yad*] is called by its name because of the 14 [*yud dalet*, spelling *yad*] sections[E]...[F]

About the Author

Rabbi Isaiah ben Avraham HaLevi Horowitz (c. 1565–1630) was born in Prague and lived in Poland and Frankfurt before settling in *Eretz Yisrael*. He was known as the Shelah Ha-Kadosh, the Holy Shelah, from the acronym of his most famous work, Shnei Luḥot HaBrit [The Two Tablets of the Covenant]. Horowitz was brought up learning from many great Torah scholars of his time and excelled in *halakhah* [Jewish law] and Kabbalah. His major work combines *halakhah*, homilies, and mysticism with the overarching theme of how to live an ethical life. This was greatly influential after Horowitz's death and likely inspired many Hasidic teachers who followed.

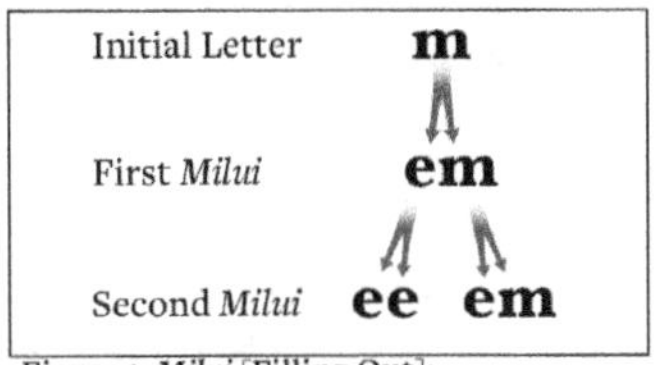

Figure 1. *Milui* [Filling Out]: Spelling English Letters

Comments

There are many different tools that Jewish interpreters use to find meaning in a text. Kabbalists such as the Shelah often work with Hebrew letters. The methods used in this text, *milui* and *gematria*, are just two tools in a much larger set.

The question sometimes arises, do these interpreters really believe all of their findings on a literal level? Some people are skeptical because inherent in these interpretive methods is the choice of the rabbi to lean one direction or another. For example, with *milui*, some letters can be spelled with either two OR three letters.

So where does that leave us? In earlier times the rabbis often believed that deep truths could be found by combining and analyzing the Hebrew letters. For many modern readers, even spiritual people, this may sound far-fetched. One way I approach letter-play is by thinking of it as an art and not a science. It is a way to derive beauty from the Hebrew and show the synchronicity inherent in even small details of life and scripture. It is like a delicious dessert at the end of a hearty meal. The Shelah may have seen the "findings" of Hebrew letter manipulation as objective, like a science. However, it still took tremendous creativity and artistry to deliver these results.

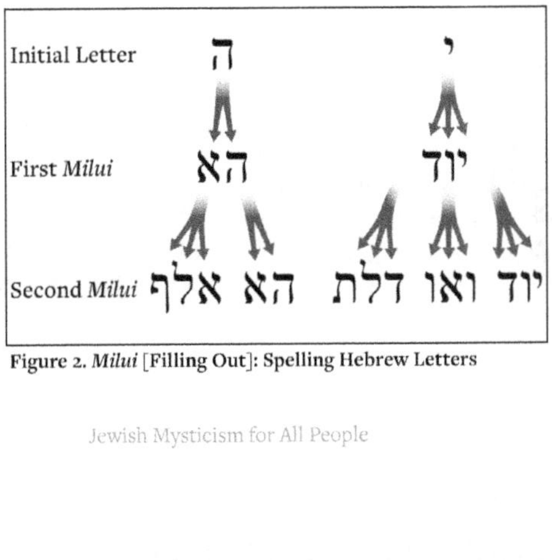

Figure 2. *Milui* [Filling Out]: Spelling Hebrew Letters

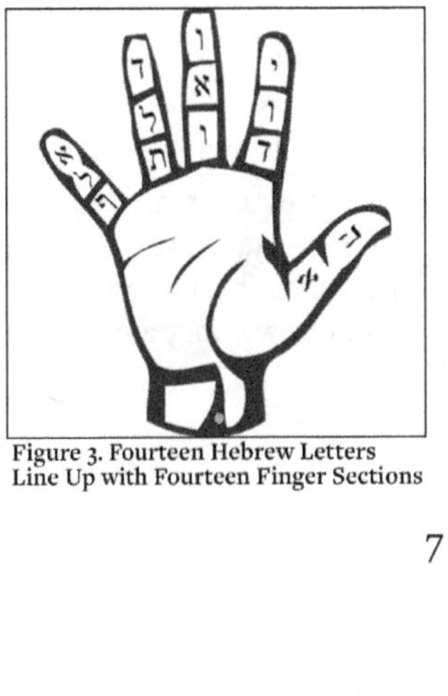

Figure 3. Fourteen Hebrew Letters Line Up with Fourteen Finger Sections

Book: Sefer HaYashar[1]

About the Author

Rabbi Abraham Abulafia (1240–c. 1291) was an ecstatic kabbalist who was born in Zaragoza, Spain. His style of mysticism is called Prophetic Kabbalah and was influenced, in part, by Islamic mysticism. Abulafia fervently disseminated his teachings and tried to reach both Jews and Christians. He stands out in his era because of his vivid descriptions of mystical states, something which was often kept hidden by other rabbis—even in mystical writings. Abulafia's writings were excluded from subsequent Spanish schools of Kabbalah, partly because he was proclaiming himself as prophet and Messiah. Despite this, some of his insights were anonymously cited by many influential Kabbalists and continue to have an influence today.

If, however, he has felt the Divine Touch and perceived its nature, it seems right and proper to me and to every perfected man that he should be called "master," because his name is like the Name of his Master[A], be it only in one, or in many, or in all of His names[B]. For now he is no longer separated from his Master, and behold he is his Master and his Master is he: for he is so intimately adhering to Him that he cannot by any means be separated from Him, for he is He.[C] And just as his Master, who is detached from all matter, is called... the knowledge, the knower, and the known, all at the same time, since all three are one in Him: so shall he, the exalted man, the master of the exalted Name, be called intellect, while he is actually knowing: then he is also the known, like his Master[D]: and then there is no difference between them, except that his Master has His supreme rank by His own right and not derived from other creatures, while he is elevated to his rank by the intermediary of creatures[E].

A. In this text, Abulafia is describing the experience of mystical union. Abulafia makes reference to a Talmudic passage (b. Sanhedrin 38b) which states that the angel Metatron is known by same name as God. This is in reference to the verse Exodus 24:1 where God says to Moses, "Come up to *YHWH*." The Talmud, wondering why God did not say, "to me," interprets this as referring to Metatron, who also goes by the name *YHWH*. Exodus 23:21 is also brought into the discussion where God says He will send an angel to guide the Israelites and says "My name is in him," refering to the angel. Metatron is considered the highest angel in Merkavah mysticism, an esoteric spirituality which the early rabbis practiced. Here, the author is implying that the mystic attains the level of Metatron and also gains the same name as God. **B. Implied in this** statement is many forms of realization. To be called by the name Elohim, for example, would be one type of enlightenment, while to be called by other names of God would be other forms. **C. A complete union** takes place between the mystic and God. The phrase "he is He [hu hu]," meaning the seeker is God in that state of realization, is found in Islamic mysticism, known as Sufism, in Arabic [*huwa huwa*]. **D. In God, the** perceiver and the perceived are united, as is the act of perception. When the mystic unifies with The Absolute, he reaches a state in which he is unified with all he is perceiving, a state of non-dual awareness, in which he becomes awareness itself. **E. According to Moshe** Idel, who translated this passage, the term "intermediary" refers to the *Sephirot*. Thus, in this view, Abulafia is stating that despite the fact that the seeker and God are one, God did not need intermediary steps in order to reach the state of unity, whereas the mystic goes there by means of the stages of emanation between the physical world and God. This last phrase can also be translated as "by created beings and by their means," which would refer to humans. In this perspective, the spiritual seeker needs to rely on other people, such as teachers, in order to reach that enlightened state.

Comments

There is a disagreement amongst Jewish studies scholars as to whether the concept of mystical union exists in Judaism. Gershom Scholem, the founding scholar of the study of Jewish mysticism, wrote in 1971, "[*devekut*] is not union, because union with god is denied to man even in that mystical upsurge of the soul, according to kabbalistic theology." In Scholem's view, the Jewish mystical path ends with "communion," which is more like intimacy and closeness than union itself. However, Moshe Idel, Scholem's most esteemed student, disagreed. The text on this page was part of a broader study by Idel on Abraham Abulafia. We can see from this description that there is a sense of union in mystical Judaism, at least amongst certain teachers. Later on in Jewish history, union is articulated by some Hasidic teachers as well. Despite these examples, however, there are many cases in which *devekut* is seen more as attachment to the Infinite than as becoming God. In this way, the statements from Abulafia are particularly striking and edgy, at least within the context of Kabbalah.

Reflection

1. Is it possible for human beings to attain a state of consciousness where they become god?
2. What ethical considerations play into our descriptions of our mystical states? For example, if we say someone becomes god versus being close to god, does that make a difference in the power they are given by those around them?

[Commenting on the section of the book of Exodus where Moses notices a burning bush and turns towards it:] The literal reading of this section is that Moses understands three things: (1) the fire, (2) the angel, and (3) the Divine Presence. At the beginning he saw the fire that was taking hold of the bush, but the bush was not consumed. He saw this while awake, with his physical eyes. When he saw the bush burning with fire, he recognized that it was fire and thought it was earthly fire from sulfur. When he was thinking that, but the bush was not being consumed, at that point he wanted to go closer [to investigate]. As it says, "I will turn aside and see this great sight.[A]" That is to say, "I will see this wondrous thing: if the bush is different from other plants, or if the fire is different from other fires." If he had thought that this was heavenly fire he would not have gone closer.[B] After he saw this fire, his consciousness was strengthened when he saw the angel.[C] As it is written, "An angel of *YHWH* appeared to him in a flame of fire from within the bush." The reason it is written [in that way] is because he saw the flame first and afterwards the angel within the fire.[D]

A. Exodus 3:3. Rabeinu Baḥya is showing the progression that Moses went through from the physical, to the angelic, and then to God. This verse that he cites initially from Exodus is a moment in the original text where the burning bush catches Moses' eye. Bahya's interpretation is that the bush caught his eye specifically with something that appeared to be physical. This appearance of physicality is not explicit in the original context but the sense that the burning bush initially draws Moses in is certainly present in the biblical account. **B. Moses thought the** fire was an unusual kind of physical fire. This was how God coaxed him gradually to come closer, by not overwhelming him or scaring him with a Divine encounter from the beginning. **C. In this translation,** the words consciousness and mind are used interchangeably. The mind is that part of us that perceives the world. Strengthening consciousness means that the mind needs to grow stronger in order to be able to perceive more of reality. To be aware of the physical we need a certain strength of consciousness. That consciousness has to become stronger in order to perceive the angelic realms. As we will see, consciousness has to develop even more capacity to perceive the *Shekhinah* [Divine Presence]. **D. Exodus 3:2. This** verse describes the angel appearing from within the flame. This is an image that can have an array of meanings drawn from it. As an interpreter, Baḥya siezes on this description and uses it to continue on his point that this was a step-by-step process from perceiving reality to perceiving Divinity. The fact that the angel appears from within the flame, for Baḥya, means that Moses had to start with the physical flame and then progress to the angelic. It is possible that the original meaning of the verse was that the angel was appearing as the fire. The phrase "in a flame of fire" can also be translated, "as a flame of fire."

About the Author

Rabbi Baḥya ben Asher ben Ḥlava (13th century) was a Spanish biblical interpreter, kabbalist, and preacher. He is one of two teachers referred to as Rabeinu Baḥya, "Baḥya our teacher," the other being Baḥya ibn Paquda (11th century). Baḥya ben Asher completed his most popular work, a commentary on the Torah, in 1291. His Torah commentary, featured here, interprets the text using literal, homiletical, rational, and kabbalistic perspectives. His writings reflect a period in Kabbalah when the Zohar was being composed. The Zohar is the magnum opus of medieval Kabbalah that appeared in the 13th century. Rabeinu Baḥya often cites some of his contemporary Kabbalists such as Joseph Gikatilla who, according to one theory, were part of the circle that wrote the Zohar.

A Comparative Look

Psychologists Stanislov and Christina Grof's book *Spiritual Emergency: When Personal Transformation Becomes a Crisis* details the ways in which spiritual experiences can become overwhelming. Often, mystical experiences leave us with new insights and heightened sensitivities to our world. However, sometimes these experiences can be so powerful that they can lead to something akin to mania or even psychosis. In their book, the Grofs look at this phenomenon from a variety of cultural and religious perspectives. Like Kabbalah, many spiritual paths including Buddhism and Kundalini Yoga caution students from moving too quickly. In addition to this, the work of the Grofs shows the ways in which even a spiritual emergency can be transformative if dealt with in the right way. It is ideal for people to use caution when working with powerful mystical energies, but if things get out of control there are ways to integrate that process in a way that can lead to growth and positive results in the end.

After his consciousness was strengthened by seeing the angel, he saw the glory of the *Shekhinah* in a prophetic vision. As it says, "*YHWH* saw that he turned to see and *Elohim* called to him.[E]" Since this was the beginning of Moses' [ability of] prophecy, the Holy Blessed One wanted to initiate him little by little to bring him up from level to level until his mind would be made strong. A parable: to what is this similar? To someone who is sitting in a dark house for a long time. If he suddenly goes out to look at the sun, his vision will darken. He therefore needs to look at the light little by little until he gets used to it. Just as this happens with the light of the sun, this is the rule and the reason itself [for what happens with] the light of consciousness.[F] Matters of the mind correspond to matters of nature. What happens to the mind is like what happens to the senses. The powers of the soul, are they not connected with the powers of the body?[G]

E. Exodus 3:4. Moses was brought up stage by stage until he was ready to hear God's voice. Mystics and prophets are most often not born as such. They may have a natural capacity, but it takes refinement in order to get there. In this case, God brings Moses to that level very quickly, but the central message is the same: it is wise to grow to more expanded stages of consciousness one step at a time. The verse cited here is used by Rabbeinu Baḥya because it mentions God, and not the angel speaking to Moses. Also, in Kabbalah, the Divine name of *Elohim* is associated with the *Shekhinah*. This may be one reason why Baḥya links Moses' encounter specifically with the *Shekhinah*, and not another name/manifestation of God. This system of Kabbalah did not exist at the time Exodus was written and many biblical scholars believe that the usage of Elohim was associated with a particular author's account of this narrative. **F. Here, referencing a** famous parable from Plato the Greek philosopher, Baḥya lays out his central message more clearly. Just like sunlight can blind us, the light of consciousness has the capacity to obscure the mind if we are not prepared to encounter it. It is unclear exactly what Baḥya was eluding to but common phenomena in this type of literature are what today we would call ungroundedness, a spiritual emergency, or psychosis. **G. The mind follows** the same rules as our body. Just as eyes need to adjust to the light, so does consciousness. Our minds cannot jump from the ordinary to the Divine. They need to evolve to that point, little by little.

If You Are Having a Spiritual Emergency

If your spiritual practice has led you to a place that feels overwhelming and that you are not able to come down from, (1) follow the Practices for Grounding on this page and (2) find a guide who can help you through this. Some psychotherapists, psychiatrists, and clergy have experience in this field.

The Spiritual Emergence Network has an online registry where you can find referrals. Spiritual Emergencies are distinct from psychosis but being under the care of a psychiatrist and taking psychiatric medications can be helpful for integration in certain circumstances.

Practices for Grounding

If you find yourself starting to feel light-headed, scared, or overwhelmed while doing a spiritual practice, do the following:

- Take a break from that practice
- Eat a well-balanced meal that has heavier foods like potatoes, beets, or meat.
- Rest if you are tired. Avoid stimulants.
- Go for a run or do other physical activity.
- Focus on the soles of your feet and envision energy going from your head, through your body, and into the ground.

Know that there is light beyond the three levels of soul.[A] It is the light of the Infinite. Even though the mind does not perceive it, the striving of contemplation pursues it. By means of this striving the mind grasps it—in the sense of "attaining but not attaining.[B]" This is because in actuality it is impossible to comprehend [the light], because it is beyond the three levels of soul.

A. Rebbe Naḥman is describing different layers of the spiritual and inner worlds. The three levels of soul he articulates are *nephesh*, *ruaḥ*, and *neshamah*. In Kabbalah, these three levels of soul are within each person but also correlate to layers of the Tree of Life. The three souls are inherent within all people but also become actualized as a person develops and matures. In a way that mirrors this process, mystics journey through the levels of the Tree of Life. Rebbe Naḥman is describing a stage of the journey that is even more subtle and ineffable than the other layers. This is the light of the Infinite itself, which is both all of reality and beyond all reality, including the Tree of Life. **B. Zohar 1:16b. The** nature of perceiving the Infinite Light is paradoxical. We can, in a sense, understand it and perceive it. But, in another sense it is beyond all conception. The term "attaining but not attaining," a phrase used in the Zohar, articulates this point. There is a sense of grasping this light beyond lights, but it is not grasping in the conventional sense of the word. Rebbe Naḥman is communicating through paradoxes because it is impossible to describe this kind of experience in any other way. If the reader is confused by this description, that is because only by making contact with this refined light can we understand the nature of grasping and not grasping simultaneously.

About the Author

Rebbe Naḥman of Bratslav (1772–1810) was an ecstatic mystic with a deep knowledge of esoteric and exoteric Jewish texts who lived in modern day Ukraine. The great grandson of the Ba'al Shem Tov (regarded as the founder of Hasidism), he is known for his ingenious Torah teachings, stories, and for being the first major reviver of the Hasidic tradition since its founding.

A Comparative Look

Various mystical schools describe different layers and levels in the spiritual journey. The 9th century Zen teaching that folk musician Donavan sang about in the 1960's goes, "Before a man studies Zen, to him mountains are mountains and waters are waters; after he gets an insight into the truth of Zen through the instruction of a good master, mountains to him are not mountains and waters are not waters; but after this when he really attains to the abode of rest, mountains are once more mountains and waters are waters." Here we see that the last stage is not like the second. It resembles the first, in fact. The Rebbe Naḥman teaching does not say that the first and third stages are the same, but nonetheless we see the sense of distinct stages in that journey.

Author A.H. Almaas, one of the founders of the Diamond Approach, teaches a system that has more resonance with our text. In his system there are stages that correlate with more classical mystical experiences, such as union with the Divine, and there are stages that are more subtle and ineffable—beyond comprehension in comparison even to the mystical stages.

Christian mystic Bernadette Roberts also articulates an experience that went beyond any she previously had as a nun. After learning how to attain union, many years later she opened up into an entirely new process which was beyond anything she had previously known.

Every person should have abundant compassion for [their] physical body. [One should] reveal to it each insight and illumination that the soul perceives, so that the body will also understand them.[A] [This is] the notion of: "And from your own flesh do not hide.[B]" "Flesh" specifically, so you do not turn your gaze from being compassionate to your own physicality... People should have great tenderness for the body [in order] to refine it, so that [the soul] will be able to make known to it every insight and spiritual realization. At all times, every person's soul is perceiving and comprehending profoundly transcendent matters. The body, however, does not know about them. So every person should tune into the very substance of the body, to witness and to refine it until the soul will be able to enlighten it with all that it sees and grasps at each moment.[C]

A Comparative Look

This teaching has resonance with several body-centered spiritual approaches. For one, Focusing, a mindfulness technique developed by Eugene Gendlin in the 1960s, guides people into emotional awareness by having them feel into bodily sensations. Gendlin understood that what goes on in the subconscious mind is not always apparent to the conscious awareness. However, the body and its sensations, such as tightness, warmth, or coolness, can be used as a bridge between the conscious and unconscious. This process, over time, can lead to a general loosening of the knots of the body, and through it, the mind. Abraham Abulafia, a medieval Kabbalist, uses the metaphor of "untying the knots" of the soul to refer to spiritual progress. A similar image is taught in Tibetan Buddhism. Through working with the sensations of the body in a compassionate and attentive way, the psychospiritual blockages can be released and the brighter light of soul/mind/consciousness can shine through.

Practice

Next time you are feeling a knot in your stomach, chest or throat, see if you can take some time to show it compassion. Get in a comfortable position, whether that is lying down or sitting. You could even be walking if that's what feels best.

With your inner sense of touch, turn your awareness to that tense spot in your body with the intention of just feeling it as it is. You do not need for it to change or go away, but rather just hold it there with your loving gaze and let it be exactly how it needs to be. Sit with it for as long as you are able or for as long as you need. Notice how it feels. Is it hot? Cold? What is the knot's shape? What is its size? How tight is it? Does it loosen at all as you sit with it?

Notice if there are any changes to how it feels as you accompany this knot. Feel free to journal or draw your experiences and any insights you have in the process.

A. There are two main messages in this text. First of all, caring for our bodies is very important when living a spiritual life. It can be tempting for people who want to find God to try and divorce themselves from physicality. This certainly happened in the late 18th and early 19th century when Rebbe Naḥman was living. However, as his great grandfather the Ba'al Shem Tov had advised, the author is teaching about the benefits of balance and bodily health. **B. Isaiah 58:7. The** verse quoted here is also cited in a letter the Ba'al Shem Tov wrote to his disciple when he berated him for being overly ascetic. The original context of the verse varies greatly from this interpretation. In Isaiah, which is from the Hebrew Bible and dates to over 2500 years ago, hiding from one's own flesh refers to not helping one's own kin when they are in need. The Ba'al Shem Tov and later Rebbe Naḥman lift these words from their original context and find new meaning in them for their teaching. **C. The second main** message in this text has to do with refining the body to facilitate realization. Not only is physical health important, but care and attention for the body actually allow it to grasp the profound insights of the soul. When the body is treated with care, as opposed to anger or impatience, it is able to receive more from beyond. The term for "soul" which is used here is *neshamah* in Hebrew. *Neshamah* also means breath. This is reminiscent of the book of Genesis, the first book of the Bible, where God breathes life into Adam, the first human, to animate him (Genesis 2:7). Another way to view the term "*neshamah*" is as a higher form of consciousness. In English, the word soul can sometimes denote something removed from us, like an unreachable pure part of our being. However, in Jewish mysticism, the *neshamah* is often seen as something we come into contact with. When we prepare ourselves in the right way, such as through refining our bodies and meditating, we can be graced with an experience of our higher mind.

Truly, at the time when one is nullified completely, which is the state of—it is all good, it is all one—then, in reality, suffering is negated.[A] But, it is impossible to be permanently in the state of nothingness. In order to do that, a person would [need to] transcend human boundaries.[B] Therefore, becoming nothing must be in the manner of "running and returning."[C] That means that after nullification, when consciousness returns to the brain—which is the vessel of consciousness—it is impossible for the brain to receive the mind in that state of nothingness. The brain is a [finite] vessel! The state of nullification is equated to the Infinite, which is connected to completion—where it is all one, it is all good. Because of this the brain feels anguish and suffering[D]...

Afterwards, even though one has returned from the state of negation, there is still a trace that remains from it.[E] Torah insights are made by means of this [trace]. For, in the state of complete nothingness, one realizes that all [types of] suffering are [actually] very great, good things. Through this [insight], one is filled with joy. And joy is the vessel [for receiving] new Torah insights.[F]

A. Rebbe Naḥman is describing a type of spiritual state in which consciousness is completely absorbed into nothingness, known as nullification. Nothingness is associated with the uppermost *Sephirah* of *Keter* and is an extremely lofty and advanced state of realization. It is a point at which, among other things, suffering ceases to exist and everything is unified. States such as this are commonly referred to in Western spirituality as "non-dual," a term which originates in Hinduism. **B. As long as** we are in human form, we are not able to exist permanently in this state of transcendence where all is good and all is one. This is not the only Jewish view of transcendent states, but it is certainly a very common one: we humans are not meant to be permanently abiding in the Beyond. It is our nature to taste transcendence and then to return to more ordinary states of consciousness. **C. Ezekiel 1:14. See** the Keter Shem Tov 1:61:1 text on the bottom half of page 19 for further explanation on this verse. **D. In the state** of nullification, the mind becomes infinite, consciousness becomes one, and it is all good. The brain cannot hold this vastness however, because it is finite, and what results is a painful headache as a result of the integration process. **E. The term trace,** or *reshimu* in Hebrew, is borrowed from an earlier kabbalistic tradition. Initially this term was used to describe the trace of Divinity that was left in the world after the Infinite withdrew Itself in order to leave space for the physical world. In a beautifully self-reflective and experiential way, Rebbe Naḥman uses this concept to describe the Divine energy that remains in us after we have a transcendent experience. **F. This trace of** Divinity is experienced as the joy we feel. After having an experience of oneness and goodness in even the suffering we experience, joy remains, though we are no longer absorbed in the nothingness. This joy is a container, or "vessel," that can receive new realizations. The Torah insights Rebbe Naḥman is referring to are new ways to understand verses from the Jewish wisdom texts. However, the types of realizations can be broadened quite easily to the inner wisdom we receive as part of a mystical experience.

A Comparative Look

In Buddhist systems of enlightenment and Hindu forms of liberation, the awakening is often permanent. In many of these schools, the ultimate attainment is a permanent freedom from suffering. Rebbe Naḥman is articulating something different. His system is one in which it is impossible for someone to permanently move beyond suffering as long as they are living. It is important to remember that mystical systems that develop in separate cultures do not necessarily mean the same thing by "transcendence." There are many expanded states of consciousness that may be accurately labeled as realization. That is to say, different Buddhist and Hindu forms of realization may not be what Rebbe Naḥman is describing here. However, it is noteworthy that being absorbed into a state of nothingness, an extremely high form of expanded consciousness, is only part of a two way process. Part of the journey is towards the transcendent but the other part is to return with a trace of that realization in normal consciousness. What flows from that is new insights into reality and into our lives. Rebbe Naḥman does not touch on this here, but there is a strong current in Judaism of living out the wisdom that we acquire. In this way, the state of nothingness, associated with the highest *Sephirah*, is only a leg in the journey. In an interesting way, this mirrors the Buddha's path after he had attaining enlightenment. He taught his realizations of the Four Noble Truths and Eightfold Noble Path to students for the rest of his life. The path of the realized master who puts off complete enlightenment for the sake of helping others awaken is most strongly articulated in Mahayana Buddhism.

(*Pronouns Changed*)

It is a great mitzvah to be joyful at every moment, to conquer sadness and bitter darkness and keep it away with all your might![A]... Our human nature is to draw ourselves to melancholy and depression because of the afflictions and events of this time.[B] We are all filled with suffering, so we need to compel ourselves with great strength to be joyous at all times and to make ourselves happy in any way we can, even with nonsense words![C]...

However, it is also very good to have a broken heart. But, it should only be at a particular time. We should set a time each day to break our hearts open and have a conversation with God.[D]... But each day we need to be happy because from a place of brokenheartedness it is easy to come to depression, more so than erring through joy leads to debauchery. It is less of a distance to go from a broken heart into melancholy.[E] Therefore we should always be happy, but have a special time to be broken-hearted.[F]

A. The Hebrew word *mitzvah* literally means commandment but can also mean "good deed." Rebbe Naḥman is saying it is a great religious act to maintain happiness and stay away from depression. **B. Rebbe Naḥman endured** a great deal of suffering in his life. This included the death of many of his children and first wife, the opposition he faced from some Jews both within and outside the Hasidic world, the several year bout with tuberculosis which inevitably killed him, and his mental anguish which today could be diagnosed as Bipolar Disorder. **C. Bringing oneself out** of unhappiness, in this part of his discourse, can be done by any means available. This includes silliness. In the 21st century in Israel, followers of Rebbe Naḥman dance ecstatically on the streets with techno music playing in the spirit of this teaching. **D. Rebbe Naḥman's spiritual** practice of *hitbodedut* involves pouring out our hearts for one hour each day to God in our own language. The idea presented here is that we should be intentional with dealing with our suffering and take time each day to open up to it. **E. The dangers of** happiness do exist, such as going overboard in the midst of joy and later regretting our actions. However, it is easier to slip into a problematic situation with sadness, according to Rebbe Naḥman, which is why he warns against it. **F. The essence of** the teaching is to find a transformative outlet for our suffering and to be happy the rest of the day.

Related Jewish Sources

Menaḥem Mendel of Kotsk, the 19th century Hasidic Master said, "In God's eyes, there is nothing more whole than a broken heart." Having a broken heart and being present with it allows us entry into a type of healing we could not access otherwise.

The great poet and singer Leonard Cohen[2] sang in Anthem, "Ring the bells that still can ring, forget your perfect offering. There's a crack in everything, that's how the light gets in."

Reflection

Rebbe Naḥman is advising people to be very intentional about working with negative moods. The rest of the time it is incumbent upon us to be joyful. There are similarities and differences to the Piaseczner's teaching on page 15. Both texts point towards an intimate moment with The Absolute in order to find comfort in times of difficulty. Also, in both teachings there is an emphasis on at least some element of positivity. For Rebbe Naḥman it is to be happy 23 hours each day. For the Piaseczner, it is studying Torah and teaching, even while crying. Both of these Rabbis lived very difficult lives, beyond what many people today could imagine. If you were writing a guide for how to deal with sorrow and how to balance it with joy, what would you advise? What does your inner *tzadik* say is the ideal way to work with suffering in our times?

Book: Esh Kodesh³ Section: pp. 178–179

A. The rabbinic tradition speaks of God's tears in many instances. God was said to weep, for example, when the Holy Temple was destroyed. In the Talmud, God is described as weeping in His inner chambers (b. Ḥagiga 5a). God does not weep in public, however. Studying Torah has always been a rabbinic and Hasidic method for coming close to the Divine, a spiritual connection known as *devekut*. Here, the Piaseczner is telling us we can draw close with Torah study and push our way into the inner chambers. In this way, neither we nor God cry alone. **B. Intense emotions can** be overwhelming. When we experience them in isolation and without the proper tools, we can break down. But, when we weep with the support of the Source of Life we find stability and vitality. **C. To weep and** study Torah with God is to participate in holy suffering and holy *devekut* all at the same time. That is the way that suffering can be uplifted in this perspective, through intimacy with The Holy One.

About the Author

Rabbi Kalonymos Kalmish Shapira (1889–1943) was the Hasidic rebbe of the Warsaw Ghetto, which existed during the Holocaust. A descendant of the Seer of Lublin and the Maggid of Kozienice, two early Hasidic Masters, Shapira became the Rebbe of Piaseczno at the age of twenty. Often referred to as the Piaseczner Rebbe, he founded a yeshiva in 1923 and focused his work on pedagogy and the creation of a circle of students to help rejuvenate the Hasidic movement. During World War II, refusing to leave his community in Warsaw, he saw many close family members die. Despite this, he remained as Rabbi and worked in relief kitchens that served 1500 people per day. He also continued to teach and give sermons which related to Torah and the ineffable suffering of life during the Holocaust. His last book which he titled "Torah Insights from the Years of Wrath 5700–5702 [1939–1942]" was buried in 1943. It was found after the war and published as *Esh Kodesh* [Holy Fire]. The section featured here was written in March 1942, shortly before the Warsaw Ghetto was destroyed.

> God, blessed be He, is to be found in His inner chambers weeping, so that one who pushes in and comes close to Him by means of studying Torah, weeps together with God, and studies Torah with Him.[A] Just this makes the difference: the weeping, the pain which a person undergoes by himself, alone, may have the effect of breaking him, of bringing him down, so that he is incapable of doing anything. But the weeping which the person does together with God—that strengthens him. He weeps—and is strengthened; he is broken—but finds courage to study and teach.[B] It is hard to raise one's self up, time and again, from the tribulations, but when one is determined, stretching his mind to connect to the Torah and Divine service, then he enters the Inner Chambers where the Blessed Holy One is to be found: he weeps and wails together with Him, as it were, and even finds the strength to study Torah and serve Him.[C]

Reflection

In one sense, the words of the Piaseczner are about a personal relationship with the Creator who is in agony when creation is in turmoil. In another sense, "weeping with God" can be a metaphor for meeting our pain with the awareness, compassion, and intention that is always available in our world. There are many ways to process negative feelings. The idea here, in the most universal sense, is to feel accompanied in that process. When times are rough, what helps you feel like you are weeping with Spirit Itself? Is it the company of loved ones? A journal? Meditation? Prayer? Or is it studying Torah and crying with the Compassionate One?

About the Author

Rabbi Israel ben Eliezer (c. 1698–1760) is considered the founder of the Hasidic movement. He was known as the Ba'al Shem Tov and lived in what is now Ukraine. Keter Shem Tov, Sefer Ba'al Shem Tov, and Tzava'at HaRivash are different collections of his teachings compiled after his death. An herbal healer and expert in amulets, the Ba'al Shem Tov is remembered partly for the many miracles attributed to him. His namesake means "Master of the Good Name," and it was believed he had access to the innermost secrets of Kabbalah, which allowed him, among many other gifts, to hear Divine decrees and to revive those who had recently died. The Ba'al Shem Tov, or Besht for short, spent many years in relative seclusion in the Carpathian Mountains before gathering a small group of students. His teachings emphasized direct connection with God, joy, and simplicity. His students and their disciples would go on to form and spread Hasidism, a popular spiritual movement which, within a few generations, became extremely influential amongst Eastern European Jewry. Hasidism exists until today and has developed an extensive canon of stories, teachings, and songs attributed to the Besht.

In tractate Menahot in the Talmud, Reish Lakish said, "Sometimes the neglect of [the study of] Torah is its foundation...[A]" It is hard to understand how ignoring Torah can possibly support it. The Ba'al Shem Tov explains it [with the verse], "The living creatures were running and returning." Everything burns to return to its root. Through eating, drinking, and business dealings a person neglects the study of Torah and the service of God. [However,] at that point the soul rests from its burning and is strengthened so it can return [later] to an even higher *devekut*.[B,C] And about this the Ari said, "'Sometimes the neglect of Torah is its foundation' is the mystery of 'the living creatures were running and returning.[D]'"

And understand!

Reflection and Practice

Is there a particular practice that sets your soul on fire? Perhaps it is a type of meditation or dance. Maybe it is reading a mystical text or the Bible late into the night. Integrating these words from the Ba'al Shem Tov means knowing when to take a break from a practice that sets your soul on fire. This is the practice of not practicing. It may seem counter-intuitive at first, but it is extremely beneficial for those times when we connect very intensely with God. Mystical development is a lot like lifting weights. When we first start, we lift less. Each time we push ourselves, we create actual micro-tears in our muscle tissue. We need to take time off in order to let our muscles heal. And, as they heal, they grow and strengthen! Next time we work out we might be able to handle a little more weight. And on and on. This is the progression of "running and returning" in both weight-lifting and spirituality. Great moments of connection with God fill our being with light, but that energy stirs things up in us a little bit as well. If we give time for those inner shifts to settle and find harmony, our consciousness strengthens and expands. Both the striving and the resting are complementary parts of the path.

Here is the practice: if you find yourself burning with an intense spiritual experience, enjoy it! And, take some time off from the spiritual practice or situation that led you to that state. Eat some healthy food. Drink some water. Spend time with friends engaging in more ordinary activities for a while. Stay aware of your spiritual state and observe it as it moves through you. Eventually, you will return to your baseline state of consciousness, maybe with new insights, greater compassion, or even heightened intuition. Once you're feeling grounded and back to your old self, reengage with that spiritual practice. And repeat!

A. **b. Menahot 99a-b.** In the Talmud, this statement originally meant that sometimes that which seems opposed to Torah study actually promotes it. The medieval commentator known as Rashi writes that a person who leaves his studies in order to escort a deceased person to the grave is rewarded by God as though he were studying. That is to say, "neglecting" Torah study for the sake of actualizing its principles is not neglecting the Torah at all—it is actually supporting it. The Ba'al Shem Tov takes this teaching in a more mystical direction.

B. **Ezekiel 1:14. Citing** a verse, the Besht explains that, in order to properly integrate the fire of Torah, a person needs to take breaks. The verse cited is referring to one part of a vision the prophet Ezekiel had in which the "living creatures," a type of angel, were moving closer to and farther from the Divine throne. The phrase "running and returning" takes on a new meaning of encountering God and then coming back to the everyday world and integrating that experience. In this way, the initial quote from the Talmud is reinterpreted. The "neglect of Torah" now becomes eating, drinking, etc. However, it still supports Torah, because one needs to give the soul rest so that it may regain its strength and later reengage. This way, it may attain an even higher spiritual level, and progress in a two-steps-forward-and-one-step-back fashion.

C. **The term *devekut*,** literally translated as "attachment," here means "spiritual state" or "mystical connection."

D. **The Ari is** an acronym in Hebrew for Elohi Rabbi Yitzḥak, the Godly Rabbi Isaac. The Ari was a 16th century Kabbalist who taught in *Tzfat* [Safed] in *Eretz Yisrael*. His teachings shaped the next several centuries of Jewish mystical practice and thought. Here, his quote is being brought in because it links the two texts cited above.

The matter of a humorous word before study [mentioned in the Talmud].[A] The *hayot* [angels] are "Running and returning.[B]" This is the mystery of a person being in contraction [*katnut,* lit. smallness] and expansion [*gadlut,* lit. largeness]. And, by means of joy and a humorous word, a person goes out from contraction and into expansion to learn and to cleave to God.[C] Thus it is written of these two jesters that were removing people's sorrow through humor.[D] Then they would bring them closer and elevate them. Also, it is written, "And he took his two [*shnei*] youths [*ne'arav*] with him, and Isaac [*Yitzhak*] his son." That is because by means of holy laughter [*tzhok*] we can elevate the years of youth[E] [*shanim ne'arut*] along with ourselves.

A. b. Shabbat 30b. There is a story in the Talmud of a teacher named Rabba who would begin his lessons with humor. Eventually, he taught in a more stern way, however. The Ba'al Shem Tov is interpreting the role of humor in facilitating Torah study through his mystical lens. **B. Ezekiel 1:14. The** image of the angels running and returning from the Divine Throne in Ezekiel's vision is used here, and more generally in *Ḥasidut,* to describe going back and forth between ordinary states of consciousness and expanded ones. The term *katnut* literally means smallness and denotes an ordinary mind, which compared to the expanded state is narrow and contracted. The related Hebrew word *katan* can mean child, which has relevance for the Besht's interpretation at the end of this teaching. The word for expansiveness is *gadlut*, from the word *gadol*, which means "large." **C. For the Besht,** Torah study was a mystical practice. It was not just about learning teachings in the conventional sense, but was a means to connect deeply to God. Humor allows us to be elevated with joy and to reach a place where we can engage with sacred study from a place of expanded mind. In a more everyday sense, if people are sad or downtrodden it might be hard for them to get engaged with learning. A funny moment can help turn that around. **D. b. Ta'anit 22a.** There is a Talmudic story of two righteous brothers who a rabbi meets in the market place. They tell him that, as jesters, they cheer people up who are depressed and when people are fighting try to make peace between them. The Ba'al Shem Tov uses the term "elevates" to describe their peacemaking, and connects it to the elevation of the mind which humor can bring for students. **E. Genesis 22:3. This** verse from the Bible describes Abraham bringing his son Isaac up a mountain to sacrifice him, at God's request (though in the end God told him not to). Abraham brings two young servants with him for the journey. The Besht uses a play on words to tie this verse into his teaching. Isaac's name *Yitzḥak* shares the same Hebrew root as the word for laughter, *tzḥok*. The word for "two-of," *shnei*, as in "two of his youths," sounds like the word for "years," *shanim*. The word for "his youths," *ne'arav*, is related to the word "youth," *na'arut*, which when paired with "years" becomes the years of youth. That is related to the word for constriction (see footnote B), which is related to the word for child. When it is all put together, the verse is read to mean that Abraham elevated the constricted mind [aka the mind we have in the years of youth] with laughter. That's one way to ascend the mountain up to God!

Comments

We come across different types of transformative practices in Jewish mysticism. Some involve digging deep into negativity in order to transform it at the root. Other methods, like this one, involve aiming straight for positivity. In truth, these practices are like remedies. Depending on our present ailment, we will be in need of a different practice. This kind of practice, which the medieval Christian mystic Meister Eckhart termed *via positiva* [the positive way], has advantages for preparing for study. In the example that the Besht brings about the Talmudic rabbi who starts his class with a joke, a *via positiva* practice is beneficial because it is quick-acting. A moment of humor has the capacity to connect us to joy almost instantaneously, even in the midst of real suffering. And, when we can find humor and snap out of a negative mood, engaging in a sacred practice to connect with ultimate reality is easier. No wonder that, along with facing darkness, early Hasidism emphasized joy!

Practice

This teaching describes one way of bringing on happiness: telling a joke. In reality, there are almost limitless ways of cultivating joy. Part of the art of happiness is to bring on good feelings in a way that does not detract from us at the same time. For example, drinking alcohol can bring joy, but in excessive amounts can bring sorrow. The same can be said for social media and movies. What is your favorite way to find a joy that uplifts without negative side effects?

Comments

The way the Ba'al Shem Tov describes reality is echoed in the writings of contemporary philosopher Ken Wilber. Wilber developed a map of stages of consciousness that a mystic progresses through on their way to enlightenment. The last stage, he says, is not a line on the chart but is rather the paper that the chart is written on. When we come to realize the true nature of reality, we see that it was there all along, in every stage of our journey. If we were to map this onto the kabbalistic tree of life, the Infinite would not be above the highest *Sephirah* of *Keter*, but would rather be the very material upon which the tree was written (Figure 4). In the chart, the white background is *Ein Sof*, the Infinite. It is there in every stage of the journey. But, as the Besht points out in our text, we are not experientially aware of that reality until we get far enough along.

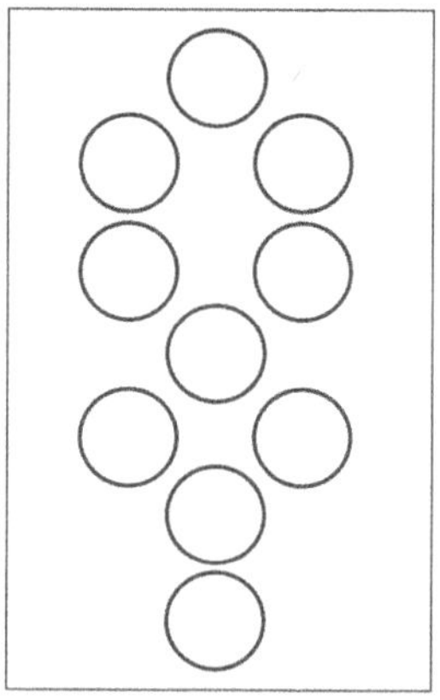

Figure 4. The Ten *Sephirot* and *Ein Sof*

"God's glory fills all the earth.[A]"
"There is no place devoid of God.[B]"

Wherever a person is, His Blessed Glory is found. But if so, why is prayer received through angels [that take it] from realm to realm?[C] It should be said that the Holy Blessed One did this to show to humanity that He is distant, so that [humans] would make great effort to be close, as the Ba'al Shem Tov told [in a parable]:

There was a king, a great, wise man who made an optical illusion [that looked like] walls, towers, and gates. He commanded that people would come to him by way of its passages and towers. He ordered [his workers] to distribute the king's treasures at each and every opening. There was one person that went to the first opening, took money, and left. There was one [who made it to the second opening and went back]...[D] [Eventually] his beloved son tried very hard to make it all the way to his father the king. It was then he saw that there was not [actually] a separating divider between him and his father, because it was all an optical illusion.[E]

A Ba'al Shem Tov Story

There is a rich body of legends told about the Besht. As to whether they are "true" in a literal sense or not, there is a wonderful Hasidic saying, "If you deny every miraculous tale you are a heretic, but if you believe all of them you are a fool." Here is a famous story that relates to the perspective that prayers travel from realm to realm: There was a simple, uneducated man who went to a synagogue during the High Holidays. He wanted to participate in the prayer service, but the people there prayed in a very rigid way and tried to say all the words of the prayer book absolutely perfectly. They were precise in their prayer to the point of arrogance and focused much more on the technical details of how to pray, than on the actual experience of talking to God. This simple man walked in and just wanted to connect. He walked into the center of the sanctuary and said, "God, I don't know how to pray but I know how to whistle." He opened his heart and let out a whistling prayer.

[*cont'd next page*]

A. Isaiah 6:3. This verse is originally from a vision the prophet Isaiah saw of the angels praising God in worship. This was one of the statements they declared. Before the Ba'al Shem Tov, the verse was often interpreted as God's Glory being present in the world, but God being beyond the world. The Ba'al Shem Tov's innovative interpretation is that physicality itself is God in a concealed form. This view came to be one of the defining features of the Hasidic paradigm. **B. Tikunei Zohar 91b.** This verse from the 14th century kabbalistic text is part of a description of the Divine Body, one way the *Sephirot* manifest. The preceding section describes how Divinity is found in each and every portion of the Divine Body, and so no place is devoid from God. Here, the Ba'al Shem Tov interprets it to mean, similarly to above, that God is everywhere on Earth. **C. If we know** that God is everywhere, then why does prayer have to go through several stages in order for God to hear it? The point about the angels here is that there are many layers, chambers, realms and worlds that prayer has to go through in order to reach God. There is therefore a tension between God being everywhere and God being so far away. Jewish beliefs in angels have been varied, but there is a sense here that angels are messengers between our world and God. **D. In Jewish parables,** the king is almost always representing God. There are different stages people go through in order to attain God consciousness. As we journey, there are rewards along the way. Some people might walk to that first gate and say "Wow, this is amazing!" and take that treasure and leave. The gift might be a sense of self-discipline, depth of thought, awakened intuition, and so on. That can be enough for some people, or they may go on to the next openings, each with their own rewards. **E. The beloved son** here is the *tzadik*, the mystic. This person goes all the way to the central chamber to find God. The seeker journeys through what can be compared to the stages of the angels in their realms. The seeker ultimately finds that the whole journey, every realm, was actually God. The palace itself was an illusion, it was just the king there all along. There is no place devoid of God.

The parable is understood as such: the Holy Blessed One is hidden in several garments and veils, and [simultaneously] it is known that "God's glory fills all the earth." Each movement and thought is entirely from God, and so too are all the angels and celestial chambers. Everything is created and formed, if you will, from God's blessed Essence, in the same way as the caterpillar, whose garments are from and within itself.[F] Thus there is no barrier separating the person from God. By this awareness, "All the workers of iniquity are scattered."[G]

F. **The parable of** the king can also be told as a caterpillar and cocoon. The cocoon may appear to be its own form, distinct from its maker, but it is not actually separate from the caterpillar. The creation of the cocoon is the very same essence as its maker, but it appears in a different form. In this way, even along the journey, which seems like a distance to travel, God can be found along every part. The realization, however, comes only on later stages of the journey, so at first it seems like both prayers and humans need to travel a long way to reach God. G. **Psalms 92:10. This** verse can be taken to mean literal, human enemies of God being scattered because of their misdeeds. Here, however, the message is that when we think we are separate from God we sin.

A Ba'al Shem Tov Story [continued]

Everyone there was shocked and they kicked him out. He walked outside, ashamed, and it was then that he saw the Ba'al Shem Tov. The Besht was not only a mystic, but also an intuitive, and had a sense of some of the deeper things that were happening. They both walked back into the synagogue and the Ba'al Shem Tov told the people of the congregation that all of their prayers, the ones they said with the exact right pronunciation, and melody, and timing, etc., those prayers had been hovering within the synagogue. They did not ascend to God. They were stuck in the sanctuary, unable to move on. When this simple man had whistled, the Besht said, it opened up the gates of Heaven and all of the prayers were received. This person had a heartfelt connection and it was this element that allowed his prayers to journey from one world to the next, and to take the other prayers along with them.

Book: Keter Shem Tov Section: 1:61:1

The notion of "running and returning[A]" is that, even in physicality, [one should] "warm oneself by the light of sages.[B]" That is to say, one should not [try to] warm oneself from a distance nor get [too] close to the burning coals. Be cautious with the coals so you do not get seared.[C]

A. **Ezekiel 1:14. This** quote from Ezekiel's vision is of angels running back and forth to the Divine Throne. Running and returning is often used in reference to spiritual integration in Hasidic mysticism. That is, the spiritual path is not always in the forward direction. A person needs to take breaks in order to integrate new insights, energy, and expanded states. In this text, the source of the spiritual growth is from teachers. One must "return" to a resting state in order to integrate the experiences of "running" towards the sages, their teachings, and their transmissions. B. **M. Pirkei Avot** 2:10. This teaching is from the 3rd century CE and may originally be a caution against the biting words from sages. The full teaching is, "warm yourself before the light of sages, but beware of being singed by their glowing coals, for their bite is the bite of a fox, and their sting is the sting of a scorpion, and their hiss is the hiss of a serpent, and all their words are like coals of fire." Here, the Ba'al Shem Tov reads the glow of the sages to be a form of spiritual energy that can be transmitted from teacher to student. The Hebrew term translated as sages is *ḥakhamim*. It literally means "wise ones." By spending time around teachers like this, we can progress in consciousness as well as wisdom and knowledge. C. **Because these mystical** teachers can transmit a lot of profound insight and mystical energy, one should be careful not to be overwhelmed by them. It is good to be close enough to be able to grow. However, mystical teachings are like fire: if we get too close we can get burnt.

A Comparative Look:

In the Kundalini Yoga tradition, which originates in India, one way a teacher passes on transformative Kundalini energy to a student is through *shaktipat*. *Shaktipat* is a transmission of the energy to the student often through eye contact with the teacher or touch. Kundalini is known as an extremely powerful transformational force that can both awaken but also psychically injure a person if they do not go at the right pace and take the right precautions. Stanislov Grof, a transpersonal psychologist, writes about his experiences with the profoundly mystical and controversial Yogi Swami Muktananda[4]. In several instances, Grof received *shaktipat* and fell into dramatically expanded states of consciousness that he had only previously experienced through LSD. There are other accounts of Kundalini awakenings, such as in *Farther Shores* by Yvonne Kason, which have caused the emergence of mental illness when proper self-restraint was not taken.

Comments

Have you ever met someone who could really see the good in people? Truly, we all have that ability within us. Someone who is connected to love and equanimity can do a lot of good as a healer. The idea is that, from the perspective of deep reality, we are perfect just the way we are. And, paradoxically, when we have moments of awareness and self-compassion, we can grow and transform. A good healer, rabbi, guide, or therapist has the ability to see us as we are and in that process allow our true nature, little by little, to emerge.

Practice

The metaphor of the tree is not accidental. The Ba'al Shem Tov spent a great deal of time in nature. In fact, it is widely held that his spiritual life was deepened tremendously by time he spent living in a cabin in the woods. The practice of connecting with nature can be as simple as spending time outdoors, but preferably in a place that feels less urban. Try taking time each day, for one week, to be in nature: by trees, a body of water, a field, mountains, etc. After that week, see how you feel. It is probably worth continuing!

It says in the Talmud "*Tzadikim* are like trees that are planted in a pure place.[A]" When we plant something in the earth it draws all the energy that is there into the seed, and yields fruit. So too, in our reality, the *tzadik* draws sparks from the soul of everything in the world, and raises them up to the Creator.[B]

A. **Kiddushin 40b. In** the Talmud, this line continues on to say that the branches of the *tzadik*, unlike the trunk, hang over an impure area. Those branches are cut off, but the *tzadik* remains on pure ground. That is to say, even a righteous person transgresses from time to time and goes through suffering in order to be refined. The Ba'al Shem Tov focuses on the first part of that metaphor and takes it in a transformational direction.

B. **A tree uses** the energy around it in order to develop and ultimately bear fruit. The "pure place" in which the *tzadik* is planted is like the earth in this metaphor. A tree needs earth to bear fruit. Similarly, the *tzadik* is rooted in the spiritual essence of all that is around. The term "sparks" is a reference to Lurianic Kabbalah, which sees the mission of humanity to elevate the Divine light that has been scattered back to its rightful place in the spiritual realm. The Ba'al Shem Tov has this in mind but his teachings saw a more personal quality to kabbalistic principles. The *tzadik* is one who, despite anyone or anything's outward appearance, can connect with their inner nature and help them transform. This sense of uplifting the world would be called *tikkun* in Lurianic Kabbalah. In that system it has to do with repairing the cosmic sphere for the sake of metaphysical wholeness. Here, it includes that meaning but also refers to the kind of inner change that we might call healing, growth, or an "aha moment."

"You shall love your neighbor as yourself. I am YHWH.[A]" This verse means that how you behave towards your friend, with love and harmony, "as yourself I am YHWH." In other words, that I, God, will be like you.[B] This is the mystery of "YHWH is your shadow.[C]" Just as a person behaves below with his friend or neighbor, with love and good qualities, so behaves the Supreme King.[D] Like with shade, every move we make the shadow does in parallel.[E] This is how God is with us. This is the meaning of "You shall love your neighbor," because "like you I am YHWH," acting towards you as well with love and all good things.

A. Leviticus 19:18. This verse comes from a section in the Torah where the words "I am *YHWH*" appear after many of the instructions. The meaning in its original context may have been "because I *YHWH* say so." The Besht is lifting this one verse for his teaching about the relationship between our actions and God's. **B. The Besht is** splitting up the verse so that "As yourself I am *YHWH*" becomes its own unit. The Hebrew phrase *kamokha* can be translated "as yourself" or "like you." With the Besht's teaching, the phrase becomes "Like you I am *YHWH*." The meaning of this is spelled out with the next verse quoted. **C. Psalms 121:5. The** Hebrew term "*tzel*", meaning "shadow" or "shade" in its context in the book of Psalms represents protection. It is a metaphor for God shielding someone from the light of the sun and moon which are seen there as aggressors. Here, the Besht sees the shadow as a one-to-one relationship between human and Divine action. **D. When we act** with kindness, this arouses kindness in the Divine world. In kabbalistic terminology this is called *itaruta delitata*, awakening from below. Our actions on Earth impact the goodness that flows into our lives and into the world in general. **E. Kabbalists teach that** everything in our world has a correlate in the spiritual world. The Divine world and the physical world mirror one another and move together like the body and the shadow.

A Comparative Look

In our times, many people use the word "karma" to refer to the way our actions come back to us. Originally a Sanskrit term, karma was often associated with the nature of one's rebirth in Hindu, Jain, and Buddhist teachings. Today, however, many people use it to refer to the notion of "what goes around comes around." Whether we believe in karmic retribution or not, treating other humans well will surely lead to more peace, harmony, and happiness in our lives.

Related Jewish Sources

Not only do humans and God reflect one another, so do humans and humans. The book of Proverbs 27:19 says, "As face answers to face in water, so does one man's heart to another."

Rashi comments on that verse saying that we see our face when we look into the water. In the same way, if a person knows they are loved by the other, their heart mirrors that feeling back.

Relatedly, the Mishnah says (Pirkei Avot 4:1): "Who is honored? The one who honors others." If we want to receive respect in life, the best thing to do is give it.

Sometimes, when we fall down a level by our own doing, or when the world causes us to fall from our standing, God knows we need that.[A] But the descent is for the sake of ascent in order to come to a high plane.[B] As it is written "He will lead us beyond death.[C]" And it is written, "Abraham went down to Egypt,[D]" and "Abraham went up from Egypt.[D]" [Here] Abraham is the soul and Egypt is the husks.[E]

A. Sometimes we stumble in life. We do something that is not in-line with our highest Self or we are in a period of time where we our spiritual connection feels like it is missing. Perhaps we are faced with something difficult in our lives like the death of a loved one, and this causes us to behave in ways that are not healthy for us as a result of the grief. This kind of thing happens to all people at some point, and for the vast majority of us, stumbling is a regular part of life. The Besht says that this is not simply a negative thing. God knows that we need to go through that. Although we feel badly and disconnected from Spirit, the Divine is with us in the process and is aware that this is part of our personal development. **B. Descent for the** sake of ascent is a major Hasidic principle. In this text, it is describing a process of personal transformation. The downward direction we may be traveling spiritually can ultimately bring us back not just to where we started, but actually to a higher plane than we could have reached otherwise. If we work with negativity in a conscious way, we can use that difficult occurrence for the sake of transformation and benefit from it. **C. Psalms 48:15. This** biblical verse is from a poem describing enemies at the gate. People know that God is protecting God's City. The kings who have come to conquer the city are fleeing because they are afraid. The Psalm ends with this verse about God leading us forever. Though the meaning of the Hebrew phrase *al mut* is uncertain, it is often translated as "eternally," as in, "He will lead us eternally." Psalm 48 may have arisen in connection to an actual battle but was likely viewed as a metaphor in ancient times as well. The Ba'al Shem Tov reads the verse as "beyond death," *mut* being very similar to the Hebrew word for "death." He interprets this verse to mean that a person falling from their spiritual standing has a danger of descending and never coming back up again, a kind of permanent spiritual death. However, though it may feel that way, there can be a descent for a sake of ascent and we can be led beyond this low point, this near-death, for the sake of a higher attainment. **D. Genesis 12:10 and 13:1**, respectively. See the page on Zohar 1:83a, footnote B, for the mystical metaphor of Abraham's descent to Egypt. **E. In The Ba'al** Shem Tov's view, influenced by Kabbalah, Abraham is the soul that journeys into negativity. The husks or "shells," *kelipot* in Hebrew, are a kabbalistic metaphor for the demonic realm called the *Sitra Aḥra* [other side]. The metaphor in Lurianic Kabbalah is part of a creation narrative in which, as the world was being created, there were vessels, akin to clay pots, being filled with Divine light. At some point, the vessels shattered and both the shards and the light were scattered. The light remained connected to the shells (i.e. the husks) of the vessels, like olive oil would cling to a shard of hardened clay. The task of the Kabbalist was, through using meditations combined with ritual acts, to separate the husks from the light and elevate them both to the cosmic realm. In the process, the shard would be transformed into something positive. Here, the Ba'al Shem Tov is describing a personal rectification in which we can transform our own spiritual shortcomings, our "husks," through the process of descent and ascent.

Practice

There are many methods that people can use to do the work of consciously going into negativity when it arises. The Ba'al Shem Tov's great grandson, Rebbe Naḥman of Bratslav, teaches a method called *hitbodedut*, which means "self-seclusion." It involves praying alone in our own vernacular, just saying the words that are on our heart, not written in any prayer book. Ideally, one finds a place in nature, but it can be anywhere indoors as well that has privacy. Rebbe Naḥman advises taking time aside every day for one hour to speak out what is deep inside, to pour our soul out to God. Part of the practice, as it was handed down to me, is to actually speak from the perspective of our feelings. Instead of saying, "I am feeling angry now," we say something that captures that feeling like, "I AM SO MAD AT YOU!!" The idea is to direct the feelings towards God. God can handle whatever we say, so there is no need to hold back! This practice has the effect of allowing us to get really deeply connected with our inner lives, especially with negative states, to articulate them so they can be transformed. With practice and perhaps with the help of a mentor we can learn how to use this method to transmute our interior world and allow both our negative and positive feelings to be gateways towards what lies beyond us.

A Comparative Look

Within Christian mysticism there is a model of transformation that is inspired by Saint John of the Cross, the 16th century Carmelite Monk.

He wrote a poem called The Dark Night of the Soul in which he outlines three major stages of spiritual growth. The first stage is when a person is beginning to feel a connection with God. We feel alive, like our souls are awakened. The second stage, however, is the dark night, where every spiritual gift previously earned seems to be taken away. This is a period of difficulty and suffering, where God seems very distant.

Part of the work of that stage is to continue on the path, to keep striving to work through that darkness. The third stage is when a person finally makes it through the obscurity and difficulty and arrives at a new level of connection that was far more profound than the original first stage. This third stage is called union. It is said that if it was not for the dark night, if it was not for the experience of going through all of that obscure unknown, a person would not be able to reach the realization of union in the third stage.

"[They who dwell in His shade shall return,] they shall bring grain to life and blossom like the vine, [its scent will be like the wine of Lebanon]."[A]

All produce that change from their created state and are diminished, their initial [higher] blessings are lost. We bless them with [the catch-all food blessing] *shehakol*.[B] But, in the case of grain and wine, [after they are broken down, they transform and] change to a higher level. We give them their own [higher] blessing of *hamotzi* [who brings forth bread] and *hagafen* [who creates the fruit of the vine].[C] So too is the *ba'al teshuvah* from love [the person who leaves a life of *mitzvot* but then, out of love, does repentance and returns to communal life].[D] He changes for the better, so that willful wrongdoings become merits for him and he establishes a blessing for himself in the process of changing, like grain and wine.[E]

A. **Hosea 14:8. This** verse from the Hebrew Bible is originally meant to describe the process and aesthetics of returning to God after going astray. The metaphor is of grain and wine, two staples of the Israelite diet, flourishing just as a people returned from exile would flourish. In the Bnei Yisaschar's interpretation, the grain and wine symbolize a specific form of *teshuvah* [repentance/return]: *teshuvah* from love. B. **In Jewish practice,** different blessings are said over different foods before they are eaten (See chart below). Each blessing begins with the words, "Blessed are you, *YHWH* our God, King of the Universe..." Over produce that grows from the earth like a potato, for example, the blessing ends with, "who creates the fruit of the earth." Over produce that grows from trees it ends with, "who creates the fruit of the tree." For meat, milk, and most types of "broken down" food—such as juice—the blessing ends with "for everything is brought into being with His word." The "for everything" blessing is a catch-all blessing and can actually be said on any type of food, but it is preferable to be more precise when possible. The more specific the blessing, the higher the holiness. With most fruits and vegetables, if they are broken down—such as when one makes apple juice—one ends the blessing with "for everything..." In other words, most produce becomes "diminished" when it is ground up; it goes from its specific blessing to the catch-all blessing. C. **There are two** important foods which get a more specific and holier blessing after they are broken down. When grapes are crushed, fermented, and turned into wine they go from a "fruit of the tree" blessing to the "fruit of the vine" blessing. This latter blessing can only be said over wine or grape juice. Similarly, when a grain of wheat, barley, rye, spelt or oats is crushed, mixed with water, fermented, and baked it goes from a "fruit of the earth" blessing to the blessing of "who brings forth bread from the earth." This latter blessing is very specific and can only be said over bread. So, when grapes and grains are crushed, they go through a transformation process and attain a more specific, holier blessing than before. D. **A *ba'al teshuvah*** literally means a "master of return/repentance." In the Bnai Yisaskhar's era this was someone who left the community of religious Jews but who later came back. It is said in the Talmud that a *ba'al teshuvah* can stand in a place where even a complete *tzadik* [righteous person] cannot stand (Berakhot 34b). Like grapes and grain, the fracturing event and subsequent transformation through *teshuvah* leads a person to a greater level than they could have attained otherwise. E. **There are two** categories of *ba'al teshuvah*, one who returns out of love and one who returns out of fear. According to the Talmud, when one does *teshuvah* out of fear, that person's intentional sins are counted as accidents and are essentially neutralized. When one does *teshuvah* out of love, however, the intentional sins are made into merits and metamorphosize from negativity into positivity. In other words, when someone does an act of loving return, they get to a higher spiritual place as a result of the negativity they encountered. They grow from that experience.

Heirarchy of Food Blessings

Blessing	English Translation	Food that Blessing Covers	
Hamotzi and *HaGafen*	"Who Brings Forth" and "Fruit of the Vine"	Bread and wine/ grape juice respectively	SPECIFIC
Mezonot	"Various Kinds of Sustenance"	Foods, besides bread, made from grains	
HaEtz	"Fruit of the Tree"	Produce that grows on trees	
HaAdamah	"Fruit of the Earth"	Produce that grows from the ground, like vegetables	
SheHaKol	"For Everything"	Meat, dairy, eggs and everything else	GENERAL

About the Author

Rabbi Zvi Elimelekh of Dinov (1785–1841) was a Hasidic master who lived in Galicia, modern day Poland. A deep student of Kabbalah, he was a disciple of many great Hasidic teachers of his time. He is often referred to by the title of his most celebrated book, the Bnei Yisaskhar, which is a commentary on all of the months and holidays of the Hebrew calendar. The text featured here is found on a section about the holiday of Purim. A similar teaching also appears about the High Holidays.

Comments

The main message of this text is that when something bad happens to us we have the capacity to transform that negative event and its accompanying thoughts and emotions into positive growth. This means that we can actually become better for having gone through that difficult time. In my experience, this theory of transformation is only as valuable as the practices used to employ it. Whether we are feeling into the pain in our bodies, journaling to express it, praying sincerely from our anguished state, or using any other method, actually feeling our suffering us important. If we want to hear its wisdom we need to lean into it. Within this process, however, there is often a need to take breaks. It is wise to find a balance between actively engaging with a difficult state and finding comfort or small moments of relaxation and contentment. Any positive practices of cultivating pleasure to take our minds off of the pain can support our overall engagement with it. At times like these, seeking out guides and supports can be crucial. Through these approaches, help from guides and loved ones, and the support of the universe, a person will see themselves be transformed for the better.

It is also important to remember that if someone comes to you because they are suffering, it is usually best to be a listening ear and help them in their process. Teachings like the one in our text should come at the right time. When a loved-one is in crisis, it may not be the best time to talk directly about the philosophy of growth through hardship.

About the Author

Rebbe Levi Yitzḥak ben Meir of Berdichev (c. 1740–1810) was a third generation Hasidic Master and one of the most famous of his era. He served as both a rabbi who would determine matters of law as well as a Hasidic rebbe. Reflective of this dual role, Levi Itzhak, also known as The Berdichever, taught in a way that was highly accessible. He was a spiritual leader for the general population, not just for a select few, and the recordings of his teachings in the Kedushat Levi reflect this.

Comments

The teachings of the Kedushat Levi came forth near the beginning of the Hasidic movement. At that time, there was a great deal of passion and spiritual fervor amongst *Ḥasidim*. There were teachers and practitioners who had a very ecstatic mindset, who were very actively expanding and exploring consciousness. Among those were The Berdichever's fellow students in the school of the Maggid of Mezeritch, some of whom were retreating from the world for the sake of their own spiritual lives. The Maggid's son, for example, was known as "Abraham the Angel" because he was seemingly not of this world. He did not want to be a rebbe, a leader and teacher for others. He would rather invest in his own path of *devekut*.

In truth, there are many different types of mystics. Some are mystic servants who relinquish part of their own journey for the sake of others. Another variety we could call the mystic journeyer who focuses on the spiritual realms and less on the physical. Though this text emphasizes the role of mystic servant, those who work in a much more focused way with consciousness, though more rare, are also an honored part of the wider world of spiritual striving. The important distinction to make for ourselves, if we are drawn towards the second variety, is whether we want that because it is truly our heart's desire and purpose, or whether we are trying to escape or avoid worldly realities.

YHWH said to Moses, "Go down, warn the people not to break through to *YHWH* to gaze, lest many of them meet their end. And the priests as well, that draw near to *YHWH*, they should sanctify themselves lest *YWHW* breaks out upon them." Moses said to *YHWH*, "The people cannot come up to Mount Sinai because you charged us, saying, 'put boundaries around the mountain and sanctify it.'" *YWHW* said to Moses, "Go, get down! And you should go up with Aaron, but the priests and the people should not burst through to go up to *YHWH*, lest God break them apart."[A]

Rashi explains that [God told Moses to descend a second time because] one should admonish people [before a forbidden action and come back and admonish them at the time they are committing the action]. It seems that Moses our teacher, peace be upon him, believed in the words of the Blessed Creator with great and complete faith. With great zealousness, he would fulfill the words of the One immediately upon hearing the instruction from the Divine mouth. Moses was thinking that just as he believes in the words of the Creator and would not transgress against them, so too was the faith and disposition in the hearts of the Israelites.[B]

A. Exodus 19:21–24. These verses from Exodus describe Moses on Mount Sinai speaking to God. Moses is receiving revelation. Here, God tells him to go down and warn the people not to come near and Moses wonders why he would need to do that, since they had already been warned. God tells Moses, "Go, get down!" in stronger language to emphasize the need.

B. Rashi is saying that Moses is being told to admonish the people as a warning for a second time because this is the proper way to warn about a forbidden action in the rabbinic mindset (from which Rashi is writing). The Berdichever interprets that Moses needed this second instruction from God to "get down!" becasuse he himself would not need two warnings because he was so connected to God. In other words, Moses was unable to grasp that the Israelites did not possess his same degree of faithfulness.

A Comparative Look

Sri Ramakrishna Paramahansa, the 19th century Hindu mystic, tells this story: There was an infinite field beyond a high wall. Four friends tried to find out what was beyond the wall. Three of them, one after the other, climbed the wall, saw the field, burst into loud laughter, and dropped to the other side. These three could not give any information about the field. Only the fourth man came back and told people about it... None of the first three persons had the patience or capacity to turn back and tell their friends what was happening inside. Only the fourth could check himself, thinking of the countless people living outside who were unaware of this place of joy. So he climbed down, told everyone about this joyful place, and shared the joy with the others in the enclosure.

But, in truth, we are not on as high a level as Moses our teacher, peace be upon him, who God knew "face to face."[C] He would constantly perceive, at each moment, the expansiveness of the Infinite. He had strong faith to keep the command that went out from the mouth of God and not to transgress His will, Heaven forbid. He was constantly in *devekut* with the Creator and was at a lofty spiritual stage.

This is the hint in the verses... It was as if Moses said to God, "Why should I return to tell them again?" Since You commanded to them once, then of course they will not transgress Your work. It was foreign in Moses' eyes for a person in this world to transgress the command of the Creator. Moses was on a high plane and thought that it was impossible for a person in the community to transgress the commandment of the Infinite.

This is what is meant by, "God said to him, 'Go, get down...'" God was saying to Moses, "You are on a high level and you are always in *devekut* with me. It is hard for you [to understand] how it is possible for someone to go against my command. Go, get down!" That is to say, descend from your rung and see that at a lower level a person can transgress my instruction. You should therefore go a second time and testify to them.[D]

C. **Deuteronomy 34:10. Moses,** regarded in Jewish tradition as the greatest prophet who ever lived, attained the spiritual stage of seeing God "face to face." In the Hebrew Bible this description is clearly special and profound. It indicates a very intense intimacy with the Divine but it is not explicit that this connection never ends. The Berdichever interprets being "face to face" with the Infinite as being in constant connection, constant *devekut* with God. What flows from this state of connection is following Divine guidance. If we are so aware of the Divine in the world, at each and every moment, being good and living according to our true purpose is natural.

D. **In one sense** God is telling Moses to get down from the mountain to tell the Israelites not to sin. But, in a deeper sense, God is telling Moses to descend from his mystical connection in order to be able to relate to other people. Most people tend to understand others through projections of their own inner world. It is not different with the prophet Moses who cannot see the Israelites clearly. His incredible spiritual attainment has value for being a prophet but it is hindering him in this moment from being a perceptive leader. When we are so high up that we cannot relate to others we are supposed to be helping, that is a good indication it is time to descend.

Related Jewish Sources

The Turkey Prince, a parable from Rebbe Naḥman recorded in the early 18th century, relays a similar message about the importance of meeting people where they are.[5]

Once the king's son went mad. He thought he was a turkey. He felt compelled to sit under the table without any clothes on, pulling at bits of bread and bones like a turkey. None of the doctors could do anything to help him or cure him, and they gave up in despair. The king was very sad...

Until a Wise Man came and said "I can cure him." What did the Wise Man do? He took off all his clothes, and sat down naked under the table next to the king's son, and also pulled at crumbs and bones. The Prince asked him, "Who are you and what are you doing here?"

"And what are you doing here?" replied the Wise Man. "I am a turkey," said the Prince. "Well I'm also a turkey," said the Wise Man. The two of them sat there together like this for some time, until they were used to one another. Then the Wise Man gave a sign, and they threw them shirts. The Wise Man-Turkey said to the king's son, "Do you think a turkey can't wear a shirt? You can wear a shirt and still be a turkey." The two of them put on shirts. After a while he gave another sign, and they threw them some trousers. Again the Wise Man said, "Do you think if you wear trousers you can't be a turkey?" They put on the trousers. One by one they put on the rest of their clothes in the same way. Afterwards, the Wise Man gave a sign and they put down human food from the table. The Wise Man said to the Prince, "Do you think that if you eat good food you can't be a turkey any more? You can eat this food and still be a turkey." They ate. Then he said to him, "Do you think a turkey has to sit under the table? You can be a turkey and sit up at the table." This was how the Wise Man dealt with the Prince, until in the end he cured him completely.

About the Author

Rebbe David Solomon Eibeschitz (1755–1813) was born in the Ukraine and led various Eastern European communities until he moved to *Eretz Yisrael* in 1810. A scholar of Jewish Law and Kabbalah, Eibeschitz studied under well-known Hasidic teachers of his time. The Arvei Naḥal is a Hasidic commentary on the Torah.

Comments

There are some spiritual teachers who are fantastic examples of peace and love but who do not seem to experience suffering like the rest of us. We can find accounts of people like this in religious history but also in present-day. In my experience, teachers that seem to be larger than life may be good examples of love and spiritual connection, but they are often less skilled in helping people work with day-to-day struggles and negative emotions in an integrated way. John Welwood, a Buddhist psychologist, coined the term "spiritual bypassing" which he defined as using "spiritual ideas and practices to sidestep personal, emotional 'unfinished business,' to shore up a shaky sense of self, or to belittle basic needs, feelings, and developmental tasks." In other words, people can use spiritual practices and teachings in order to avoid working with underlying issues. Someone can be very in touch with high spiritual energies without having addressed emotional baggage and personal qualities. If a teacher comes from this orientation, it will be difficult for them to teach others what they do not know or practice themselves. The Arvei Naḥal's perspective is directed at these teachers and offers an optimistic view that it is never too late for them to do the more worldly work. However, though every teacher has this capacity, for students it is wise to be aware of this most human of tendencies and to be cautious about getting too close to a guide who is avoiding their own dark side.

For a person who has a trace of evil within, God invites him, through the trace, to look at and listen to that negative element and repair it.[A] Through [being engaged with] this process, he can facilitate transformation in someone else who is acting in an evil way.[B] This is not so with someone who is [spiritually] expanded beyond the physicality of this world. In that case, he does not have any hint of evil and [therefore] he does not have any connection whatsoever with people who are sinning. So, he is unable to help them.[C]

This is what we have spoken of [elsewhere], that from one perspective this *tzadik* who completely went out beyond nature is incomplete. That is to say, it is not within his power to return wicked people to the good.[D] But, certainly, this *tzadik* who transcends nature, and is [therefore] not amongst those who bring acquittal to the guilty,[E] he is not [irreversibly] at a loss. He should therefore make a descent for the sake of ascent.[F]

A. **A trace of** evil or negativity is something within us that, if we were to let it find full outward expression, would cause harm to ourselves and/or others. For example, this could be a desire to eat unhealthy food or to be dishonest for the sake of personal gain. Instead of acting on that urge, we can see it as an invitation to look more deeply at that element of ourselves. Through contemplating that part of us, we can allow it to transform.

Comments

The terms "evil," "wicked," "sin," and the like are used by this teacher to describe what I would frame as misalignment. In my view, there are no pure "sinners" just as there are no true *tzadikim*. We all have some positive and negative qualities. I understand the lessons of this teaching to be especially valuable for spiritual teachers, but they are also applicable to each of us in some way. In being more present with our inner challenges we can be more intimately connected to this world and each other.

B. **When we are** actively engaged with our own negativity, we can help people who are overpowered by their impulses. For people who are acting ethically, being connected with inner urges can allow them to help people whose desires are being played out in the world in destructive ways. C. **It is possible,** says the Arvei Naḥal, to be enveloped in spirit to a degree where we do not struggle with traces of evil. However, this self-removal from the world will hinder us in aiding others. If our spiritual practices take us to an elevated state in which we are not connected to this world any longer, we will not be able to resonate with people who struggle with their inner negativity. D. **Though this *tzadik*** is on a high spiritual level, there is a sense of incompleteness. This is because a *tzadik*'s role is not just to be spiritually elevated, but also to do service in the physical world and help others. E. **The phrase bringing** "acquittal to the guilty" means bringing blessings to those who are caught in negative patterns. Someone who is in touch with their internal struggles but is not overcome by them can be of great service to those who are overcome by them. F. **If a *tzadik*** has become expanded beyond this world, it is still possible to reenter everyday life. The concept of *yeridah letzorekh aliyah*, descending for the sake of ascending, here refers not just to the inner journey, but the path of the spiritual teacher who descends into material reality in order to elevate others.

Comments

The Arvei Naḥal is providing reassurance to those who are hesitant to engage with the world and common people, that they will not be drawn into sin as a result. I appreciate the Talmudic quote brought at the end of this text in the sense that it is trying to calm the anxieties of spiritual leaders who are reentering the world of their students. However, I believe that all people are capable of missteps. That is not something we need to fear. In the words of Dr. David Lertzman, my teacher of blessed memory, "The only mistake is one that isn't learned from." Mistakes are an opportunity to grow and, to take this text one step further, will help the *tzadik* connect even more with the ones who are struggling.

That is, from time to time he should intentionally step down from his level and become intermixed with the concerns of the world. Through this, he will be connected to the evil people and can elevate them. [He may think that] descending to the place of desires is dangerous, like if people were to tell him, "Sin, in order to bring blessing to your comrades!" In fact, he was given assurance from God, as the Sages said, "All who bring merit to the masses will not come to sin.[G]"

G. b. Yoma 87a. Someone who has cultivated a life removed from physical desires may have fears about reentering the world. One could possibly be tempted into an improper action. The Arvei Naḥal quotes the Talmud to say that, in fact, people who do the holy work of elevating others have Divine protection from transgressing. The Arvei Naḥal brings this quote to teach specifically about *tzadikim* who reenter the world. The Talmud, in it's original context, however, is speaking broadly about anyone that brings merit and blessings to the public.

About the Author

Elimelekh of Lizhensk (1717–1787) was a popular Hasidic Master of the third generation of Hasidism. A disciple of the Maggid of Mezeritch, he is known for refining and popularizing the term *tzadik* to mean mystic-leader of a community. He and his brother Zusya spent several years wandering from village to village in self-imposed exile as a way to identify with the exile of the *Shekhinah*, and thus the brokenness of the world. Elimelekh trained many of the greatest teachers of the next generation of Hasidic leaders including the Apter Rav and the Maor VeShemesh. He taught at length about the life of the *tzadik* and different paths that *tzadikim* took in their personal journeys and in their leadership. His sermons were recorded by his students in the Noam Elimelekh.

Comments

This articulation of the *tzadik* is one of many varieties that the Noam Elimelekh describes. In Jewish thought it is not common to describe a stage of enlightenment which does not cease. However, this text articulates just that. Shabbat is said to be a taste of the world to come. The world to come is seen by some as heaven on earth, part of which is reward and pleasure for all. Today, when Shabbat is practiced with intention, where we eat the best food, put our cellphones away along with the cares of the workweek, and spend time with people whom we love and enjoy, it can feel like we have found a taste of that perfected world. To live in shabbat consciousness all week is no easy task. As well, it is arguably not the wisest way of being in a world that still has work to be done. In my most generous interpretation of descriptions of these kinds of *tzadikim*, they still do the work of helping others but can do so from a place of acceptance and ease. And, for those of us who have not made it to shabbat consciousness all the time, a regular practice of unplugging, not doing work, and finding rest, refreshment, and enjoyment can help us bring that sense of peace into the rest of our lives.

It says in the holy Zohar that the *tzadik* is called Shabbat:[A] this is because during the week he has the soul that other people have on Shabbat.[B] But what additional rung does he have on Shabbat? One can say that the soul is added in holiness until he brings pleasure to the Blessed Creator[C]... They give him a portion "without constrictions.[D]" The *tzadik* is always connected and united with the higher worlds that have no end. The constriction and boundary of this world has a limit, and it is in the hand of the *tzadik* to connect all the worlds to the Infinite... But, there is [also] a [kind of] *tzadik* that is not constantly in the state of *devekut* to the upper worlds. He still needs to work on his personal attributes with fear and humility. He needs to descend from his *devekut* in order to improve them. Yet, he is still, because of his inner life, not committing a sin in his descent below.[E]

A. Zohar 2:94b. This passage, in its original context, is describing different types of souls and the purpose for which they descend into the world. The soul of the *tzadik* is said to do holy work in the world, which is equated with the work of Shabbat, not the mundane work of the week. "The *Tzadik* is Shabbat," is the exact phrase in the Zohar itself, which the Noam Elimelekh is reiterating in different words. **B. It says in** the Talmud that on Shabbat we are given an additional soul (b. Beitza 16a). This phenomenon can also be seen as a hidden part of our soul emerging. In Hasidic thought, this phenomenon is seen as a type of expanded consciousness. The Noam Elimelekh reads the Zoharic passage to say that the *tzadik* is called Shabbat because of the expanded consciousness available to them, even during the work week. **C. If the *tzadik*** has Shabbat Consciousness throughout the week, what happens on Shabbat? One way to interpret the state of "bringing pleasure to the Blessed Creator," is that it is an even more refined mystical experience than Shabbat Consciousness. The Noam Elimelekh does not elaborate beyond this description. Another way to interpret it is through the notion of bringing pleasure to God, which is communicated elsewhere in Hasidic literature (e.g. Avodat Yisrael, Re'eh 5, by the Maggid of Kozhnitz). There, it refers to God creating the world to enjoy Israel doing Divine Service. Perhaps observing Shabbat, for someone continually connected to Shabbat Consciousness, is such a high level of service that it brings enjoyment to the most subtle realms of existence. A third possibility is that there is an inherent tension in practicing Shabbat for someone who is already experiencing it in their minds at all times. The idea of bringing pleasure to the Creator, which can happen when anyone observes Shabbat, might be a way for the Noam Elimelekh to rhetorically dispel this difficulty (See *Devotion and Commandment* by Arthur Green for more on the tension between early Hasidic mysticism and Jewish law). **D. b. Shabbat 118a.** This section of the Talmud is describing anyone who takes delight in Shabbat. They are given a boundless portion, meaning a large reward or freedom from exile, which are both equated with the experience of Shabbat itself. Here, the Noam Elimelekh is interpreting this passage to refer to the *tzadik* who experiences each day as Shabbat, as a day of reward, peace, and pleasure. The role of this *tzadik* is to connect the world of boundaries, which is the physical world, to the Divine, where there are no limitations. The *tzadik* achieves this by being a human being, inherently limited and embodied, while also spiritually in-line with the world of unbounded freedom. **E. The other kind** of *tzadik* is not constantly in a state of Shabbat Consciousness. This second type is still working on personal limitations. Though the Noam Elimelekh does not describe it in this passage, other sources in this book such as the Arvei Nachal and Kedushat Levi texts critique the *tzadikim* who are so elevated that they cannot relate to everyday people. Here, this teaching merely distinguishes between types and acknowledges that there are different kinds and, indeed, different levels of *tzadikim*.

"Abraham went up from Egypt... into the South.[A]"

Rabbi Shim'on said, "Come and see: All is a mystery of wisdom. Here beckons an allusion to wisdom and rungs below, to the depths of which Abraham descended, knowing them but not clinging, returning to vitality.[B] He was not seduced by them like Adam, who upon reaching that rung was seduced by the serpent and inflicted death upon the world...[C]

"But of Abraham, what is written? 'Abraham went up[D] from Egypt,' ascending, not descending, returning to his domain, the supernal rung he had grasped before.[E]

A. Genesis 13:1. In the Bible, this verse describes Abraham leaving Egypt and journeying back into the Southern lands of Canaan. He had experienced a difficult time in Egypt, with Pharaoh taking his wife Sarah as a wife for himself. Ultimately, Pharaoh was punished by God and Sarah returned to Abraham. Along the way, Abraham had acquired wealth there and returned to where he had been before, the South, richer than when he had ventured to Egypt. Here, the Zohar is interpreting Abraham's descent to Egypt as a descent into the "Other Side," a kabbalistic term for the evil realm or demonic world. **B. Egypt is *Mitzrayim*** in Hebrew. This comes from the same root as the word *meitzar*, which means a narrow place. In Jewish interpretation, Egypt is commonly seen as representing a place of difficulty, evil or suffering. Abraham's journey into Egypt was a journey into the *Sitra Aḥra*, the Other Side, which is the dark realm of the spiritual world. He had previously encountered the Divine World and attained the level of *Ḥesed*, lovingkindness. From that place, represented as "The South," Abraham started to explore the dark world. He went into Egypt and came out again, representing his succesful journey to the Other Side and back.

Comments

While ancient Egypt is a very powerful symbol for struggle, suffering, and evil in Jewish tradition, it is somewhat problematic in today's world where Egypt is a nation and not just a past myth. When I read texts that use this metaphor, I separate the symbol of Egypt in the mythic system from both its real-world history and its current existence. Egypt's symbolic status in the Jewish imagination is not connected to Egyptian history after the biblical era including present-day Egypt, other than the shared name and geography. It is also worth noting that Pharaoh and Egypt are mentioned in the Quran in disparaging terms, and modern-day Egypt is 90% Muslim. There is clearly a distinction made in the Muslim faith between Egypt of the past and the present.

C. There are some people who enter into the Other Side and get trapped there. According to the Zohar's view, Adam misapprehended the *Sephirot* in his encounter with the snake, a being of the Other Side. As a result, *Shekhinah* was separated from the rest of the Tree of Life and acted from the Tree of Death. After the sin of eating the forbidden fruit, Adam is punished with death as his, and thus all humanity's, inevitable end. **D. The word in** Hebrew *veya'al* literally means "went up." It is the term used to this day when referring to traveling to the *Eretz Yisrael*. In the Zohar's read, the term has a special significance. It is not just going to the physical promised land, but also leaving the Other Side to "go up" to the Divine realm of *Ḥesed*. **E. Different characters in** the Bible represent different *Sephirot* in Kabbalah. Certain characters are a *merkavah* for a *Sephirah*, which literally means a "chariot" for that quality. Abraham is a chariot for *Ḥesed*, which means that he brings lovingkindness and the expansive energy of Divine blessing into the world. When he realizes the reality of *YHWH* and follows Divine guidance into the land Cana'an, he attains that level. Abraham was the main vehicle, according to the Zohar, through which *Ḥesed* was initially revealed in the world. It is from this rung that he journeyed into the Other Side and returned.

About the Author

The Zohar is the central text of Kabbalah. Written as an account of the adventures and teachings of 1st century rabbis, this text was first published in the 13th century in Spain. The Zohar views the Torah as a code for much deeper secrets involving the *Sephirot*ic world and its interactions with our world. The text is at once theosophic, describing the cosmic realm, theurgic, teaching how we can affect the spiritual world, and experiential, describing, in a veiled way, the life of the mystic.

A Comparative Look

1. Kabbalah and other forms of Jewish mysticism all have certain visionary elements. In this mystical orientation, journeying to other worlds could be what is known in English as Astral Travel, a visionary journey to another dimension. In *Of Water and the Spirit*, Malidoma Some describes his initiation rite in the Dagara tribe of Berkina Fasau. He tells the story of entering into another world through a magical portal created by an elder. He entered into that place with a rope tied around him. His main instruction was to not get stuck, though it was very alluring. All the initiates went through the ordeal but some did not survive because they tarried in that non-physical place.

2. The process of journeying into the Other Side [*Sitra Aḥra*], the lower/demonic world, might also be called Shadow work. Psychologist Carl Jung coined the term The Shadow to describe our inner dark side. The poet Robert Bly describes the shadow as a bag we carry around where we keep those parts of us that society (including our parents and other social influences) has deemed unacceptable. Each culture will have its own version of the shadow, but common shadow traits are violence and taboo sexual urges. The shadow can also include impoliteness, messiness, aggression, or, in some cultures, passivity. Eventually, for so many of us, the weight of the shadow can get very heavy. But, with conscious intention, we can do the work of listening to our shadow side and befriending it in a way that we can learn to hear its voice. According to author John Monbourquette, one way to identify our shadow is to see what we judge in others. We all project our shadow onto the world.

[*cont'd next page*]

A Comparative Look [continued]

When we can identify a trait that we judge, such as pride, we can try and find that quality in ourselves and see what we can learn from it. Over time, this process allows us to unpack that bag we have been carrying around and gain more energy and self-knowledge. Monbourquette quotes Carl Jung as saying, "It is not by looking into the light that we become luminous, but by plunging into the darkness."

Related Jewish Sources

Long before Kabbalah, Abraham was seen as a symbol of love. One *midrash* [a rabbinic interpretation of the Hebrew Bible] recounts that he would leave his tent open on both sides and would run to welcome anyone who passed by (Bereishit Rabbah 48:9). Another oral tradition says that Abraham was so intent on hosting others that he would never eat a meal alone. He would only eat if he was feeding someone else at the same time. As well, another *midrash* relays that during Abraham's life the world was like a building on fire. People had been passing by it for years but Abraham was the first one to stop and see what was happening and inquire if there was an owner. That is when God revealed himself to Abraham. As you can see, in Jewish tradition Abraham was seen as the embodiment of lovingkindness who helped bring *Ḥesed* into the world.

The event transpired to reveal wisdom, for he endured firmly—fittingly—and was not seduced.[F] He rose erect, returning to his domain..."the South," supernal rung to which he had been linked before...[G]

"Come and see the mystery of the matter: If Abram had not gone down to Egypt and been refined there first, he would not have become the share of the blessed Holy One.[H]"

F. This event not only left Abraham unscathed it actually "revealed wisdom" in the world. The process of encountering the Other Side bore fruits for Abraham and everyone else. **G. In the Zohar,** words and phrases from the Torah are often seen to represent elements of the spiritual realm. In this case "The South," the region in the south of Cana'an is code for *Ḥesed*. Abraham returned there, spiritually, after his descent. **H. Abraham was transformed** through his encounter with the demonic realm. If it had not been for his journey into that constricted place, he would not have been able to become God's servant in such a profound way. Encountering the Other Side is challenging and dangerous, but the fruits of this mission are beyond equal.

Comments

Another way of relaying this teaching is to say that a good mood is like a runway upon which insight and spiritual connection can land. In truth, spiritual moments can come to us at any time. In a real sense, though, they are beyond our control. We cannot force a spiritual moment. However, there are ways of being that make them more likely to come our way. Though the *Shekhinah* can land even on rocky terrain, a joyful mood is a much more inviting destination.

There is a story told about Gary Player who is widely regarded as one of the greatest golfers of all time. He was practicing hitting shots from a sand-bunker at a golf-course in Texas when someone came to watch. In Player's own words, "The first shot he saw me hit went in the hole. He said, 'You got 50 bucks if you knock the next one in.' I holed the next one. Then he says, 'You got $100 if you hole the next one.' In it went for three in a row. As he peeled off the bills he said, 'Boy, I've never seen anyone so lucky in my life.' And then I replied, 'Well, the harder I practice, the luckier I get.'" So too with spiritual practice. If we do the inner work we can never be sure that it will lead us into transformation or transcendence. However, the more we practice the luckier we get, and the more likely *Shekhinah* is to land if we build her a runway.

The Divine Presence does not dwell in a place of sorrow, but it does dwell in a place of joy.[A] If there is no delight there, the *Shekhinah* does not rest there. As it says, "Now, get me a musician. [And as the musician played the hand of God came upon him].[B]" The spirit of God was on him. This is the *Shekhinah*, and of course it does not rest in a place of sadness. How do we know this? From Jacob. When he was sad because [he was mourning] over Joseph, the *Shekhinah* removed herself from him. When joy came to him from the good news about Joseph [being alive], immediately "Their father Jacob's spirit was revived.[C]"

A. The Divine Presence, which is the *Shekhinah*, is the *Sephirah* that is closest to our physical world. It is said to "rest" or "dwell" in certain moments and places. When it is connected to us, blessing flows from the Divine world. According to this passage, human joy creates a context in which the *Shekhinah* can dwell. **B. 2 Kings 3:15.** In this section of the Bible, the prophet Elisha wishes to hear the voice of God so he calls on a musician to play for him. The "hand of God" descends upon him when the music plays, which an early rabbinic Aramaic translation renders as the "spirit of prophecy." The Zohar reads this as the *Shekhinah* resting with Elisha. In essence, the music brought the prophet to a state of joy which allowed him to hear God's voice and prophesize. **C. Genesis 45:27. Joseph's** brothers sold him into slavery and told Jacob, his father, that Joseph had died. Jacob was in a period of deep mourning for many years. When he heard that Joseph was still alive he regained his strength. The Aramaic translation is that the "spirit of prophecy," was returned to Jacob. Thus, the same language is used in these stories of Elisha and Jacob. On this verse, the authoritative medieval commentator Rashi writes that, at this moment, the *Shekhinah* rested with Jacob. The Zohar's read, backed up by traditional sources, is that in moments of joy we can connect with the Divine Presence.

There are a few levels of faith.[A] There is the faith of the head, above it is the faith of the heart, and as the Yesod HaAvodah wrote in the name of the *tzadik* Rabbi Leib of Dokar (a student of the Maggid of Mezeritch), "For [the distance] from the trust of the head to the trust of the heart is farther than the distance of the Heavens from the Earth.[B]" But there is another [even] higher level from them: the faith of the limbs. [This is] where trust in *YHWH* is imbued in one's bodily tissues.[C] As scripture says, "All my bones will say, '*YHWH*, who is like you?[D]'" In other words, all the organs and even the bones will feel that there is none besides God.

We observe that even a person whose faith is luminous, if a dangerous beast should jump him, he would still get very scared. The reason for this is because trust is not permeating his limbs. However, the one who has faith manifested, with roots all the way to the physical body, will not be afraid from anything.[E]

A. The word faith in Hebrew, *emunah*, can also be translated as "trust." Often, when we use the term "faith" in Western Culture, we think about believing or not believing that God exists or if the Bible or other sacred texts are true. In this teaching, like in many other Jewish sources, the term *emunah* is not about faith in God's existence but rather whether we trust in God's guidance in our lives. It is about believing that God is faithful and reliable. A way of saying this in contemporary terms is, "do we trust in the unfolding of reality, and that, even if it seems difficult, there is something valuable for us in every moment?" If so, we are connecting with *emunah*. In this translation, the words trust and faith are used interchangeably. **B. There are different** body-centers that correlate to different kinds of trust. We see from this quote that attaining the faith of the heart, where we can actually feel our trust, can be a very long journey. However, each type of trust is attainable through spiritual seeking and discipline. **C. The term "limbs"** can be used in place of "body-parts" or the body in general. To have faith of the limbs is to have a deeply ingrained trust in Reality itself from moment to moment. It is an embodied belief in God's guidance in our lives, each day and each hour. **D. Psalms 35:10. In** this biblical quote, the phrase "all my bones," is akin to saying "my whole being, even the essence of my body." In Hebrew, in fact, the word for bone, *etzem*, also means essence. The Slonimer's interpretation is that the trust has been developed to a point that it is felt even in one's bones. Even the most foundational parts of our body are aware, deeply, that everything comes from the Divine. **E. Even if we** are someone who has an extremely profound intellectual trust—a head-centered trust—we can be thrown off when something negative comes our way. This is an indication that our faith has not been fully integrated into the level of physicality. When it is embodied in such a deep way that it can be felt in the bones, this *emunah* of the limbs, this trust of the body, will give us the capacity to face what comes our way with openness.

Comments

See reflections on Arvei Naḥal text on page 26 in comments section about human perfection and imperfection.

About the Author

Rebbe Sholom Noah Berezovsky (1911–2000) is a modern day Hasidic Master who served as the Slonimer Rebbe from 1981 until his death. Born in Belarus, Berezovsky helped revive the Slonim Hasidic community in Jerusalem after the Holocaust. The Netivot Shalom is the collection of his teachings. Because of its profound spiritual insights, it has achieved wide readership within and beyond the Hasidic and Orthodox communities. It has also become popular because of its clarity and the fact that Berezovsky wrote it in Modern Hebrew. The Slonimer *Ḥasidim* are known, amongst other things, for their unique and complex wordless melodies [*nigunim*] that switch between musical keys, which they sing together on Shabbat and Holidays.

Comments

One of the teachings the Slonimer Rebbe is presenting is the difference between a theoretical and an experiential trust. A related schema that can be found elsewhere in Hasidic thought is a particular interpretation of the three *Sephirot* of *Ḥokhmah*, *Bina*, and *Da'at* [wisdom, discernment, and knowledge]. *Ḥokhmah* is seen as the spark of insight. This is that first flash of an idea that sometimes seems to miraculously dawn upon us. It can be a thought like, "kindness brings people together." This is a valuable insight, but left unexamined it will not be integrated more deeply into our being.

In the second stage, *Bina*, we do the work of discernment and consideration. We contemplate the idea, thinking of its different angles, we turn it over in our minds. In what ways am I kind? How much do I value togetherness? I am currently feeling upset, would I rather express my anger harshly or with compassion? We spend time with that first spark and through this process the fire grows inside of us. The third stage, *Da'at*, knowledge, is when we are united with the insight. That is to say, we do not just think it, we live it. Through the process of contemplating the idea that "kindness brings people together," we arrive at a place where kindness arises naturally from within us when we are wanting to build connection with others.

About the Author

Rebbe Zvi Hirsh of Nadvorna (1740–1802) was a Hasidic Rebbe in the third generation of Hasidism. A student of the Maggid of Mezeritch and some of the Maggid's students, he also taught the well-known Hasidic teachers Zvi Hirsch of Zydachov and Menaḥem Mendel of Kossov. Besides his collection of teachings, Tzemaḥ HaShem LeZvi, Zvi Hirsch wrote an alphabetized work of moral living called Alpha Beta which gained wide readership.

Comments

To receive is to give. When others want to be generous to us, assuming it is genuine, then it is a very kind act to accept their gifts. Whether it is a physical present, a compliment, or a place to stay, being a gracious recipient completes the circuit of that offering and allows love to flow. The same reciprocity happens when we give. To give is to receive. We can gain a tremendous amount of satisfaction by being kind, compassionate, and generous to others. In fact, it is one of the surest routes to feeling good.

"You shall eat and be sated, and bless YHWH your God[A]"

The analogy is that of a flowing spring. The more you draw from it (by priming the pump), the more strongly its waters flow and offer their blessing. Our sages referred to a "river that grows from its own shores.[B]" If you don't draw from it, it recedes into its own source. When Israel merit receiving the Divine flow and draw it forth from God, the Divine name itself is blessed.[C] "You shall draw water in joy from the wellsprings of salvation.[D]" Those wellsprings need to be saved! Their salvation comes about as you draw their water. Our eating and being sated is a commandment to act: "You shall eat and be sated." "And bless," a commandment to speak.[E]

A. **Deuteronomy 8:10. This** section of the book of Deuteronomy is where Moses is telling the Israelites that God is giving them good land to inhabit. After they eat and are satisfied they should bless God for the land they have been given. The Talmud interprets this to be a commandment to say a blessing after the meal (b. Berakhot 21a). As we shall see, Rabbi Zvi Hirsch sees multiple commandments in this verse. B. **b. Nedarim 40a.** This quote from the Talmud originally was asserting that a river does not increase from rain but rather from water that flows into it from its "shores," meaning tributaries. Our text is interpreting it to mean that if we, as people, draw from the river's banks that it actually increases the flow. C. **The meaning of** this analogy is that God wants us to enjoy the bounty that is being offered in our world. Our enjoyment of this blessing, whether it is spiritual or physical, actually brings pleasure to God, who created this world to give love to every creature. D. **Isaiah 12:3. This** verse is part of a prophecy for Israel to be redeemed from Babylon and brought back to its land. In its original context, it is saying that being delivered back home is like getting water from a wellspring. Our text flips this metaphor around saying that it is not us who need salvation but the wellspring, which is the channel for Divine flow. By enjoying the offerings which God brings us, we actually give blessing and goodness to God. In this view, Divine abundance is not static. It is responsive and appreciative—it gushes at our enjoyment. E. **Apropos what is** described in footnote A, the "commandment" that God gives us, then, is not just to bless God after we eat. According to the Tzemaḥ HaShem LeZvi, God commands us also to eat and be satisfied. In that way, partaking in the delights of this world allows sacred blessings to flow more freely.

About the Author

Rebbe Mordekhai Yoseph Leiner of Izbica, Ukraine (1800–1854) was the founder of the Ishbitza-Radzyn Hasidic dynasty. Known as the Ishbitzer Rebbe, his collection of teachings is recorded in the Mei HaShiloaḥ, a title which references a wellspring symbolizing God's help in Isaiah 8:6. The Ishbitzer's teachings were relatively unknown until the last fifty years in which they have gained popularity for their radical non-duality and daring interpretations.

"And why do you raise yourselves above the community of God?[A]"

Here, Koraḥ's claim was that there is no aggrandizing one Israelite over another because God is amongst them. That is to say, God abides in all of them equally.[B] This is described in a *midrash*, "In the future the Holy Blessed One will make a round dance of the righteous.[C]" A round dance is in a circle where nobody is closer [to God] than anyone else.[D]

Koraḥ was claiming that it is like that right now. But, King Solomon said about this, "A wise king sifts the wicked and places the wheel over them.[E]" That is to say, through the coronal and the crown he gave them, that is the crown of the Levites, through which he gave exalted status.[F]

Concerning this, "He placed a wheel upon them." That is, God answers[G] them, "Why, when I granted you a higher status, did you not argue that it is not right to aggrandize one person over another?[H]"

A. **Numbers 16:3 This** verse is from a section of the Torah where Koraḥ, from the tribe of Levi, along with others, is challenging the authority of Moses and Aaron. In its original context, this dispute may have been specifically about the status of priests vis-a-vis Levites and other Israelites. B. **The Mei HaShiloaḥ** sees Koraḥ's dispute as a claim against hierarchy in general. God is within each Israelite equally. Moses and Aaron should not be any higher up than the others. C. **b. Ta'anit 31a.** The Talmud recounts that in the World to Come the righteous will dance around The Holy Blessed One in the Garden of Eden. They will all point at God and declare that This is the One upon whom they waited for redemption, quoting Isaiah 25:9. D. **A *maḥol* can** be translated as "dance," but is related to the word *ḥul* which means circle. The image in the *midrash* cited in footnote C is of God being in the middle of the dancers as they encircle Divinity with their movement. The Ishbitzer is saying that Koraḥ's message that we all should be equal is reflective of a time yet to come. In a perfected world, we will all be equal and there will be no more hierarchy. In a sense, his message was correct but the world was not ready for it. In another sense, as we shall see, Koraḥ was being hypocritical. E. **Proverbs 20:26. This** verse, in its original context, alludes to the process of cracking the husks of wheat with a heavy mill wheel and then using the wind to separate the unneeded chaff from the good grain. Proverbs compares this to how a wise king deals with bad people. They are like the chaff that gets blown away. The book of Proverbs is traditionally ascribed to King Solomon.

Comments

See reflections on Arvei Naḥal text on page 26 in comments section about human perfection and imperfection.

F. **Here, the Mei** HaShiloaḥ interprets the verse from Proverbs through a play on words with the word *mezareh*, which means "sift" but is similar to the word *zar*, which means crown. He points out that, although Koraḥ was arguing for the end to hierarchy, he was a Levite, which was a higher caste in their society than an Israelite. G. **The word for** "placed" in Hebrew, *vayashev*, is etymologically related to the word *meshiv*, which means answers. The Ishbitzer interprets the second part of the verse with another play on words to mean that God answered Koraḥ and those with him by highlighting their Levite status. H. **In this reading,** God responds to the rebels and crushes their rebellion, like with the the wheat mill, by showing them that their call for equality is not so pure. Koraḥ and his fellow rebels were not living examples of the change they wished to create. In the end, they did not succeed.

Comments

The story of Koraḥ (see explanation of text) is often interpreted as being about an anti-God and anti-Moses rebellion by a wicked group. What is interesting about this reading is that the Ishbitzer is saying that, in reality, Koraḥ's claim is what we should all be aspiring to. In the future world, when everything is perfected, the structures of hierarchy will pass. Rav Kook articulates this in his poem "From a Distant World" by saying that everyone will have so much love in their hearts that we will not need top-down leadership to keep the order. When it comes to decisions, as we see from the round dance, we will be as in a circle, with God resting between us. The two key parts of this teaching, though, are that (1) Koraḥ was not the right person to bring it, and that (2) it was not the right time. We need to really be examples of change we are bringing. It can be tempting to want to jump to an ideal solution but if we want that to be real and if others are going to trust in it, we need to be living it. Also, if we are going to be able to reach this place, this utopian vision of the world, where we can exist on Earth together in beauty and equality, we will need to evolve there in a harmonious way. It is not about jumping to the absolute, it is about the step-by-step work that allows us to be integrated. That is true in the outer world as well as our inner lives. For example, we might have an aspiration to feel deeply connected to God at all moments. But, what is our situation right now, and how do we work with that in a way that is authentic and connected without bypassing our current stage? Similarly, we all want harmony in the world, but what is the best way to get there? What is our next step in that goal? FInding thoughtful and realistic pathways to societal change can help us grow more naturally towards the beautiful world we are all yearning for.

In truth, the quality of Abraham our father, peace be upon him, is the attribute of lovingkindness in its proper place.[A] The world of love is a clear world. Thought cannot comprehend the nature of its dimensions and goodness at all...[B] Indeed, he directed the fullness of his stature to serve the Creator with great love until his whole body was made a chariot for the qualities of love. He made His Godliness and the dissemination of this quality in the mouths of humans commonplace.[C] According to the Sages, [Abraham said to God] "In the past God was called God of the Heavens, and now I have habituated your name in the mouths of humans and [therefore] God is called God of the Earth.[D]" In other words, Abraham showed every human being that the [Divine] attributes of lovingkindness extend even into physicality.

About the Author

Ze'ev Wolf of Zhitomir (d. 1797) was a Hasidic teacher and a senior figure in the circle of the Maggid of Mezeritch. His book, Or HaMeir, contains a wealth of collected teachings from early Hasidic masters. Highly critical of pretend-piety, he brought a strong mystical voice and advocated for the spread of Hasidism in a more elitist manner than many of his contemporaries.

A Comparative Look

Being a Chariot

In *Mama Lola: A Vodou Priestess in Brooklyn,* Anthropologist Karen McCarthy Brown describes Hatian Vodou ceremonies in which the priest or priestess channels a spirit. The spirits are said to "ride" the leaders of the ceremony and, through them, speak to the people there. There are several different spirits who are channeled in *Mama Lola*, each with a distinct personality. By way of comparison, different characters in the Torah are said to be chariots for different Divine Qualities, but usually with more free will intact than the Vodou example. In our text, Abraham channeled *Ḥesed* and did great acts of kindness and love in the world through his connection with Sacred Lovingkindness.

Perceiving The World of Love

The Kedumah Experience by Zvi Ish-Shalom describes a dimension where everything is love. Contact with that reality allows us to realize that we and everything else in existence are loved unconditionally. The contemporary mystic Eckhart Tolle describes the moment of his spiritual awakening in *The Power of Now*. "The first light of dawn was filtering through the curtains. Without any thought, I felt, I knew, that there is infinitely more to light than we realize. That soft luminosity filtering through the curtains was love itself."

A. In Kabbalah Abraham is often associated with the *Sephirah* of *Ḥesed*, [lovingkindness]. There is a difference between lovingkindness as a quality that is manifested in the world and *Ḥesed* as it is "in its proper place," which is what *Ḥesed* looks like before it appears in our world. **B. Before it incarnates,** *Ḥesed* is the "world of love," or the "dimension of love." Abraham labored to allow this dimension, intangible and beyond conception, to be reachable in our world. The world of love, without a bridge, is unreachable to most people. **C. Abraham was a** chariot for lovingkindness. This means that he refined himself to a point where *Ḥesed* joined with his body as a doorway into our world. Like a charioteer rides a chariot to the desired destination, *Ḥesed* rode Abraham into physical reality. He became the embodiment of lovingkindness and brought the world of love into being as the quality of *Ḥesed*. **D. Breishit Rabbah 59:7.** This interpretation from a midrash is describing how Abraham brought the reality of God into the world. The midrash itself does not relate to the *Sephirah* of *Ḥesed* or the world of *Ḥesed* (as it predated Kabbalah) but it describes Abraham's role which, in the early rabbinic mindset, was to bring awareness of God to the planet. The Or HaMeir interprets this *midrash* to mean that Abraham brought *Ḥesed* from the "Heavens," i.e. the spiritual realm, to the "Earth," the physical realm. The Divine energy of love emerged in our world and God became the "God of Earth" through lovingkindness manifest.

Why did the Blessed Holy One dress up the brilliant light of Torah in stories, until it became something like tales one person would tell another? I have commented on the verse, "*YHWH* spoke to Moses face to face, like one [person] would speak to another.[A]" This means that God garbed the powerful light of Torah in "face" after "face."

There are in fact seventy "faces of Torah.[B]"

In its original state [The Torah] was just a clear light, comprising holy names, all of them none other than the single blessed name *YHWH*. That is why Torah is refferred to as "the keepings [*pekudei*] of *YHWH*,[C]" because all the teachings and narratives are really kept and hidden within that single name. But God dressed them up in face after face, so that they now appear to be the sort of tales one person would tell another. But, in truth, the opening of her[D] words would shine a brilliant light[E]...

Sometimes a marvelous bit of wisdom falls into an intelligent person's mind, something that contains a real insight into understanding God. But when you try to share that thought with another person, you are unable to reveal the wisdom that lies buried deep within your own heart. It would just be too subtle for them to understand. You therefore have to dress it up as a comment on a biblical verse or some saying of the sages. For this purpose one can employ any of the four ways of reading Scripture: the obvious, the allegorical, the homiletical, or the esoteric. Those people in any case will not be able to grasp the depth of your thoughts, however they are garbed. They therefore pay attention only to the garments themselves. "How well this one preaches! How nicely this one speaks!" They are just too unaware to pay attention to that wonderful inner wisdom and the good counsel for serving God that they could be finding in multiple levels of his preaching.[F]

A. Exodus 33:11. This verse is describing the way that God spoke to Moses, "as a man would speak to his friend." It denotes an intimacy which no other character has with God in the Torah. **B. BeMidbar Rabbah 13:16.** There is a teaching from the early rabbinic tradition that the Torah has 70 faces, or 70 facets. That is to say, there are many different ways to interpret the Torah. The Or HaMeir offers a different interpretation to the metaphor of the seventy and connects it with the verse from Exodus, which also uses the word "face." Instead of seeing the faces as different perspectives, he sees them as different layers, different depths. **C. Psalms 19:9. This** verse in Psalms also translates as the "precepts" or "statutes" of *YHWH*, and is written in the context of praising the Torah. The Or HaMeir interprets that term, which also means "keepings," to be alluding to the reality of the unity of God, as represented in the name *YHWH*, which contains all the other elements that emanate from it. **D. Each noun has** a gender in Hebrew. The word "Torah" is feminine and this translation stays true to that. **E. All the stories** of the Torah are really allegories to deep mystical truths. If we had the ability to "open" the words, meaning to see their underlying meaning, we would glimpse the Divine luminosity they are concealing. **F. We can see** the frustration of the Or HaMeir here. He is comparing a Rebbe to God and the Torah, but in the process he is communicating the difficulty of teaching mysticism. In his generation he was known as someone who did not want to water down Hasidic spirituality for the sake of popular appeal. He emphasized having a core group of strong students instead. It seems, from this description, that he found it aggravating when people would lose the spiritual message amidst the metaphor.

Related Jewish Sources

The Zohar (3:152a) speaks of the true nature of Torah:

Woe to the human being who says that Torah presents mere stories and ordinary words! If so, we could compose a Torah right now with ordinary words and better than all of them! To present matters of the world? Even rulers of the world possess words more sublime. If so, let us follow them and make a Torah out of them! Ah, but all the words of Torah are sublime words, sublime secrets!... So this story of Torah is the garment of Torah... This body is clothed in garments: the stories of this world. Fools of the world look only at the garment, the story of Torah; they know nothing more. They do not look at what is under that garment. Those who know more do not look at the garment but rather at the body under that garment. The wise ones, servants of the King on high, those who stood at Mount Sinai, look only at the soul, root of all, real Torah!

Practice

It is not uncommon for spiritual seekers to experience difficulty communicating their inner realizations to to others. Using this text as a model, you can harness the age-old method of storytelling and metaphor to build on your ability to communicate deep lessons.

First, ask yourself which part of your inner world you wish to share with others. This can be a belief, thought, spiritual moment, intuition, etc.

Second, think of an image, narrative, or other symbol that can represent your inner knowledge. Take some time to really plan it out. Write it down or draw it.

Finally, share it with a person or group you trust.

How did they receive it? Was the metaphor helpful? Do you need to adjust it in any way? You can recreate it and improve it based on their reactions.

Repeat this process with other aspects of your spiritual life and develop your teaching repertoire.

COMMENTS

Though it may be frustrating for a teacher sometimes, communicating through stories and metaphors can actually be a great kindness, and in more ways than one! First of all, parables have been, from time immemorial, excellent ways to relay ideas. For many students, this is the easiest access route to learning. Secondly, when teaching mystical material in particular, whether through texts or practices, overwhelming students can turn them off from the teachings or even be harmful. God does us a great kindness, says the Hasidic mystic the Meor Einayim, by keeping Divine light hidden in the world (Toldot 2). If it were to be revealed to us all at once we could not bear it. Having mediated access to this esoteric wisdom is the best way to access it and enable us to, step-by-step, meet it more directly.

Our Holy Torah herself is in the same situation. Her words as open in their own setting indeed shine a high and lofty light, but one so subtle that "thought cannot grasp it at all.[G]" But when the time came for the [ten] words [or "commandments"] to be revealed in the holy event at Sinai, they had to be garbed in the outer meanings and narrative tales of Torah[H]...

G. Tikunei Zohar 17a. This quote is originally said about God, meaning that the Master of Worlds is beyond all comprehension. In Kabbalah, and later in Hasidism, the Torah and God are sometimes seen as one and the same. That is to say, the essence of Torah and God are the same, not the literal scroll, or book, or stories. Just like the spiritual teacher, the essential Torah has a lot of work to do in order to communicate her deepest secrets. That is why the Torah contains stories and laws; it is an effort to metaphorically communicate deep mystical truths to those who could not access them directly. **H. The revelation at** Mount Sinai, which was the receiving of the Ten Commandments and, according to rabbinic tradition, the whole Torah, had to be done in a way that people could relate to. That is how the ineffable Torah came to be revealed in words.

Book: Pardes Rimonim Section: 22:2

ABOUT THE AUTHOR

Rabbi Moshe Cordovero (1520–1570) was an outstanding Kabbalist who lived in Tzfat, *Eretz Yisrael*. He wrote and taught in the most influential location for Kabbalah of his era and was a student of and teacher to many other historically significant rabbis. It is unknown where he was born but, based on his last name, he had Spanish roots. The book Pardes Rimonim, featured here, was Cordovero's effort to synthesize and systematize the diverse strands of Kabbalah that came before him, which he saw as coming from the same source. He completed this epic project at the young age of 27. He would go on to write other important works, including a complete commentary on the Zohar.

What does it mean when the Torah refers to [God's having] a hand or a foot or an eye, and so forth? Know and trust that all of these point at and attest to some great truth.[A] Nevertheless, not everyone can attain the essential truth of such matters.[B]

Even though we are indeed made in the image and likeness [of *YHWH*], do not think that [our human] eye is truly in the likeness of [the Divine] Eye, nor our hand in the form of the true Hand, nor our foot in the form of the true Foot. These are subtle things, deeply subtle, the source from which the flow [of Divine energy] goes forth to all existence.[C] But the essence of the Hand is not like that of the [human] hand. It is not like it in form, as was written, "To who will you liken Me, that I be equal?[D]"

A. The Torah, in many places, uses physical characteristics to describe God. At the time that it was written, many people in that region conceived of gods as having actual bodies. However, as Judaism continued to evolve and its theology changed, many commentators tried to find ways of reinterpreting these Divine appendages. Maimonides, a highly prolific and influential 12th century rabbi, argued that all of these human-like descriptions of God are metaphorical and fall short of the truly ungraspable nature of the reality of the One. In our text from four centuries later, Moshe Cordovero takes a different approach. **B. Not everyone can** realize what is meant by God's body parts. This knowledge is not easily accessible. It is esoteric, which means it is understood by a select few. **C. Cordovero is distinguishing** his view from that of Maimonides. God does indeed have a body, but it is not truly similar to the human body. It is so foundational to reality, that *shefa*, the flow of blessing that nourishes the world, originates from its appendages. **D. Isaiah 40:25. This** verse from the Hebrew Bible originally meant that God is beyond comparison on the physical earth. Here, Cordovero is using it to differentiate specifically between the body of God and body of humans. As he says, "The essence of the Hand is not like that of the [human] hand."

Know and understand that there is no likeness between God and us from the perspective of essence and form. The forms of our limbs are made in symbolic likeness to the inner Eye, [referring to] supremely concealed things, which the mind cannot know. This is rather [a case of] symbolic allusion.[E] Similarly, when one writes "Reuben ben Ya'akov," these letters are not the essential form of Reuben ben Yaakov, meaning his actual image, and shape, and essence. They are rather a recalling, [stating] that this is Reuben ben Ya'akov, a symbol, distinguished from the essence of that [actual] form called "Reuben ben Ya'akov.[F]" Because God wanted to bless us, He created many hidden limbs in the body of man, in symbolic allusion to the Realm of the Chariot [*Ma'aseh HaMerkavah*, i.e. the *Sephirot*].[G] If a person merits to purify one of his limbs, that limb will [come to] be in the likeness of the Throne, that inner supernal thing that is called by this name. If it is an eye, an Eye: if a hand, a Hand: if a leg, a Leg, and so forth.[H] How? Such a person must be guarded and careful with the sight of his eyes, that he not look at nakedness, nor at any other obscene thing, but at everything that is a sanctification of *YHWH* and His service.[I] Then that eye will become like a Throne for that thing that is called above an Eye, a Hand, a Foot, and so forth.

E. If Maimonedes believed that God's body is a metaphor based on human bodies, then Cordovero is stating the opposite: our body-parts are metaphors for True Reality. God does, in fact, have a body, but it is so far beyond our ordinary understanding that we cannot grasp it. We can know a hint of God's nature, however, through our own physicality. **F. Just like writing** somebody's name is a way of representing that person, so too are our bodies a symbolic allusion to the Divine body-parts. They do not share the same essence but they point to that reality. **G. Beyond the readily** accessible physicality of each part of our bodies is an underlying subtle manifestation. Each part of our physical selves corresponds to part of the Tree of Life, the Divine body. Cordovero refers to this as the Realm of the Chariot, which a reference to an earlier system of Jewish mysticism which originates at the beginning of the first millennium CE. At that time, the practitioners of Merkavah [chariot] mysticism did not work with the doctrine of the *Sephirot*. However, Cordovero viewed Jewish mysticism as one continuum and uses a term from that era. **H. If a person** manages to tap into the subtle potential of each body part then it will become like a seat for that *Sephirah*. The Divine quality associated with it will rest there. For example, the right hand is associated with *Hesed* [Lovingkindness] and the left hand with *Gevurah* [Power]. **I. The practice, according** to Cordovero, to become a throne for the *Sephirot* is to use our bodies for sanctified purposes. The hands, according to this teaching, should be used for holy and kind acts and not for doing anything immoral or anything that takes people away from their relationship with God.

A Comparative Look

The idea that different parts of our body correlate with spiritual qualities is found amongst several traditions including Hinduism. In its most well-known version in the West, there are chakras, or energy centers, that are found in the central axis of the body between the bottom of the pelvis and the crown of the head. Practitioners work with these energy centers to awaken different inner potentials in their journey towards liberation.

In the Kedumah system, a new spiritual path that draws heavily on Jewish mysticism, practitioners tune into the body in order to connect with their mental and emotional states, and ultimately into more subtle realities. Kedumah teachings point to the Divine qualities that can be encountered along the journey and felt experientially in the body.

Reflection

Cordovero's method of connecting to Deep Reality through the body is by using our physicality for holy purposes. The example he gives is not to look at nakedness or obscenity in order to purify our eyes. In this information age, many of us encounter a great deal of content every day or even every second. It is beneficial to consider what we take in through our senses and if that information is good for us to be exposed to. Be it the steady cycle of news, discussion boards, or pornography, we can consider Cordovero's teaching more deeply and ask how we can orient our bodies towards the good and the holy. Consider these questions:

1. Are there elements of your online life that you know are not beneficial for you to engage in? If so, what are they?
2. Have you had the experience of taking a break from these? If so, what were the results? If not, try taking one week off from a type of information you could do without and record the results.

Being mindful of what we expose ourselves to is part of the Jewish way of being more conscious and awake.

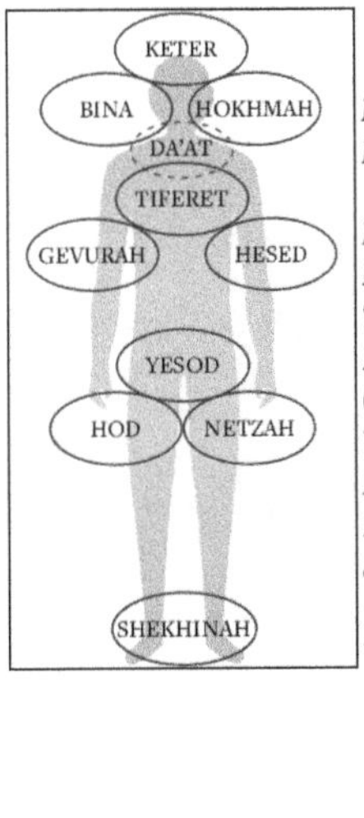

Keter: Crown of Head
Hokhmah: Right Hemisphere of Brain
Bina: Left Hemisphere of Brain
Da'at: Throat
Tiferet: Heart
Hesed: Right Arm
Gevurah: Left Arm
Yesod: Genitalia
Netzah: Right Leg
Hod: Left Leg
Shekhinah: Feet

Figure 5. *Sephirot* Aligned with Body Parts

Another reason [why the Infinite is called the Infinite] is because inquiry into It has no end. It is not like other paths of investigation that have a conclusion or agreement on a final result.[A] Indeed, the inquiry into Divinity is endless. That means there is nobody who knows Its essence at all except by means of the *Sephirot* which manifest [only] a part of Its greatness.[B] In fact, [from the realm of the] *Sephirot* and beyond there is no understanding [possible], due to the depth of the subject [one seeks to] attain.[C] That is why the Infinite is described as Infinite.

A. **This teaching is** referring to a layer of reality that goes beyond the *Sephirot. Ein Sof* is the Infinite, and it is the Ultimate Reality that exists before even the spiritual world. The Infinite is called as such partly because it is impossible to understand it in its totality. The journey is never-ending, so to speak, when a mystic makes contact with the Infinite. This perspective is in alignment with the common view many Jewish mystics hold that the spiritual journey has no end.

B. **The world of** the *Sephirot* is part of the spiritual world, but is a middle dimension between the physical world and the Infinite. Through the *Sephirot*, the profundity of *Ein Sof* can be partially grasped.

C. **In fact, compared** to comprehension of ideas, both the *Sephirot* and the Infinite are beyond are grasp. There are three levels of understanding being articulated here. There is common understanding, like understanding a math problem. Then there is *Sephirot*ic understanding which has more of an indescribable quality than the material world, but which can still shed light on the reality of the spiritual world. Lastly, there is understanding of the Infinite which can never be grasped as a concept.

Comments

A Native American teacher of mine refers to God as "The Sacred Mystery." In that sense, God is truly beyond our grasp. In Buddhist philosophy, states of realization that are beyond the intellect are known as "non-conceptual." That is to say, the mind cannot comprehend them intellectually. The Jewish term for that is *lemala meta'am veda'at*, which means beyond reason and knowledge. We can never fully understand the Infinite.

In the book of Genesis it says that Adam, the first human, was created in God's image (1:27). That means that we are also sacred mysteries. Rabbi David Ingber points out that we might think we know ourselves or someone else, but there is always more to know, and people always have the potential to change. When we meet new people, it is valuable to keep this in mind, because it is tempting to put people into categories. "I don't know" is a good attitude to have when being introduced to someone, welcoming strangers, remeeting people after having a falling-out, or when engaging with others in general.

When God speaks to Moses for the first time at the burning bush in Exodus, God uses the name "I will be as I will be." In that conversation, Moses is reluctant to be God's messenger and feels that he might not be believed or that he is not articulate enough. The use of that specific Divine name is a hint to Moses and the reader that, just as God is continually unfolding in the world and beyond our comprehension, that we too have the capacity to overcome past habits and tendencies, and to embrace our inner *tzadik* and hero. As it so happens, the name "I will be as I will be" is associated with the *Sephirah* of *Keter*, which is said to be "half-embedded in the Infinite" and is the most removed from reason and knowledge of all the *Sephirot*.

Elijah[A] began, saying, "Master of Worlds, you are one, and not in a sequence.[B] You are higher than the highest, more concealed than the concealed, thought cannot grasp you at all.[C]

You are the one who emanated ten adornments which we call *Sephirot*, through which to conduct the hidden worlds not revealed, and the manifested worlds.[D] Within them, you concealed yourself from humanity.[E]

You are the One that connects and unites them.[F] Since you are within [them], if someone separates one from the other ten, it is equivalent to dividing You up.[G]"

A. This book, like the Zohar, is set in the early Rabbinic period as a conversation between rabbis from that era. Here, the prophet Elijah is speaking to God in front of the group. Since ancient times, some Jewish teachers have recorded encounters with the Biblical-era prophet who was believed to never have died. Elijah is often a source of secret wisdom in these texts. **B. God is one,** unified. That means that God cannot be divided into parts. As well, God is not in a sequence, meaning that God is the sort of One after which there can be no "two," because God is all-inclusive. **C. God exists beyond** that which can be understood by thought. It is impossible to comprehend Divinity by using our intellect. **D. Deep Reality manifests** through the *Sephirot*, which act as intermediaries between the Divine and the rest of existence, which includes both the spiritual and physical worlds. **E. Through the *Sephirot*,** human beings can get a glimpse of the Infinite. Just as Spirit comes into our world through them, so too can we gain access to that Holy Source by means of these rungs. **F. The Infinite manifests** the *Sephirot* but is not really separate from them. Neither are they, ultimately, separate from one another. **G. If someone were** to try and make one of these *Sephirot* separate from the others, perhaps to call it an independent spiritual power, that would be the equivalent of saying the God is not one. The *Sephirot*, in this system, remain as united as the Infinite. They are not independent of God nor of one another. The truth remains that there is only one indivisible Ultimate Reality.

About the Author

This text was written by an anonymous Kabbalist in the 14th century CE. In the Middle Ages it was considered part of the Zohar, the magnum opus of 13th century Kabbalah. However, academic scholarship has shown it to be a later work that was subsequently added to that text. The Tikkunei Zohar consists of 70 sermons interpreting the first word of the Torah, *breishit*, which in English is rendered, "In the beginning." This book was revered by many later Jewish mystics, including the Hasidic masters. Rebbe Naḥman of Bratslav is cited as saying that "A thousand books would not be enough to illuminate the secrets contained in the Tikunei Zohar."

A Comparative Look

Although Judaism is often considered a purely monotheistic tradition, certain elements of Kabbalah are not so cut and dry. Kabbalah developed, beginning in the 12th century, after Maimonides' rational theology had become very influential. His view of the Divine was that God was completely beyond categorization and description, and that any comparison between our world and God was a metaphor that was bound to fall short. Unfortunately, this left many people feeling too distant to the Divine. The kabbalistic system offered both an Ultimate Reality that was indescribable, called the Infinite, and many intermediary spiritual manifestations that could be accessed, known as the *Sephirot*. In having one foundational reality and ten emanations that were also heavenly powers, the Kabbalists stepped into a realm that bordered on henotheism, which is a belief that there are many gods (or heavenly powers) who are emanations of one Ultimate Reality. This was tricky territory for Kabbalists living in a monotheistic culture. The last line of this text makes sure to differentiate between independent Divine powers and Divine powers united in the One. This is the key difference between polytheism and henotheism as well. In the Hindu system, there are many gods. However, for many Hindus there is a sense that all the gods are manifestations of the Ultimate. For those who worship Shiva, for example, all the gods are seen as manifestations of His essence. Similarly, in the Bhagavad Gita (11:15), the warrior Arjuna sees a vision of the God Krishna with other Gods, demigods, and other Divine beings within His body. Kabbalah and Hindu theology are certainly distinct from one another, but we can see a similarity in how they differentiate between the Ultimate, the spiritual world, and the physical world, and see all of them as being united in One reality.

Comprehension refers to and depends on matters of wisdom and mind. That is to say that it is [either] possible to grasp the idea or it is impossible to grasp it because of its depth.[A] But [regarding] the Holy Blessed One, who is beyond intellect and wisdom, it is not at all fitting to say about Him that it is impossible to understand Him because of the profundity of the idea. [That is] because He is not in the category of comprehension at all![B]

One who says about God that it is impossible to conceive of Him, he is like one who says about a sublime or deep idea that it is impossible to touch it with the hands because of its sophistication!

Everyone who hears will laugh at him, because the sense of touch only applies to physical things that can be seized by the hands.[C]

This is precisely how intellect and understanding are thought of with regards to the Blessed Holy One, like a physical action.[D]

A. If we are talking about things that can be understood intellectually or conceptually, we can say that if they are not grasped it is because they are really deep and difficult.

B. If we are talking about the Infinite, however, it is not fair to say that it is too deep to be understood by the mind. In fact, Divinity is something that is so refined, it is not in the realm of the conceptual whatsoever. It is beyond all reason and understanding.

C. The Alter Rebbe is saying that, in fact, people would not talk about grasping an idea with their hand because that would not make sense. Ideas are not physical, they are conceptual. In the same way, talking about understanding something non-conceptual does not make sense either. You cannot use the intellect, a powerful but limited vehicle, to comprehend something that is beyond all conception.

D. The Infinite is beyond intellectual comprehension just like thought is beyond physicality.

About the Author

Rebbe Schneur Zalman of Lyady (1745–1813) was the founder of the Chabad Hasidic dynasty. He excelled in the study of Torah from a young age and eventually became a disciple of the Maggid of Mezeritch. He played a very significant role in spreading early Hasidism to Belorussia. A multi-talented individual, the *Alter Rebbe* [old rabbi], as he is known, composed melodies, wrote highly influential legal volumes, and articulated the most systematized version of Hasidic philosophy to date in his book The Tanya.

Comments

While this teaching does not say it explicitly, there must be some method of gaining knowledge of the Infinite that is not through the intellect. A way that is very commonly spoken about in mystical circles, including early Hasidism, is through direct encounter, through what can be called a mystical or spiritual experience. This is a moment or series of moments where we have a feeling or perception that goes beyond the mind. We might touch in on it for an instant or in some cases much longer. It can be alone or in a group. In either case, it is something that is very difficult to communicate in words, especially to those who have not had that same encounter. A common way this can be perceived is as a feeling of bliss that comes while in meditation or prayer. We can have a realization of the beauty in the world and an insight that comes with that. The mystical path of experience is ineffable, beyond words and also beyond concept. There are many roads towards those types of encounters. There can be a more mind-based pathway, such as Torah study, which explores profound ideas and learning as a spiritual practice. Through the mind we can ascend beyond normal conceptual understandings. The experiential route could also be through emotions, by refining our inner affect to experience the bliss of God or transcendent love. As well, we can journey through the path of embodiment wherein a person uses their physical sensations as an anchor as they explore consciousness. In these different paths, the vehicle—mind, heart, or body—can gradually be transformed into a conduit that can receive Divine energy and insights. It might take time to find what's right for us, but each person will have a pathway or combination of methods that is most aligned with who they are.

It says in the Zohar, "What is Shabbat? [It is the] name of the Holy Blessed One who is perfect from every side.[A]" Because He is whole in every possible way, of course there is nothing lacking with [Shabbat].

One does work because there is a need. Without [work] there would be a lack, so one completes what is missing through it. So truly, [on] Shabbat, which is complete in every way and does not lack anything, one does not need work to fill any lack.[B] And that is why our Sages said that [on Shabbat], "In your eyes, it should be as though all of your work is done and nothing is lacking.[C]" On Shabbat, His Blessed Godliness expands and reveals Itself amongst the Children of Israel[D]—and it is complete on all sides, in every possible sense. If someone indicates otherwise, God forbid, he shows that he is not of that community, and that [Divine] infusion is not within him.[E]

A. Zohar 2:88b. In the Zohar, this statement reflects how the Sabbath and its three traditional meals include all of the *Sephirot*. The Friday night meal corresponds with the top *Sephirah* of *Keter*, Saturday lunch with the middle levels of *Ḥokhmah* through *Yesod*, and the small Saturday later-afternoon meal with the lowest *Sephirah Shekhinah*/ *Malkhut*. Since Shabbat is a consummation of the whole *Sephirot*ic world, it is itself a Divine name. In this passage, the Chernobyler highlights the perfection of Shabbat and, in an emblematic Hasidic turn, talks about inner completeness and what it means to be spiritually whole on Shabbat. **B. This is an** essential message of Shabbat. We work during the week with an attitude that the world is incomplete. But, on the Sabbath, we step into a sacred time where there is nothing lacking. Everything is as it should be and we do not need to add anything to our world to make it better. **C. Mekhilta, Yitro. This** quote is from a *midrash* from the 1st to 2nd century CE. It is reflecting on the verse in the Torah that says, "Six days you shall work" (Exodus 20:9). The *midrash* asks if it is possible to do all of one's work in six days. It answers by saying one should rest on Shabbat as though all of the work is completed. The Chernobyler quotes the *midrash* in a way that is true to its original meaning. **D. The Children of** Israel here refers to the Jewish people. The name Israel itself is first found in Genesis 32:29 and is ascribed the meaning "One who wrestles with God." Contemporary Jewish authors such as Rabbi Arthur Green use this sense of the word to interpret Children of Israel/Israelites to include any people who are actively contending with the Divine. In other words, spiritual seekers of any background can be called Israel. In the context of this teaching, people who are aligning with Shabbat can experience the expansion of the Infinite within them when those times of rest arrive. **E. Through the mystical** lens of this text, on Shabbat, the awareness of God, and thus completeness, is awakened. If someone acts as though the world is not complete on that day, then that person is showing that the realization of Divinity is not alive within them.

About the Author

Rebbe Menaḥem Naḥum ben Zvi of Chernobyl (1730–1787), also known as the Chernobyler, was a student of the Ba'al Shem Tov and the Maggid of Mezeritch. He was well-educated in the renowned yeshivas of Lithuania and was influenced by the Kabbalah that preceded him. The Meor Einayim [lit. Illumination of the Eyes] is a collection of his teachings compiled by his students and published in 1798. It is a classic of early Hasidism.

A Comparative Look

Matthew Fox is a contemporary Christian Mystic who teaches a path he calls Creation Spirituality. One of the foundational teachings of Creation Spirituality is drawn from the medieval German Catholic mystic Meister Eckhart.

Eckhart wrote about four pathways, or *vias*. The first two, *via positiva* and *via negativa*, speak to the dynamic between Shabbat and the rest of the week according to our text. The *via positiva* practices aim to evoke positive spiritual states directly. They are things like singing joyous songs, expressing gratitude, and using breathing and body movements to center and calm ourselves. *Via negativa* practices go into negative feelings in order to be with suffering and ultimately come to understand it more deeply and allow it to transform. These are practices like sitting with difficult emotions, making heart-felt requests in prayer, and reflecting on our missteps in life. Within this framework, the Meor Einayim's teaching is saying that Shabbat is a *via positiva* day and the rest of the week is where we can have more *via negativa*. On Shabbat we embrace all that is good and holy in the world and during the rest of the week we try to improve ourselves and our surroundings so we can, in the long-term, be in a world that is more wonderful any day of the week.

[*cont'd next page*]

A Comparative Look [continued]

Relatedly, the philosopher Ken Wilber talks about the difference between a spiritual state and a spiritual stage. A spiritual state is where we experience the world in a new way, like a mystical experience. After we touch into that awareness, we return to our ordinary reality. A stage, on the other hand, is the form of consciousness through which we normally encounter the world. We can do work that increases the frequency of states, and we can do work that gradually raises our spiritual stage. Sometimes these practices overlap and sometimes they do not. In light of this teaching from the Chernobyler, the week is when we do the work of growing in our spiritual stage. On Shabbat, we have the intention to enter a state in which everything is good just as it is for one day. To help us attain that, tradition teaches that on Shabbat we should eat our best food, rest more than usual, have sex with our partner, and generally partake in other *via positiva* practices.

In actuality, it is not just everyday work that is prohibited on Shabbat, but even the work of the Tabernacle. That is to say, the Tabernacle that is described in Exodus, "And I will dwell within the Children of Israel.[F]" The Holy Blessed one dwells within the Children of Israel and a person needs to be a [human] sanctuary to God.[G] If he is not pure from the filth of his transgressions[H] and is [therefore] preventing himself from being permeated with God's presence, on Shabbat he should remove this matter from his heart, so he will not be saddened by it. He should instead keep Shabbat according to its customs, and rejoice in God before whom he is a great pleasure and joy! We find that even the work of the Tabernacle, when one does something in order to become a [human] sanctuary, even that is excluded from Shabbat.[I]

F. Exodus 29:45. In the Torah, the Tabernacle is a portable temple. When it is built and used correctly, God says that He will dwell there, amidst the camp of the Israelites as they travel. **G. Here, the Meor** Einayim is saying that human beings are like Tabernacles. God dwells in each of us if we create the proper container within. When we are aligned within, in the right way to contain the Divine presence, God can dwell within us. **H. The Chernobyler's view** is that the soul becomes obscured through misdeeds. If a person's inner essence is too obscured then the light of God cannot reach there.

Comments

While I feel deeply connected to the Meor Einayim, I do not resonate with this way of thinking about the soul. The term "filth of his transgressions" is a harsh use of language compared to many spiritual teachings from our era. I see human shortcomings as misalignments rather than "filth." I share the Chernobyler's view that as we do inner work we can connect with God on a deeper level. However, I find it more helpful to orient towards freeing up emotional and spiritual energy through inner alignment rather than cleansing the dirt of impure deeds from the soul.

I. In the process of self-work the job is never really done. We can never be totally pure or finished with our spiritual process. Especially for people living in and working in the everyday world, and not as monks, the reality of daily life is surely to show us what we still need to work on, both inwardly and outwardly. The Chernobyler here is saying that we should not continue the work of self-improvement on Shabbat. We should rather say to ourselves, "my inner world is perfect just the way it is," just as we would say that about the outer world on Shabbat. In this way, we can enter into Shabbat Consciousness and have one day each week when we are living as though everything is good and just as it should be.

Reflection and Practice

The Meor Einayim was living in a traditional Jewish setting in which people were saying daily prayers during the week that oriented them towards what they were needing and lacking. On Shabbat, the prayers were much more oriented towards gratitude and praise for God's greatness. His spiritual orientation towards Shabbat works well in this context. It is good to have a balance of inner striving and rest. Consider these questions for yourself:

1. What are practices of striving that help you progress on your path?
2. What are practices of resting that help you feel a sense of gladness and gratitude with yourself and with the world?

Here is the practice: Divide your week up based on times for striving practices and resting practices. Try this schedule out for two weeks, or a whole month if you can. What do you notice? If this approach does not feel aligned for you, you could try dividing a single day up into striving and resting times and take note of the impact.

Even though the Torah was not given before the flood [of Noah], it was still in this world. [This is] because the power of the Maker is in the made [i.e. the natural world].[A] It was not given with clothing as it was later at the giving of the Torah [at Sinai] when it was garbed in the garments of this world.[B]

There were a special few [before the flood] that were fulfilling the Torah as it is on High. They were perceiving it with expanded consciousness to the point that they grasped its true inner essence, as it was before it was revealed [as a book]. [These were people] like Methusela, Enoch, and Adam the First that were students of Torah [embedded in nature].[C]

A. **There is an** ancient legend that God consulted the Torah before creating the world. The Torah served as a blueprint for reality itself. This Torah existed prior to creation and is known as the *Torah Kedumah*, the Primordial Torah. The legend evolved over time and here the Meor Einayim is referring to it without naming it directly. The Chernobyler's view is that wisdom and Godliness can be found in the very fabric of the world. The Meor Einayim, though different than the original legend, also believed that the Torah was God, so from his vantage point the Torah was everywhere because God made the world, and so God's essence is imprinted throughout.

B. **Before the giving** of the Torah at Mt. Sinai, and (in the context of this text) specifically before the flood of Noah, the Torah was not in the form of a scroll or book. That later Torah was communicated in a language that was more accessible to most people. It wore the clothing of our world, which is a Jewish mystical way of saying that it was not as esoteric or concealed as the Torah implanted in nature. It is possible this text is hinting that there are more layers one needs to get through in order to access the essential Torah. The Torah of Sinai is both more accessible and also requires more inquiry in order to attain its essential nature.

C. **There were very** advanced spiritual people who were able to tune into the inherent wisdom and Divinity of the universe even before the Torah was given. There are rabbinic stories that describe some of these biblical characters studying Torah. Here, the Chernobyler is characterizing them as mystics who studied the text of reality. Sometimes commentators use biblical characters in order to communicate ideas that they do not want to say outright. It is possible that the Meor Einayim and his contemporaries were wrestling with the notion of a specific sacred text in which to find Divinity, since they were having experiences that the Infinite was everywhere and in all times. Using these early characters to describe that experience is one way of dealing with that tension without needing to describe it outright— which may have had negative social consequences. This kind of concealed messaging is known as esoteric writing and often happens when authors live in a cultural/historical context where speaking freely and in plain language carries considerable risks.

A Comparative Look

Some Native American and First Nation peoples used and still use vision quests as initiation rites into adulthood. Part of the experience is spending time alone in the wilderness and receiving a message or having contact with an animal or spirit guide. Through this experience the initiate receives wisdom from the natural world. Another example of this can be found in the book *Of Water and the Spirit* by Malidoma Some from the Dagara people of Burkina Faso. Part of his initiation rite involved sitting in front of a tree for many hours until the tree transformed into the image of a giant woman before his eyes. Hazrat Inayat Kahn (1882–1927), an Indian teacher who taught a universalist Sufi mysticism in the West wrote in *The Way of Illumination:* "There is One Holy Book, the sacred manuscript of nature, the only scripture which can enlighten the reader. Most people consider as sacred scriptures only certain books or scrolls written by the hand of man, and carefully preserved as holy, to be handed down to posterity as divine revelation. Men have fought and disputed over the authenticity of these books, have refused to accept any other book of similar character, and, clinging thus to the book and losing the sense of it have formed diverse sects. The Sufi has in all ages respected all such books, and has traced in the Vedanta, Zendavesta, Kabala, Bible, Qur'an, and all other sacred scriptures, the same truth which he reads in the incorruptible manuscript of nature, the only Holy Book, the perfect and living model that teaches the inner law of life: all scriptures before nature's manuscript are as little pools of water before the ocean. To the eye of the seer every leaf of the tree is a page of the holy book that contains divine revelation, and he is inspired every moment of his life by constantly reading and understanding the holy script of nature. When man writes, he inscribes characters upon rock, leaf, paper, wood, or steel. When God writes, the characters He writes are living creatures. It is when the eye of the soul is opened and the sight is keen that the Sufis can read the divine law in the manuscript of nature; and they derived that which the teachers of humanity have taught to their followers from the same source. They expressed what little it is possible to express in words, and so they preserved the inner truth when they themselves were no longer there to reveal it."

Reflection and Practice

1. **A theoretical question:** Is the whole world equally filled with Divinity? Are there certain places, objects, or times that have more?
2. **A personal question:** Where do you find wisdom and how do you connect with insight? Is it in books? In one particular book? In people you know? In nature?
3. **A practice:** Choose one source of wisdom that you do not consult as often and spend time with it. Be present with that source, ask it a question, wait in silence and see what arises.

It is known, that which the Sages taught in the Mishnah, that [to serve God] "with all your heart," means with both of your natures. [That is to say,] with your good inclination and your evil inclination.[A] How can we understand loving God with the evil inclination?

As it is known, the Blessed Creator made the world to have qualities of light and dark.[B] That is because each day includes darkness and light. At the beginning it is night and afterwards comes the light of day. Both of them form a whole even though they are opposites. Night and day [together] are called a day...[C]

So too in a person. The aspect of darkness [arises] first in him. Before the light of consciousness enters him he is in contraction and darkness. This is a place of judgments.[D]

A. M. Berakhot 9:5 states that we should bless God for that which is good as well as for that which is bad. The Mishnah quotes Deuteronomy 6:5 which reads, "You shall love *YHWH* your God with all your heart, with all your soul, and with all your abundance." The Mishnah then states, as the Meor Einayim reiterates, that "with all your heart," means both your good inclination and your evil inclination. The heart in the biblical era was associated with the mind. Also, biblically, love is often paired with giving and service to another. So, in Deuteronomy, the meaning of loving God "with your whole heart," may have been to serve God with your whole mind. The Meor Einayim's reading, influenced by the Mishnah's interpretation, is that the heart contains two drives. One is towards compassion, justice, kindness, discipline and other "good" parts of humanity. This is called the "good inclination." The other drive leads us towards desire, selfishness, laziness, sexual impropriety, violence, and other things called "evil." This other side of every human is called the "evil inclination." In this framework, how can we understand serving God with both of these parts? With the good inclination it is obvious. But, if the bad inclination is taking us away from a moral and loving life, how can it be harnessed for a conscious life?

B. In this metaphor, light is equated with the good inclination and dark represents the evil inclination. Light and dark are both present in the world and God, as the Creator of all that is, is the source of both.

C. The beginning of the Jewish day starts when evening comes, just after sunset. That means the Jewish calendar flows from dark into light. Despite the fact that a day contains both night and day, it is just called "day." As we will see, this is actually a spiritual orientation or a spiritual level that we can reach when both light and dark are in the service of light.

D. Before we begin a spiritual life it is as though we are in a state of contraction and the light of true Reality is obscured. The term "judgments," does not only refer to being judgmental or judging oneself, as it often means in English. Rather, judgments, *dinim* in Hebrew, are associated with the misalignment of the *Sephirah* of *Gevurah*. *Dinim* denote evil, desire, and negativity more broadly. Before our soul begins to awaken, we can be subject to this inner negativity without having the same awareness and ability to work with it.

Comments

We can look at this journey from darkness to light as developmental phases. When infants are born, according to psychological theorist Jean Piaget, they do not have a sense of self. Initially, they do not even realize that they exist. There is a fair amount in common between that state of being and the refined non-dual spiritual states. Part of the developmental process is for the infant to form an ego, a sense of self. This process comes in stages. There is a gradual development of a sense of separateness from reality, a sense of self, a sense of pride and shame. One could say that this very luminous new-born gradually descends into the darkness of the dual world. Another way of saying it is that their unlimited sense of self becomes more contracted. Slowly, slowly, over the years we gain an ego, a sense of separateness, with the accompanying strong urges. They are essential for our functioning but do not always bring out the best in us. In many ways, the mystic tries to return to our original state of being—to move through, move beyond—to transcend the desire nature, the ego, and the separateness. The difference between the advanced mystic and the baby is that the mystic still has an ego and can function in the world. Advanced spiritual practitioners, however, are not subject to their ego and urges to the extent that is common to adults that have not spent time introspecting and pursuing self-awareness.

Comments

This is not necessarily how I would describe life before we start a spiritual path. There is a lot of light in children and in people who are not consciously pursuing a mystical life. But, certainly, we could say that a person enters into more expansion as they progress along the path, and the journey is from more darkness to more light.

All of this good and evil is embedded in a person so that he will have a choice...[E] Each person needs to subjugate[F] the evil to the good, to make them as one whole so they will both be called the aspect of "day,[G]" even the darkness that is there from the beginning. "The night will shine like the day," for him.[H]

E. If we did not have both light and darkness within us we would not be able to truly choose how we wanted to be in life. If we were all light, we would not have the ability to do real inner work, because there would be nothing to overcome. **F. The word "subjugate"** could also be translated as conquer or subdue. What the Meor Einayim means here is that we conscript our negativity to be in service of the good. For example, we can channel our sexual energy into a healthy relationship, as opposed to harmful sexual encounters. Or, if we are feeling violent, this may indicate that we are being encroached upon by people in our lives. We can find ways to set boundaries with our words in a peaceful way, until we reach a place of harmony.

G. When a person can find a way to tune into both the inner negativity and inner positivity so that they can work in tandem towards goodness, this is the level or the aspect called "day." When both light dark are working in harmony, when we can find a way to allow the "evil" parts of us to find healthy expression alongside the good, then both darkness and light are ultimately oriented towards the light. **H. Psalms 139:12. This** verse in Psalms, in its original context, is expressing a similar sentiment to this teaching. The Psalmist is expressing that *YHWH* will be with him no matter where he is, whether in the Heavens or in the pit. For *YHWH*, darkness is like light, and the Divine can be found anywhere. Here, the Meor Einayim is using it to say that in this stage of a person's spiritual existence, the night will shine like the day. Even the negativity can be luminescent when it is harnessed for the sake of growth and goodness on the spiritual path.

Comments

A way we might talk about this today, instead of using the word "subjugate," is to say that we can find balance between the our light and our shadow. We can connect with those parts of us that judge or lead to addictive patterns. In listening deeply to their voices we allow them to find expression and transform.

Comments

There was a phase in my journey where I became aware of a great anger and hatred that been buried within me. For most of my life, from late childhood onward, I had been a peaceful, agreeable, and easy-to-get-along-with person. At the same time, I suffered from social anxiety and the fear that others were judging me based on small mannerisms and word-choices. When the awareness of this boiler pot of inner rage dawned on me, I was a little taken aback. It fit my definition of a "negative emotion." Surprisingly, as I stayed present with the anger and hatred, I found they had real wisdom and valuable energy to share. They gradually began integrating into my persona. Contrary to my initial nervousness around being consumed by rage, the most noticeable impact was increased confidence. I had to befriend the powerful impulses of these "dark" or "evil" qualities—to use the language of the Meor Einayim—in order to live a more courageous and authentic life. I could still be peaceful but I no longer had to betray parts of myself in the process. It turns out, the "negative" aspects of ourselves have amazing gifts to give us. When we are living in right relationship to our whole selves, we can truly access our innate luminosity.

Book: Ohev Yisrael

Section: BeShalaḥ 7:8
(Pronouns Changed)

About the Author

Rebbe Abraham Joshua Heschel of Apt (d. 1825) was a Polish Hasidic Rebbe (not to be confused with his prolific great-great-grandson who lived in the 20th century and had the same name). Known as the Apter Rav, he was the disciple of Elimelekh of Lizhensk, an early Hasidic master who trained several other influential spiritual leaders. The Apter was known for recounting past-life memories and for publicly relaying esoteric teachings while entering trances involving wild body gesticulations. He gained a wide popular audience in his lifetime and began a Hasidic lineage that carried on for several generations. The collection of his teachings is called *Ohev Yisrael* [Lover of Israel].

A Comparative Look

Self-discipline is a difficult thing to master. The Apter Rav lists it as one of the stages of growth but does not offer practical guidance here. Two strategies found in *The Procrastination Equation* by Professor Piers Steel are in harmony with a passage in the Mishnah which says, "A good deed leads to a good dead, a bad deed leads to a bad deed," (Pirkei Avot 4:2). We are habitual creatures. If we do something that is good, we take a step in a direction that makes it more likely we will do that thing again. And, so too, with doing things that are not so good for us. So, for example, if we want to focus on studying or work but have a hard time getting motivated, it is helpful to start with the most simple task. First, we can simply aim to sit in front of the computer, and next we can open up the word processor. Step-by-step we can make a pathway that leads from one success to the other until we have completed our writing. Steel calls this "Scoring Goals." And, on the other side of the equation, we want to make sure we are not distracted from our task once we get going. We can turn off our notifications on our computer, and turn off our phones and put them elsewhere. This way we will not get tempted to go down the path of distraction and we will stay focused on our task. Steel calls this method "Throw Away the Key."

This is the true aim of spiritual work:[A]

(1) At the beginning you need to make every part of your body and [soul level of] *nephesh*—all desires and all worldly elements—subservient to the mind, which is in the brain. The mind will govern everything.[B]

(2) Next, you should do every action with knowledge and discernment. [You should act] in alignment with pleasant and wise paths of the Torah to abstain from what is forbidden. [In each situation you should] do as is commanded. [You will] settle thoroughly into that which is permitted and make it a habit.[C]

All the forces of the body and *nephesh* will be nullified by the intelligence and wisdom of the Torah until all the forces of the body and the *nephesh* will be a chariot for the Torah's insight and wisdom. At that point all the evil desires and the transgressions in particular will be despicable and repulsive in your eye. [It will be] as though this [way of being] was imprinted in your nature from the time you were born. It will not be possible to be inclined towards evil at all, God forbid, at any moment, ever![D]

A. The Apter Rav is describing a stage by stage process of spiritual progression from ordinary life to (1) self-discipline, (2) right living, (3) surrender, and (4) God Consciousness. In Lurianic Kabbalah (16th century), five levels or layers of soul were articulated. In this teaching, the Apter specifically points to three of them: *nephesh, neshamah, and haya*. **B. The first stage** is to have the mind regulate the body and *nephesh*. The *nephesh* is the embodied level of soul, most associated with physicality. In this stage, we work with physical urges until we reach a point where we are in control of our actions.

Comments

The Apter uses words like "subservient" and that the mind will "govern" over the body. I believe in having self-discipline but not in such a hierarchical view of mind dominating body. The Apter's sentiments are not unique in older Jewish teaching (and in some contemporary opinions too!), but many teachers today emphasize more harmony than subjugation of mind and body.

C. Once we are able to act out of our wishes as opposed to being subject to our impulses, we choose to do what is right. In the Apter's world that meant living according to the ethics and rituals of Jewish law. After doing this for long enough it becomes the new normal for our actions. **D. When we live** in alignment with the commandments of the Torah, the body and the *nephesh* become receptive to higher wisdom. The act of living in the right way actually transforms our natural inclinations.

Comments

The Apter is describing a permanent transformation here, where one will not ever be able to do anything evil anymore. There are other Jewish teachers who disagree with this, myself included. We are never free from the potential to make missteps as long as we are living in this world.

(*Pronouns Changed*)

(3) Then, you will be compelled to go to a higher level than that. You, [along with] all your thoughts and intentions, will be [directed] in Torah, good deeds, and prayer, fulfilling the command[s] of your Blessed Creator alone. That is to say, [you will] not just [live this way] because discernment and intelligence obligate you to hate evil and choose good. Rather, your intention will be to do the will of the Blessed and Exalted Creator.[E] As our sages taught: Do not say, 'I am repulsed by the flesh of the pig,' but rather, 'I would like it but what can I do since my Father in Heaven placed decrees on me?[F]'

And when you do things in this way, then your mind, which is the [soul level of] *neshamah*, will be made a chariot and a throne for that which is above it, which is the [soul] level of *ḥaya*.[G]

(4) You should go from level to level until you move beyond all the powers of the *nephesh* and *neshamah*. [That is] the state of complete nullification of existence in the presence of the glory of The Blessed God. And so you will be, if you will, as God was when it arose in the Divine Mind to create the world.[H]

E. After following Divine law from a place of feeling, we get to a place of surrender. Our actions are no longer about what we are feeling or wanting, but flow from an alignment with the Will of the Infinite. **F. Sifra, Kedoshim 9:12.** This quote is from a *midrash*, a collection of homilies on the Torah, dating to the first centuries of the common era. There, it is teaching that Israel is set apart from other nations but must follow God's law in order to be protected. The emphasis is on following the path for its own sake and not because of how people are feeling. Here, the Apter lifts the message of being loyal to God and takes it in a more personal-spiritual direction that has to do with living according to the will of the Creator. **G. The *neshamah* is** the layer of soul associated with the mind. When we live with our bodies and mind in accordance with the flow of the universe then our *neshamah* becomes receptive to our *ḥaya*, which is an even more refined level of soul that is said to dwell above the head. Just as our *nephesh* and body were transformed to align with our mind, our *neshamah* can be transformed to be in alignment with our *ḥaya* when we live in surrender. The *ḥaya* is associated with the *Sephirah* of *Ḥokhmah* and the foundational reality of all existence. **H. When people reach** *ḥaya* consciouness, they can understand the experience of God before the world was created. Their consciousness returns to its primordial and subtle nature as it disappears into nothingness. This is a very rare and refined state but the Apter lays it out here as part of the stages of transformation that all begin with self-discipline.

Related Jewish Sources

In his book *The Kedumah Experience* (chapter 11), Rabbi Zvi Ish-Shalom describes the last stage of the Apter's pathway in great detail. It is a phase at which the meaning generated from previous forms of growth ceases and is replaced by a pervasive sense of emptiness. It is said to be a difficult transition that ultimately leads one to a great sense of freedom and equanimity. In Ish-Shalom's description, at some point a person can experience the inherent hollowness and emptiness of who they are. When that happens, it may be frightening as their sense of essential self will slip away. Ultimately, what emerges from this hollowness is the manifestation of the true self, the spark of light that is *Ḥokhmah*, which is the essential point from which all else emanates.

Comments

Mystical lineages abound with stages of spiritual growth. You can find different versions in almost every wisdom tradition. But, what if you do not fit into these paths? What if your spirit cannot be categorized or contained in a package labeled, "stage three of personal refinement." In reality, none of us fit neatly into stages of inner transformation. There are as many paths as there are people. We can do well to learn from established mystical systems such as the one the Apter Rav articulates here. But, know that these paths were constructed based on the lives and journeys of individuals that came before. To progress spiritually and remain true to ourselves is to ask: in this moment, what is arising? What is manifesting in my own inner dimensions? How can that impulse push me beyond my edges and allow me to shift? Moment by moment, you can follow the natural path of your own personal progression. You can be aware of how others have journeyed, but if that feels weighty, intimidating, or forced, you can let it go. Maybe one day you can look back and try to categorize your own journey. For now, if you allow your inner world to evolve organically, you will be amazed at what can emerge when you abandon all notions of what "should be."

Book: Sefat Emet[9]

Section: 2:91

About the Author

Yehudah Aryeh Leib Alter (1847–1905) became the rebbe of the Ger *Ḥasidim* at a very young age. Having been orphaned by eight years old, the Sefat Emet, as he is often referred to, was raised by his grandfather—the founder of the Ger Hasidic lineage—and his grandmother. When his grandfather died, many in the Ger community wanted him to be the new rebbe, though he was only 18 years old. Four years later, when the spiritual leader that had taken over also passed away, Yehudah Aryeh Leib became the Gerrer Rebbe for the rest of his life. The Sefat Emet text is a compilation of his interpretations of the weekly Torah readings as well as the festivals. It was recorded by his students and published after his death. It is considered a classic of later Hasidic thought and, since many he taught were living in a more secular context than in early Hasidism, the Sefat Emet has found particular resonance with people today.

"All the people saw the voices [lit.: the thunder].[A]" The voice was that which said, "I am YHWH your God.[B]" Each one of Israel saw the root of his or her own life-force. With their very eyes each one saw the part of the divine soul above that lives within.[C] They had no need to "believe" the commandments, because they saw the voices.[D] That's the way it is when God speaks.

A. **Exodus 20:15. The** Hebrew word *kolot* can mean voices, sounds, or thunder. This part of Exodus is where the Israelites are standing at the foot of Mount Sinai, which God has descended upon. There is a cloud with thunder, lighting, the sound of a horn, and smoke rising up. The Sefat Emet is reading *kolot* as "voices" which are coming from God.

B. **Exodus 20:2. There** is a single voice producing the perception of all of these voices. It is the voice of the Infinite pronouncing the first three words (or five in English) of the ten commandments. In rabbinic tradition it is commonly believed that all the Israelites heard God speak at Mount Sinai. There is a disagreement as to how many words the Divine uttered or if there was just a single holy sound, but it is believed that the Israelites together received a communal revelation.

C. **Each Israelite (which** can also be more universally translated as "God-Wrestler," a seeker who contends with the Divine) connected with their absolute spiritual essence at that moment. They found their own inner Divinity and the voice which they "saw" spoke to them in their own unique way. The seeing here may be akin to synesthesia, the experience of perceiving one sense via another, like seeing sounds or tasting visions. D. **The commandments from** God were directly delivered individually to each person, right to the depth of their being. With an encounter like that they did not need any act of faith to relate to God or God's word. They had been struck by a moment of intimacy and awe. "That's the way it is when God speaks."

Related Jewish Sources

On the topic of being of the tribe of Israel, and also being a universalist, Rabbi Arthur Green, Neo-Hasidic scholar and theologian writes in *Radical Judaism*:

The fact that I belong to this sacred community does not establish my only religious landscape. Living in our era of both an open society and a previously unimagined awareness of other cultures and civilizations, I feel a sense of fellowship with seekers, strivers, and doers everywhere. This fellowship does not depend upon whether they have any interest in being considered part of my Israel or share any relationship to the legacy of that name. While I may experience them as "Israel," to declare them such would be a sort of spiritual imperialism. I recognize my fellowship with them without needing to make them over into my own. They may be Buddhist monks or "secular" ecologists, jesters in the marketplace who make people laugh or great musicians who make their spirits soar. When I pray for God to "bring peace to us and to all Israel," I find myself wanting to include them as well.

Comments

As this text describes, magical moments can happen in groups. I lead a type of contemplative prayer service that involves Qi Gong movement, singing wordless melodies called *nigunim*, listening to evocative poetry, and sitting in silence. At the end of these four practices, there is often a palpable presence residing amongst the group. I invite everyone to feel into the space using body-sensations and notice what they experience. Almost always people describe related experiences, but each unique to the perceiver. This is how the one voice of God is heard, deeply and intimately, as many.

One who attains the secret of *devekut* will attain the secret of equanimity. If he attains the secret of equanimity, he will attain the secret of meditation. After he attains the secret of meditation, this person will attain the holy spirit, and from this to prophecy until he prophesizes and declares future events.[A]

The secret of equanimity Rav Avner told me: a wise person came to one of the meditators and requested to be accepted among [them]. The meditator said to him, "My son, it is clear to God that your intention is good, truly. Tell me, have you attained equanimity?" The wise person said to him, "Master, explain your words." The meditator responded, "If one person honors you and one insults you, are they equal in your eyes, or not?" The wise person answered, "No, my lord, because I feel delight and pleasure from the one who honors, and pain from the one who ridicules, but I do not avenge or bear a grudge." The master replied, "My son, go in peace, because every moment that you are not equanimous, that your soul will feel disgrace from what is done to you. You are not invited to have your thoughts connected to the Supernal that you may come and meditate. So go and subdue your heart further, a true subjugation, until you will be non-reactive and then you can contemplate.[B]"

The cause of equanimity is attaching the mind to God. The one who is connected and joined to the mind to God, even though people do things to him, he does not feel it. He does not pay attention to "soothsayers and diviners."[C]

A. The Meirat Eynayim is describing a progression of spiritual development. These stages use words that overlap with other Jewish mystical systems but are not necessarily the same. The term *devekut* in later Hasidic mysticism refers to a mystical connection with God. Here, *devekut* is a preparation for later stages. Though its exact nature is not articulated in this text, it may involve visualizing the Hebrew name of God before one's eyes. Whatever its exact components, it is evidently a practice which connects a person to the mind of God. In this state, they will not be swayed by the world around them. Equanimity is akin to neutrality and perceiving the positive and negative as one experience. Meditation [*hitbodedut*] in this system is more advanced than *devekut*. The levels of holy spirit and prophecy are even more rarefied mystical attainments. **B. This story demonstrates** that one may not learn meditation with this school of practitioners until they have mastered equanimity. It is not uncommon for mystical systems throughout the ages to have a series of prerequisites or levels to progress through. From a practical perspective, more powerful meditations can lead to greater insight and perception but can also increase in risk. This system is acknowledging that and requiring students to train the mind before moving on. **C. Deuteronomy 18:14. When** people devote their minds to God, they are less susceptible to being thrown off by others. In the biblical context, the term "soothsayers and diviners" occurs where Moses is telling the Israelites that they are not to sacrifice children, practice necromancy, or do various kinds of divination. Here, Isaac of Acre is referring to detractors who insult the spiritual seeker. When one is connected to God, in the book of Deuteronomy, one avoids these practices. When one is connected to God in Isaac of Acre's world, one also avoids getting distracted and deterred by insults.

About the Author

Rabbi Isaac ben Samuel of Acco [Acre] (late 13th–mid 14th century CE) was a kabbalist who grew up in *Eretz Yisrael* and later spent time in Italy and Spain. His book, the Meirat Einayim, which means the illumination of the eyes, is a commentary on the mysticism of the very influential rabbi Naḥmanides (d. 1270). The book also includes material from other kabbalistic circles of the time. Isaac of Acco famously investigated Moses de Leon who had published the Zohar and had attributed its composition to Shimon bar Yoḥai, who lived more than 1000 years prior. Isaac of Acco's account of investigating De Leon is cited by modern scholars in trying to date the Zohar.

Comments

Regarding Deuteronomy 18:14, quoted at the end of this text: when it comes to divination practices, which I define as methods that harness synchronicity to help people tune into the will of the universe, I personally distinguish between helpful and harmful practices. For example, astrology and tarot, when used to assist people in having insight or greater self-knowledge, are in the helpful category. Practices such as the ancient method of reading the entrails of an animal sacrificed for that purpose, are in the other category. Jewish history has had its share of astrologers and, though the biblical injunction against divination sounds sweeping, many Jews and Jewish leaders in the past and the present have made finer distinctions between these methods. See page 50 for another teaching about equanimity.

Related Jewish Sources

Rabbi Yosef Yoizel Hurwitz of Novogrudok (1847-1919) used unique methods to train his students to be undaunted by the judgements of others. It was important that they be able to make good, ethical choices even in the midst of criticism. He would send them on ridiculous tasks in order for them to gain the experience of being mocked. For example, they would have to go to the bakery and ask for screws. If they could learn to withstand the inevitable chastisement and laughter of the shopkeepers, they they would surely be more courageous in stepping forward to do the right thing—even if it seemed out of place.

(*Pronouns Changed*)

About the Author:

Dov Baer (The Maggid) of Mezeritch (d. 1772) was the leader of the Hasidic movement after the Ba'al Shem Tov. He did not write his own teachings down but they were collected by his students and later published. The Maggid was renowned for his charisma as a preacher as well as his great learning of Talmud and Kabbalah. He inspired the third generation of Hasidic leaders to spread this new kind of mysticism and start their own communities throughout Eastern Europe.

A Comparative Look:

In Buddhism, equanimity [*upekkha* in Pali] is one of the Four Immeasurables, which are four sublime attitudes to adopt. According to the *Vissudhimagga*, the ancient treatise of Buddhist monastic practice, "neither-painful-nor-pleasant feeling is intended here by 'equanimity' (*upekkh*, lit. onlooking); for it 'looks on' at the occurrence of [bodily] pleasure and pain by maintaining the neutral (central) mode." A resonant philosophy can be found in Stoicism. Roman Emperor Marcus Aurelius (d. 180 CE), who used the Latin word "*aequanimitas*" wrote in his Meditations, "If you are distressed by anything external, the pain is not due to the thing itself, but to your estimate of it; and this you have the power to revoke at any moment."

We should think of ourselves as nothing and forget everything about who we are.[A] In prayer, we should only pray for [what] the *Shekhinah* [needs].[B] Then we can ascend beyond time, which is in the World of Consciousness.[C] There, everything is equal: life and death, sea and dry land[D]... We need to break free of ourselves and to forget our own needs in order to come to the World of Consciousness. There, everything is equal. The opposite is true when we are attached to the physicality of this world. Then, we are attached to the division of good and evil,[E] which are the seven days of creation [i.e. the seven lower *Sephirot*].[F] How can we then transcend time? In that place everything is completely unified.[G] So, when we think of ourselves as something, and ask for our own needs, the Holy Blessed One cannot make us into garments of the Divine.[H] No vessel can bear God, the Infinite. But, if we think of ourselves as nothing [we can receive Divinity].[I]

A. The Maggid works with a mystical system involving Something and Nothing, *yesh* and *ayin*. It is the goal of the mystic to self-nullify and become sacred Nothingness. Part of this path is to be selfless. **B. It is common** for people to pray for what they need. In the route towards becoming nothing, the method is to pray for the *Shekhinah* [Divine Presence] and thus direct our prayers to what is needed for Deep Reality's manifestation and alignment in the world. **C. The *Sephirah* of** *Keter* is associated with Nothingness and is beyond space and time. It is the realm in which the Divine Will first arises and is called the World of Consciousness or the World of Thought. **D. In *Keter* Consciousness** all is equal. The good and the bad are not seen as different. The "sea and dry land" is a reference to the splitting of the Sea of Reeds when the Israelites were leaving Egypt. The miracle was that God parted the sea so that the Israelites could escape the Egyptians. However, in *Keter* Consciousness, there is no difference between sea and dry land, death and life. **E. When we are** living from ordinary consciousness, there is a difference between good and bad. The Maggid is equating this with being bound to physicality.

Comments

The Maggid had some ascetic tendencies, which is to say he was a kind of mystic who, at times, practiced self-denial and affliction of the body. In my view, we can be deeply connected to the physical world and to bodily health while still cultivating equanimity. There is a difference between experiencing pain and pleasure and witnessing that pain and pleasure. The latter can be practiced while living an embodied, healthy lifestyle.

F. The lower seven *Sephirot* are *Ḥesed, Gevurah, Tipheret, Netzah, Hod, Yesod,* and *Shekhinah*. They are associated with the seven days of the week and the seven days of creation, beginning on Sunday with *Ḥesed* and ending on Shabbat with *Shekhinah*. These levels of the spiritual world, though having sacred character, are not beyond distinctions of good and evil. **G. If we are** attached to the physical and are living within ordinary consciousness, which sees separateness and distinction in the world, we are not in the world of *Keter*, of the unified consciousness beyond time. **H. To be a** garment of the Divine is to have the Infinite dwell within us. We can bring God into the world if we move beyond our own ego. If we remain in the state of *yesh*, of Something, we cannot. **I. The Infinite overwhelms** created reality. If, however, we become *ayin*, there is nothing to overwhelm and God can enter the world through us.

Comments:

Both this text and Meirat Eynayim, Ekev (p. 49) describe the experience of equanimity. The Maggid teaches one method of moving towards that, which is to pray for God and not for oneself. There are, in fact, many methods to help us acquire a more equal stance in life, with an openness to what may come. It can be tempting to want to will ourselves into not feeling pain or pleasure. However, this is a road that can easily lead to repression. My advice is to work with emotions and physical sensations in a way where we can feel them but not be overtaken by them. This can also be called practicing awareness or non-attachment. By allowing our feelings and sensations to be there as they are, we neither repress them nor push them away. Through this we develop the quality of equanimity to our inner world, which can lead us to equanimity to our outer world.

"*YHWH* spoke to Moses after the death of the two sons of Aaron when they drew near to the presence of *YHWH* and died.[A]"

Another explanation[B] of the verse is that God spoke to Moses about the manner of the death, which came about because they "drew near" to God.[C] The interpretation is that they came close to the supernal light, in holy love, and through this they died. This is the mystery of the kiss through which *tzadikim* die.[D] And this means their deaths were equal to the deaths of *tzadikim*, except for the fact that for *tzadikim* the kiss approaches them, and Nadav and Avihu approached it. And that is why it says, "They drew near to God.[E]... The text hints at the wondrous nature of the love of these *tzadikim*, that even though they felt their death was near, they did not abstain from getting close to the pleasurable, satiating, tender, beloved, and alluring mystical states when their souls were yearning. In this state, one does not see its quality, and it rules over perception.[F]

A. Leviticus 16:1. Aaron's two sons, Nadav and Avihu, were *kohanim* [priests]. They were serving in the newly built tabernacle, a portable temple where offerings were brought. They brought inappropriate offerings and a Divine fire came out from the inner sanctum, the Holy of Holies, and consumed them. While this is a literal biblical reading, the Or HaḤayim takes the encounter in a deeply mystical direction. **B. Individual commentators sometimes** give multiple explanations of the same verse, reflective of the great number of ways to interpret Torah. This Or HaḤayim passage is one of several perspectives he articulates on this verse. **C. The plain meaning** of the verse is that Nadav and Avihu "drew near" to the holy fire and were burnt. But what does this mean, exactly? The Or HaḤayim offers a mystical suggestion, that they drew spiritually close to the Divine Presence in a way that was dangerous. **D. The Talmud states** that there are 903 ways to die and the Kiss of Death is the easiest out of all of them (Berakhot 8a). When Moses dies, it says that he passes away "by the mouth of God," (Deuteronomy 34:5). This is a phrase that could mean "by the word of God," or "by the command of God," but early rabbinic tradition interprets it as the Kiss of Death (Bava Batra 17a). Similarly, it says that Moses' sister Miriam was taken by the Kiss of Death. The meaning of this way of dying to the Or HaḤayim is that God takes back the soul that he initially breathed into our bodies. It is a moment of deep spiritual connection with the Infinite as we die. The soul communes with the Creator and does not return to the physical plane. It could also be called, "death by mystical experience." **E. For righteous people** whose lives were very connected to Source, God approaches them in their final hours. With Nadav and Avihu, however, they rushed into the Tabernacle, God's dwelling-place on Earth, and were consumed in the ecstasy of that occasion. They died before their time, but it was nonetheless the Kiss of Death. **F. Love of God,** like erotic love, can be intoxicating. People can be overcome by the experience and lose sight of everything else. Our normal sense of worldly responsibilities or rationality can be overlooked for the sake of that single moment of ecstacy. Nadav and Avihu were so enraptured with Divine intimacy that they even overlooked life itself.

About the Author

Rabbi Ḥayim ben Moshe ibn Attar (1696–1743) was born in Sale, Morocco and spent his life teaching and writing in Morocco, Italy, and *Eretz Yisrael*. A rabbi and kabbalist known for his piety, he attracted large audiences for his teaching. Students of his in Jerusalem were known to do ascetic practices such as spending the nighttime in prayer for the sake of Jews in the Diaspora. Though he wrote books on rabbinic law, ibn Attar is often called the Or HaḤayim after his commentary on the Torah, his most popular book. It was especially well-received amongst Hasidic communities and there is a legend that the Ba'al Shem Tov tried to go to the Holy Land to study with him.

Related Jewish Texts

1. The *Babylonian Talmud* (*Berakhot 8a*) discusses the different types of death: **Nine hundred and three types of death were created in the world, as it is stated: "Issues [totzaot] of death," and that, 903, is the numerical value [gimatriya] of totzaot.** The Gemara explains that **the most difficult of** all these types of death is **croup [askara]**, while **the easiest is** the **kiss** of death. **Croup is like a thorn** entangled **in a wool fleece, which, when pulled out backwards,** tears the wool. **Some say that** croup **is like ropes at the entrance to the esophagus,** which would be nearly impossible to insert and excruciating to remove. The **kiss** of death **is like drawing a hair from milk.**[10]

2. The early Hungarian Hasidic teacher Moshe Teitelbaum writes in *Yismaḥ Moshe* (*Balak 4:2*): Those who live by the aliveness that is beyond nature [beyond physicality], by the light of the God who is the source of life, from where does their death come [if they are already not reliant on the physical world]? The answer is: it comes from the surge of light from the immense pleasure [at the time of death], until the soul can no longer stay in the body. At that moment it blossoms with intense desire for pure *devekut*. This is what is meant by a "kiss."

Reflection and Practice:

Do you ever think about the moment of death or the afterlife? What scenario brings you the most comfort? Some people feel nourished by thinking about a paradise that awaits, while others like the idea that we simply cease to exist after we die. Here's a more challenging practice: Is there a scenario in the after-life that you find difficult to think about?

If so, when you are in a stable and grounded state, try bringing your mind to that possibility. Can you imagine it being real? Can you accept it? If you can grapple with your worst-case scenario of the afterlife and learn to be open to what may come, you will be walking the path of freeing yourself from that fear.

(*Pronouns Changed*)

About the Author

Rav Abraham Isaac Kook (1865–1935) was the first chief Ashkenazi rabbi of British Mandatory Palestine. A prolific writer and mystical thinker, Rav Kook was also highly regarded as a legal decisor and Torah scholar. Inspired by his belief and experience in the oneness of all existence, he saw all nations and worldviews as expressions or partial expressions of Divine truth. Many of his teachings came spontaneously as automatic writings. He did not, for the most part, organize them or edit them afterwards. Rav Kook was a unique individual, true to the text presented here. As a religious leader he was often at odds with other orthodox rabbinic authorities, especially because he saw many positive elements in the secular Zionist movement which sought to resettle the land of what was then called Palestine. He saw spiritual richness in the theory of evolution and vegetarianism and believed each had a place within traditional Judaism. Rav Kook maintained that, despite the new lights coming from the secular and scientific realms, the world needed religion in order to make sure that human beings would live ethical lives.

Reflection and Practice

Find a quiet space. Get in a comfortable position, lying down or sitting up. Take a few slow breaths, as many as you need to start to feel relaxed.

Ask yourself, "What is my task in this life?"

Wait for the first thought, image, memory, etc. that arises in your mind. That is your subconscious giving you a symbolic representation of the answer to your question.

Spend some time reflecting on the symbol you receive. Write it out, draw it, feel it in your body, talk about it with a spiritual friend. See what's hiding behind that clue.

Did you get a sense of what the message was? If not, keep trying that exercise and see what comes. If you've been succesful or if you already had a sense of what you came here for, ask yourself, "What is keeping me from my life's purpose?"

The last part of this practice is to take one action step towards living more in-line with your purpose. Now go!

Each of us is called to serve in alignment with a unique understanding and perception, according to the root of our particular soul. In this [inner] dimension that encompasses worlds beyond number, you will find the treasure of your life.[A]

Do not be thrown off balance by the things that rush into you from other worlds, those you cannot absorb properly. You are not capable of tying them beautifully into the fabric of your life. Those [foreign] worlds will find their reparation in their [right] place by those who are able to build them and perfect them.[B]

Rather, you should focus your life on your own realities, your own inner dimensions, because they fill all and surround all.[C]

Each of us should say, "This world was created for me![D]" This great humility strengthens us and brings us to Divine wholeness, which stands and waits for us.[E] When you walk [the] road of life with this confidence, in your own unique way, in this righteous path that you make your own, you are filled with living courage and spiritual joy. The light of God will be revealed to you. From your own unique letter in the Torah, your power and luminosity will emerge.[F]

A. At our core, we are unique. The "soul root" is a teaching from Jewish mysticism that each of us has a core spiritual essence from which we emerge. Rav Kook is saying that if we journey deeply into our own nature we will find out who we truly are. He is telling us that our work in this world, our purpose or calling in life, stems from that foundational place inside of us. **B. There are many** other tasks to do in this world besides our own. If we try to take on something that is not ours, we will not be able to perfect it while maintaining harmony with who we really are. The term "worlds" [*olamot*] here means "aspects of reality," and in Jewish mysticism can refer to aspects of spiritual, conceptual, and physical realms. The word can also be translated as "dimensions." **C. The term "fill** all and surround all" is in reference to the paradoxical nature of the Infinite. Divinity is both beyond us [surrounding all] and within everything [filling the whole world][11]. Rav Kook is describing our own inner worlds in this way because of how absolutely all-ecompassing they are to who we truly are. They fill our whole being and surround us as well. Also, there is a sense that through deep introspection we can find God. If we really tune into who we are at our core we can get in touch with the Divine that fills and embraces all creation. **D. b. Sanhedrin 37a.** This quote from the Talmud originally references the Biblical account that all humanity was descended from a single person, Adam. In rabbinic lore, God used a mold to create the first human and uses the same mold to fashion everyone else. Since we are made from the same mold as the first person, in a sense the world was created just for us. Famously, the Hasidic teacher Simḥa Bunim used to say that we should keep a note in one pocket that says, "This world was created for me." In the other pocket we should keep a note that says, "I am dust and ashes," (Genesis 18:27). When we are feeling low we can read the first note, and when we are feeling arrogant we should read the second. Rav Kook uses this teaching in a different way. He is saying that each of us should embrace our inner world and purpose, because it was created for us! **E. This choice is** a humble choice because we are surrendering to our true nature. We are not trying to do anything but trust the path that the Infinite places before us. **F. There is tremendous** joy and strength that can be derived from being in our element. Through discovering who we really are and letting that flow out into our lives we can exist from a place of connection and wholeness. There is a kabbalistic teaching that there are 600,000 letters in the Torah that correspond to 600,000 root souls (there are, in fact, 304,805 letters). By writing about finding our own letter in the Torah, Rav Kook is referencing this teaching.

Book: Naphshi Takshiv Shiro Section: MeOlam Raḥok[12]

And from a distant world[A], full
of illuminations,
The suns there are as broad as the ocean,
And the stars, like the light of our sun[B],
On the face of the expanse of the
sapphire stone[C], There...
The news reaches me,
Like dew full of overflowing delight,
Guiding me to the hidden Eden[D],
There... the pleasure[E] is stored.
All the faces there are joyful,
Every mouth sings songs of praise,
The highest feelings fill each heart,
And... all legs dance in jubilation[F].
The past and the future are scrolled
into one[G],
Nothing hidden, everything known[H],
Every soul full of love for all[I]

A. **This poem can** be read as a vision of another dimension or of our world, perfected, in the future. One common view of Heaven in Judaism is that it is a Heaven on Earth that is the destiny of humankind. Rav Kook, the author, was certainly a believer in that future. B. **A sun as** broad as the ocean is likely referring to the sun over the horizon being as broad as the ocean as we look out to sea. This aligns with the image of stars being as bring as our sun. The imagery here evokes the concept of Divine Light. It is said to be ever-present in our world, but often concealed. In the World to Come, one way of refering to Heaven on Earth, the Divine light will no longer be concealed. C. **The color of** sapphire appears in a few very significant moments in the Bible. In Exodus 24:10 Moses, Aaron, his sons, and the seventy elders of Israel all gaze at God on Mount Sinai, who has under His feet the appearance of a sapphire stone. This occurs during the revelation, the time that is considered by tradition as the greatest nearness of the Jewish people to God. Also, in Ezekiel 1:26, a very important chapter in later Jewish mysticism, the prophet sees a vision of the Divine Throne that has the appearance of a sapphire stone. The word *rakia* also appears there in Hebrew, which is translated as expanse in this text, but can also mean heaven or sky. D. **On a simple** level, the hidden Eden is a metaphor for a beautiful world that is sometimes hidden from view. E. **On a more** kabbalistic level, Eden is a symbol for the *Sephirah* of *Ḥokhmah* [Wisdom]. Rebbe Naḥman (early 1800s) writes that, "the essence of the pleasure of the Garden of Eden is apprehension of Divine Wisdom." The direct insights into reality yield a mystical pleasure beyond ordinary physical enjoyment. F. **Not all Jewish** teachings endorse taking pleasure in elevated spiritual experiences. However, for those that do, happiness and fulfillment are commonly associated with the World to Come. As 18th century mystic Moshe Ḥayim Luzzato says, "Humanity was created to take pleasure in God, and to enjoy the radiance of God's Presence. This is the true pleasure and the greatest delight [*idun* in Hebrew, sharing the same root as *Eden*] that can possibly exist. The place of this delight is truly in the World to Come," (Mesilat Yesharim, 1). True to Rav Kook's personality and teachings, the joy described here is of a highly ecstatic nature. The praise sung by the dancers is what one says naturally when in awe of the Infinite radiance. G. **In higher levels** of consciousness, such as in the *Sephirah* of *Ḥokhmah*, time and space are not operating in a conventional sense. So too, in this edenic world, all time is as one moment. H. **Higher *Sephirot* and** spiritual stages are often described as hidden. There is a sense that Deep Reality is right beneath the surface of our normal perception, but it is concealed for most people at most times. In the Future to Come, all will be revealed. I. **Along with the** state of realization being described, there is a tremendous love being felt and expressed by everyone. Simply having an awareness of God is only part of the spiritual journey. Living with a loving heart is essential. In Rav Kook's book *The Moral Principles* he gives guidances for living an ethical life. In the first sentence of the first chapter he writes, "The heart must be filled with love for all."

Reflection and Practice

What gives you the feeling like everything is aligned? Is there a particular time or place or person that helps you feel truly alive? Asked another way, what makes you feel like you're in Heaven? Find a way to do something you really love each week.

In seeking to cultivate a conscious life, it is important to have practices that challenge us and cause us to grapple with our own shortcomings. And, it is essential that we cultivate joy and gratitude as well. Perhaps Rav Kook's experience with truly amazing moments allowed him to be receptive to such a vision of the future. It is important to experience bliss to remind ourselves of what the world could look like.

Comments

There is a story found in multiple religious traditions about the difference between Heaven and Hell. Though articulated through slightly different ways, each culture portrays a similar scene. In Hell, there is a great banquet with everyone seated at a table. The smell of the food makes them incredibly hungry. They want to eat but their elbows are permanently locked and their hands have become spoons. They can get the most delicious food into their spoon-hands, but they can never bring it to their mouths to eat. It is torture. But, what about Heaven? Surely it must be nothing like Hell! As it turns out, in Heaven they have the same banquet. They sit together before an endless table of the most delicious foods you could imagine. And, they also have spoon-hands and locked elbows just like in Hell. The difference is, in Heaven, they learn how to feed each other.

Wow, what an amazing difference a small adjustment can make! This story teaches us that the line between beauty and misalignment—between bounty and lack—can be as simple as coming together to help each other out.

Feelings for the multitudes[J]

And... the light is sown[K].

All the pasts flow like rivers[L],

Purity, illumination, strength and light,

Life renewed, freedom and liberation,

Fills... all our thoughts and activities[M].

And without teachers, guides, judges or politicians,

Everything is good, everything is clear,

There is no corruption or injustice, everything is with integrity[N],

And... the night shines like the day[O].

To a world such as this my soul longs[P],

In life such as this my spirit soars[Q]...

Related Jewish Sources

Rav Kook describes a vision of a perfected world that could also be seen as the afterlife. Within Jewish history there have been many different articulations of what happens after death. It is a religion which primarily emphasizes the art of sacred living and which highly values debate. It is therefore fitting that there are many competing viewpoints about what happens to us after we dies. One perspective is what Lurianic Kabbalists called *gilgul*, the recylcing of souls from one life to another—a Jewish form of reincarnation. In the following text from *Sha'ar HaGilgulim*, the Lurianic perspective on reincarnation is given. In this passage, it is related to the perfection the three levels of soul—*nephesh*, *ruaḥ*, and *neshamah*:

If he did not completely refine the *nephesh* the first time and he dies, that *nephesh* needs to return through reincarnation. This happens many times until he can purify it completely. Then, even though it is whole, it has not yet acquired a *ruaḥ*... Therefore it needs to die and return and then it will merit its *ruaḥ*. If he refines the *ruaḥ*, then he will need to die and afterwards reincarnate. Then the *neshamah* will arrive... If he does not refine the *ruaḥ*, the *nephesh* will need to reincarnate several times with the *ruaḥ* until the *ruaḥ* will be refined. Then that person will die and return, reincarnating the *nephesh*, *ruah*, and also the *neshamah*, until they are all refined. Afterwards, that person does not have a need to reincarnate anymore because, when the three levels of soul are refined, he is a complete human.

J. In many ways Rav Kook was a universalist. Though he saw Judaism as the superior religion, a kind of particularism not in-line with many universally-oriented people today, on many occasions he wrote in an embracing way for all people. In the same chapter on love quoted above he writes, "The love for people must be alive in heart and soul, a love for all people and all nations, expressing itself in a desire for their spiritual and material betterment." **K. This is from** Psalms 97:11, "Light is sown for the righteous, and joy for the upright of heart." This verse was often interpreted in Hasidism to mean that the *tzadik* can find hidden light and joy in the Torah and in the world through heart-felt striving. However, here Rav Kook seems to be using it in the sense that the light that may shine in the world at times is deeply implanted within people, that it is integrated. It is not just a "wow" moment, but something that engenders love in every soul. **L. In Hebrew the** word for past, *avar*, shares a root with the word for transgression, *aveirah*. Everything that has happened in the past is flowing with the beauty of a river. In this enlightened and loving place there is no bitterness from what came before it. **M. Inside and out,** the people in that vision are saturated with Divine qualities. **N. In our world,** we need hierarchy, guidance, and supervision in order for society to be a good and safe place. In a perfected world, people are so inherently good that we do not need anything besides our own loving and sincere selves to live in a just civilization. **O. Psalms 139:12. The** full verse reads, "Even the darkness is not too dark for You. The night shines like the day, darkness is like light." The Bible is describing God's presence no matter the situation. Here, this presence is manifest for all. Deep Reality shines through whether it is day or night. **P. Rav Kook acknowledges** his yearning for such a world. However, **Q. He has had** glimpses of it. This distant world can already be found in our world, it is just more hidden.

Book: Shmoneh Kevatzim Section: 7:112, Shir Meruba[13]
(Pronouns Changed)

A. **Rav Kook's Fourfold** Song walks us through the four spiritual ways that a person can "sing." It describes how we harmonize with the world, what drives and motivates us, and the goals for which we strive. The literal translation of this first part is "there is one who sings," but here it is translated as "there is that part of us." The poem here is changed to the first person plural but these four parts of us are also four types of people. B. **The song of** the self, the song of one's own soul, is sung by people who are passionate about their own journey, their inner and outer path. C. **The song of** the people could also be called the song of community. Here Rav Kook talks about the community of Israel but this way of being can be extended to any other community, family, or tribe. It is when we connect to a wider circle beyond ourselves. D. **The song of** all humanity is the song of universal love for every person on Earth. In this song we feel aligned with every culture, every race, religion, and way of life, no matter who they are or what group rivalries are supposed to exist between us. E. **In the fourth** song, our circle of alignment broadens to include every animal, plant, micro-organism, rock, and atom, as well as the spiritual dimensions. We are singing along with every single aspect of the manifest world. F. **This is a** reference to a medieval text called Perek Shirah, the "Chapter of Song." This text is comprised of the unique songs of praise of the different creatures of the natural world including animals, celestial bodies, times of day, rivers, clouds, and plants. The introduction to this text says that anyone who recites Perek Shirah in this world will get to live in and sing this text in the World to Come. Here, Rav Kook is equating the fourth song, the journey of being in harmony with all existence, with Perek Shirah, and giving his interpretation of the inner meaning of that text. G. **This last part** is a song that includes the other songs. It is when all of these songs can be sung simultaneously. That is why Rav Kook compares it to the Song of Songs in the Bible (see footnote K). The term Song of Songs can be taken to mean the "greatest of songs" or "a song that is composed of other songs." In this case, both meanings apply. H. **The phrase "sounds** of joy and gladness," originally appears in the book of Jeremiah in a prophecy of the Israelites returning to their land after exile. This phrase is also part of the Seven Blessings said at a wedding, in the blessing for bringing joy to the couple getting married. Here, Rav Kook is alluding to those feelings of celebratory elation when every part of us sings together.

There is that part of us[A] that sings the song of ourselves. Within ourselves we find everything, our full spiritual satisfaction.[B]

Then there is that part of us that sings the song of our people. We leave the circle of our individual self, finding it without sufficient breadth, without an ideal basis. We aspire toward the heights, attaching ourselves with a gentle love to the whole community of Israel. Together with her we sing her songs, we feel grieved in her afflictions, and delight in her hopes. We contemplate noble and pure thoughts about her past and her future, and probe with love and wisdom her inner spiritual essence.[C]

And then there is that part of us that reaches towards more distant realms. We go beyond the boundary of Israel and sing the song of humankind. Our spirit extends to the wider vistas of the majesty of all humanity and its noble essence, aspiring towards our collective goal, looking forward to our higher perfection. From this source of life we draw the subjects of our meditation and study, our aspirations and visions.[D]

And then there is that part of us that rises toward wider horizons. We link ourselves with all existence, with all God's creatures, with all worlds, and we sing our song with all of them.[E] It is of one such as this that tradition has said that whoever sings a portion of song each day is assured a share in the World to Come.[F]

And then there is that part of us that rises with all these songs in one ensemble, we all join our voices.[G] Together we sing our songs with beauty, each one lending vitality and life to the other: sounds of joy and gladness[H], calls of jubilation and celebration, voices of ecstasy and holiness.

Reflection:

What do your songs sound like? Which ones are the loudest and which ones are the quietest? For each song—self, community, humanity, and all existence—ask yourself:

1. How alive do I feel singing this song?
2. What is working?
3. What is not working?
4. What is my ideal vision for my relationship to this part of me/the world?
5. What is one goal I can set to get me moving in that direction?

(Pronouns Changed)

COMMENTS

What if we could activate these different parts of our being and bring them all into alignment? Can you imagine being in touch with your true self, in conscious relationship with your community, living for the benefit of humanity, and every plant, animal, and even non-living element in existence? Surely, this would be an awakened state. Rav Kook is describing a form of holistic self-actualization and enlightenment—of a great, compassionate, and flowing aliveness. In this vision, realization is not about a cessation of personal suffering nor of blissful attachment to the Inifinite, but of manifesting the potential of every sphere of life. What a life we could live and a world we could inhabit if we rose with these songs all together. This journey can only start with a single step. What is your next move?

The song of ourself, the song of our people, the song of humankind, the song of all the worlds merge in us at all times, at every hour. And this full comprehensiveness rises to become the song of holiness, the song of *El*, the song of *YisraEl*, in its full strength and beauty, in its full authenticity and greatness. *Yisrael, Shir El* [the song of God].^I It is a simple song, a twofold song, a threefold song, a fourfold song.^J It is the Song of Songs of Solomon, for the King in whom is peace.^K

I. In Hebrew, if you rearrange the letters of *Yisrael* [Israel], you get *Shir El*, which means the song of God. *Shir* means "song" and *El* is a name of God. When we sing these songs together, we reach the level of the Divine Song. **J. This phrase appears** in kabbalistic sources dating back to the Zohar. It refers to the four letters of the Divine name *YHWH*. The letter, Y [*yud*] on its own is the simple song. The first two letters YH [*yud, heh*] are the twofold song. YHW [*yud, heh, waw*] is the threefold song, and the full name of YHWH [*yud, heh, waw, heh*] is the fourfold song. The Tikunei Zohar (52a) describes how the prayers of Israel ascend through these four types of songs, and that Israel is redeemed through song. **K. King Solomon is** traditionally believed to have written the Song of Songs from the Bible. His name in Hebrew is Shlomo, which means "His Peace." The last phrase of the poem could also be translated as, "For the King who has peace." The king here can either be Solomon or God, who is also called King.

Appendix 1

Names and Associations of the Ten Sephirot

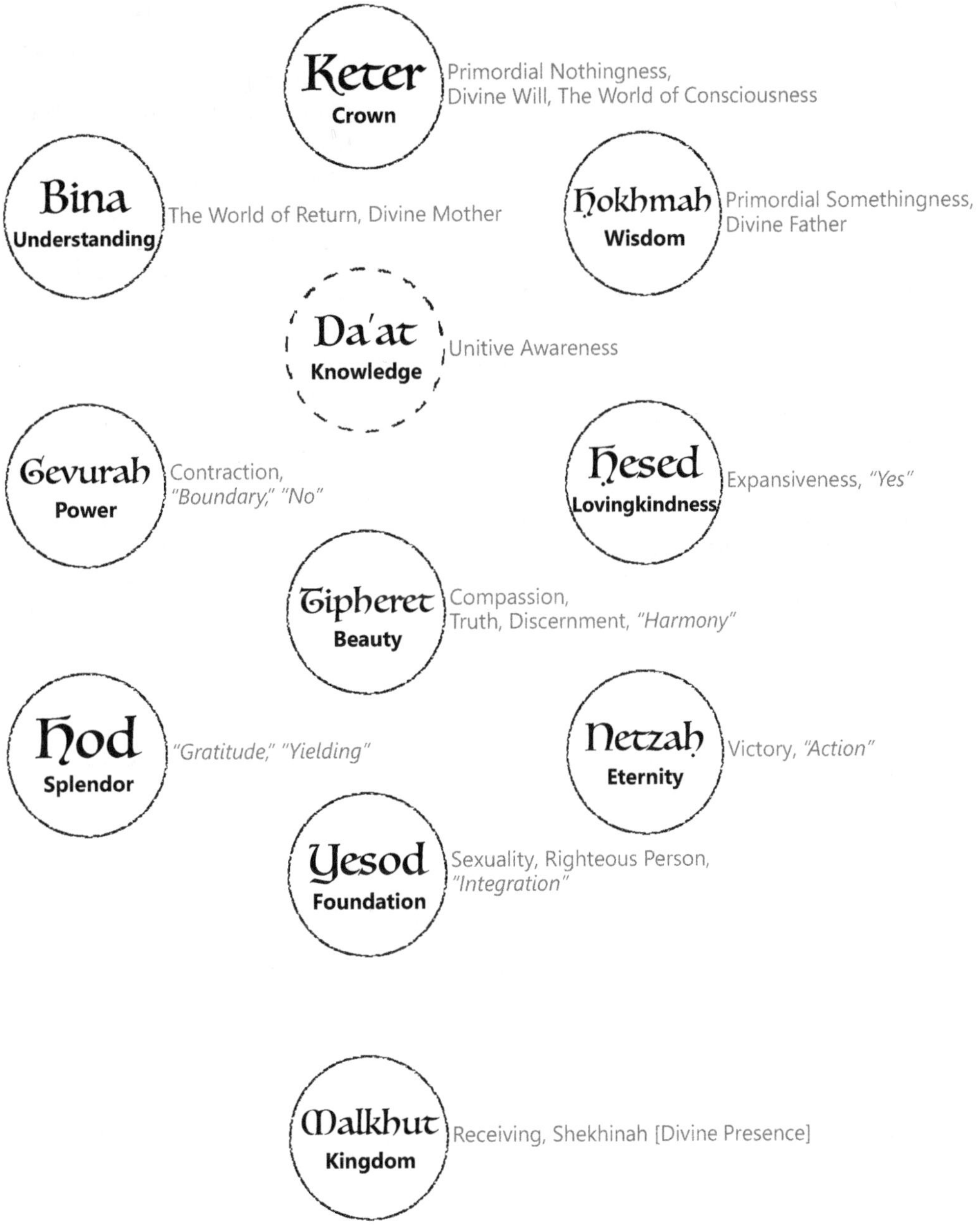

Bold text: Literal translation

Plain text: Other traditional names for this *Sephirah*

"Italicized text": Contemporary associations

Appendix 2

Timeline of Jewish Mysticism

The TaNaKH and Prophecy

(Ending in 6th Century BCE)

The main form of mysticism from this era was the prophetic lineage. It involved hearing God's voice, seeing visions, and carrying out the will of the Divine.

There are many instances of prophets being chosen by God, such as with Moses when God spoke to him from the burning bush. There are also examples of prophetic discipleships, such as the prophet Elijah who trained his successor Elisha.

Early Rabbinic Era and Merkava Mysticism

(1st Century BCE)

The foundational rabbinic texts, the Mishnah and Gemara, as well as *midrashim* and some lesser-known writings, contain fragments of a rabbinic mysticism that involved travelling through celestial chambers, seeking hidden wisdom, and encountering angels.

The goal of many ascents was to encounter the highest angel Metatron or to glimpse the Divine Throne. Merkava mystics were known to begin their ascents by sitting with their head bowed low and chanting without food for great lengths of time.

Kabbalah

(13th Century CE)

A mystical movement that explored the layers between our world and the Infinite. These layers are known as the *Sephirot.*

The earliest known Kabbalist was Isaac the Blind, who lived in Provence, France. Over the course of his life and in the next several generations, the most significant early works were written. These included the Bahir and the Zohar, primarily theosophic works interested in mapping the celestial realms. These conceptual maps show the Infinite's stage-by-stage emanation to the physical world. The map constituted steps in the the spiritual journey when travelled in the opposite direction. Ecstatic Kabbalah also flourished during this period, most notably in the writings of Abraham Abulafia. Its writings were more explicitely experiential and it held the personal encounter with the Divine as the highest ideal. Kabbalah had a great influence on all Jewish mysticism that followed.

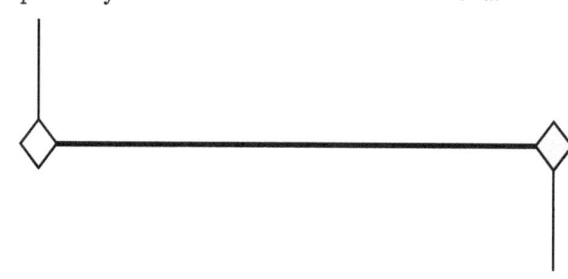

Appendix 2
Timeline of Jewish Mysticism

Lurianic Kabbalah
(16th Century CE)

Inspired by the teachings of Isaac Luria, this mystical movement was centered around the cosmology of the shattered vessels, holy sparks, and *tikkun olam* [repairing the world]. This narrative described how the initial spiritual foundations of the world were shattered. Subsequently, holy sparks of Divine light as well as unholy shards were scattered and misplaced throughout the world. In Lurianic Kabbalah, a Jewish mystic's role is to repair the cosmos by realigning the sparks and shards through elaborate visualizations paired with ritual acts.

Luria's cosmological system was extremely complex and precise. He spent seven years living mostly in a cave in Egypt before sharing it. He died at the age of 38 after having only taught for two years. Due largely to the work of his students in preserving, adapting, and passing on his teachings, he is the most influential Kabbalist of all time.

Hasidism
(18th Century CE)

This was a popular mystical movement that started in Eastern Europe and emphasized experiential spirituality, joy, simplicity, embodiment, and transformation.

The Hasidic movement classically attributes its founding to the Ba'al Shem Tov, a nature mystic and shamanic healer. Equally if not more important to the Hasidic Movement was the Maggid of Mezeritch, a student of the Ba'al Shem Tov who trained and inspired dozens of students who spread the Hasidic message across Eastern Europe in the mid 18th Century.

Our Era

We are in the midst of a new blossoming of Jewish mysticism. Exposure to eastern religions, psychology, psychedelics, shamanic traditions, as well as the integration of academic insights into Jewish life are producing many new theologies, interpretations, and practices. In all Jewish camps, but especially outside of the Orthodox Jewish world, the emerging themes are pluralistic views of gender and sexual orientation, inclusion of people regardless of ethnicity and religion, meditation (including some body-centered practices), and a general spirit of experimentalism.

Today, the major mystical trends are Jewish Renewal, Neo-Hasidism, and Post-Jewish forms. Jewish Renewal was started by Reb Zalman Schachter-Shalomi as a way to reconnect the Jewish denominations with spirituality. Neo-Hasidism began in the 20th century as teachers and students of all denominations began to explore and experiment with Hasidic mysticism outside of the Hasidic communities. Post-Jewish forms are oriented towards the transformative, contemplative, and/or ecstatic journey inspired by Jewish mysticism and are not concerned with particularistic issues of Jewish identity or peoplehood. As such, they are explicitly open to all.

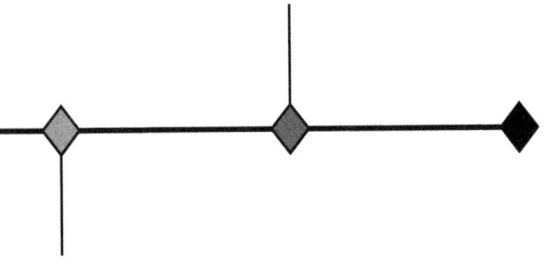

Appendix 3

Hebrew Versions of the Texts

Maor VeShemesh Sukkot 1:11

אָמְנָם הַצַּדִּיק אֲשֶׁר כְּבָר הִגִּיעַ לְמַעֲלַת הַדְּבֵקוּת בְּאֵין סוֹף בָּרוּךְ הוּא וְהוּא קָשׁוּר בְּמַחְשַׁבְתּוֹ בְּכָל עֵת עִקַּר עֲבוֹדָתוֹ הוּא בְּמַחְשָׁבָה כְּמַאֲמָרָם זִכְרוֹנָם לִבְרָכָה קִיֵּם אַבְרָהָם אָבִינוּ כָּל הַתּוֹרָה כֻּלָּהּ עַד שֶׁלֹּא נִתְּנָה. הֲגַם שֶׁלֹּא מָצָאנוּ שֶׁעָשָׂה בְּפֹעַל מַעֲשֵׂה הַמִּצְוֹת כְּהַנָּחַת תְּפִלִּין וַעֲשִׂיַּת סֻכָּה וּכְדוֹמֵיהֶן מִכָּל מָקוֹם הִמְשִׁיךְ עַל עַצְמוֹ פְּנִימִיּוּת הַקְּדֻשּׁוֹת שֶׁרוֹמֶזֶת אֲלֵיהֶם הַמַּעֲשִׂים הָהֵם עַל יְדֵי מַחְשַׁבְתּוֹ הַקְּדוֹשָׁה אֲשֶׁר הָיְתָה דְּבוּקָה בְּאֵין סוֹף בָּרוּךְ הוּא.

Shnei Luḥot HaBrit
Toldot Adam, Beit Yisrael 35

עוֹד תִּמְצָא רֶמֶז יהו"ה בְּעֶשֶׂר אֶצְבָּעוֹת הַיָּדַיִם, שֶׁהֵם מִסְפַּר עֶשֶׂר סְפִירוֹת. כֵּיצַד, הִנֵּה בְּכָל אֶצְבַּע ג' פְּרָקִים, לְבַד מֵאֶצְבַּע אֲגוּדָל שֶׁבּוֹ ב' פְּרָקִים. וַאֲשֶׁר יָצַר אֶת הָאָדָם בְּחָכְמָה, יְצָרוֹ כֵּן בְּכַוָּנָה נִפְלָאָה. יַד יָמִין תִּרְמוֹז לְאוֹתִיּוֹת י"ה, וְיַד שְׂמֹאל תִּרְמוֹז לְאוֹתִיּוֹת ו"ה. קַח אוֹתִיּוֹת יָהּ בְּמִלּוּי כָּזֶה יו"ד ה"א הֲרֵי הֵם חָמֵשׁ אוֹתִיּוֹת, וְהֵם חֲמֵשׁ אֶצְבְּעוֹת הַיָּד. וְקַח אֵלּוּ הָאוֹתִיּוֹת וְתִמַלְּאֵם שֵׁנִית כָּזֶה, יו"ד וא"ו דל"ת ה"א אל"ף, הֲרֵי בַּד' אוֹתִיּוֹת בְּכָל אוֹת ג' פְּרָקִים, וּבְאוֹת ה"א לֹא יֵשׁ רַק ב' פְּרָקִים, כֵּן בַּד' אֶצְבָּעוֹת בְּכָל אֶצְבַּע ג' פְּרָקִים וּבְאֶצְבַּע אֲגוּדָל ב' פְּרָקִים. וְעַל כֵּן נִקְרָא יָד עַל שָׁם י"ד פְּרָקִים.

Sefer HaYashar

אֲבָל אִם הִתְפַּעֵל (דְּהַיְנוּ הַנָּבִיא קִבֵּל שֶׁפַע) וְהִשִּׂיג שֶׁהִתְפַּעֵל, דִּין הוּא אֶצְלִי וְאֵצֶל כָּל שָׁלֵם לְהִקָּרֵא בְּשֵׁם מוֹרֶה, עַל הֱיוֹת שְׁמוֹ כְּשֵׁם רַבּוֹ, מִפְּנֵי שֶׁהוּא לֹא נִפְרָד מֵרַבּוֹ, וְהִנֵּה הוּא רַבּוֹ וְרַבּוֹ הוּא שֶׁכְּבָר דָּבַק בּוֹ דָּבוּק שֶׁאִי אֶפְשָׁר לְהַפְרִידוֹ מִמֶּנּוּ בְּשׁוּם סִבָּה, כִּי הוּא הוּא וּכְמוֹ שֶׁרַבּוֹ נִפְרָד מִכָּל חֹמֶר יִקָּרֵא תָּמִיד שֵׂכֶל מַשְׂכִּיל מֻשְׂכָּל אֲשֶׁר שְׁלָשְׁתָּם עִנְיָן אֶחָד בּוֹ לְעוֹלָם בְּפֹעַל, כֵּן זֶה הַמְּיֻחָד בַּעַל הַשֵּׁם הַמְיֻחָד יִקָּרֵא שֵׂכֶל בְּעֵת שֶׁיַּשִּׂיג בְּפֹעַל וְאָז יִהְיֶה מֻשְׂכָּל מַשְׂכִּיל שֵׂכֶל בְּפֹעַל כְּרַבּוֹ, וְאָז אֵין הֶבְדֵּל בֵּינֵיהֶם אֶלָּא מִפְּנֵי רַבּוֹ תַּכְלִית מַעֲלָתוֹ וְלֹא בְּזוּלָתוֹ מִן הַנִּבְרָאִים, וְזֶה הִגִּיעַ אֶל מַעֲלָתוֹ עַל יְדֵי הַנִּבְרָאִים וּבְאֶמְצָעוּתָם.

Midrash Rabeinu Baḥya
Shemot 3

וְעַל דֶּרֶךְ הַפְּשַׁט עִנְיַן הַפָּרָשָׁה הַזֹּאת, כִּי מֹשֶׁה הִשִּׂיג שְׁלֹשָׁה עִנְיָנִים, וְאֵלּוּ הֵם: הָאֵשׁ וְהַמַּלְאָךְ וְהַשְּׁכִינָה. תְּחִלָּה רָאָה הָאֵשׁ שֶׁהָיְתָה מִתְלַקַּחַת בַּסְּנֶה וְאֵין הַסְּנֶה נִשְׂרָף, וְרָאָה זֶה בְּעֵין הַבָּשָׂר מַמָּשׁ בְּהָקִיץ, כִּי כְּשֶׁרָאָה הַסְּנֶה בּוֹעֵר בָּאֵשׁ הִכִּיר שֶׁהוּא אֵשׁ וְהָיָה סָבוּר שֶׁהוּא אֵשׁ גָּפְרִית שֶׁל מַטָּה, וּכְשֶׁהָיְתָה דַּעְתּוֹ כֵּן וְלֹא הָיָה הַסְּנֶה אוּכַּל עַל כֵּן רָצָה לְהִתְקָרֵב. זֶהוּ שֶׁאָמַר "אָסֻרָה נָּא וְאֶרְאֶה אֶת הַמַּרְאֶה הַגָּדֹל הַזֶּה" (שְׁמוֹת ג, ג), כְּלוֹמַר אֶרְאֶה הַפֶּלֶא הַזֶּה אִם נִשְׁתַּנָּה הַסְּנֶה מִשְּׁאָר הָעֵצִים אוֹ נִשְׁתַּנָּה הָאֵשׁ מִשְּׁאָר הָאִשּׁוֹת, שֶׁאִלּוּ הָיָה סָבוּר שֶׁהָיָה הָאֵשׁ שֶׁל מַעְלָה לֹא הָיָה מִתְקָרֵב. וְאַחַר שֶׁרָאָה הָאֵשׁ הַזֹּאת, נִתְחַזֵּק שִׂכְלוֹ בִּרְאִיַּת הַמַּלְאָךְ, וְזֶה שֶׁכָּתוּב "וַיֵּרָא מַלְאַךְ ה' אֵלָיו בְּלַבַּת אֵשׁ מִתּוֹךְ הַסְּנֶה" (שְׁמוֹת ג, ב), מַשְׁמָעוּת הַכָּתוּב כִּי לַבַּת אֵשׁ רָאָה תְּחִלָּה, וְאַחַר כָּךְ הַמַּלְאָךְ מִתּוֹךְ הָאֵשׁ. וְאַחַר שֶׁנִּתְחַזֵּק שִׂכְלוֹ בִּרְאִיַּת הַמַּלְאָךְ רָאָה בְּמַרְאֶה הַנְּבוּאָה כְּבוֹד הַשְּׁכִינָה, וְזֶהוּ שֶׁאָמַר "וַיַּרְא ה' כִּי סָר לִרְאוֹת וַיִּקְרָא אֵלָיו אֱלֹהִים" (שְׁמוֹת ג, ד). וּמִפְּנֵי שֶׁעַתָּה הָיְתָה תְּחִלַּת נְבוּאַת מֹשֶׁה, רָצָה הַקָּדוֹשׁ בָּרוּךְ הוּא לְחַנְּכוֹ מְעַט מְעַט וּלְהַעֲלוֹתוֹ מִמַּדְרֵגָה לְמַדְרֵגָה עַד שֶׁיִּתְחַזֵּק שִׂכְלוֹ. מָשָׁל לְמָה הַדָּבָר דּוֹמֶה, לְאָדָם הַיּוֹשֵׁב בְּבַיִת אָפֵל זְמַן מְרֻבֶּה, אִם יֵצֵא פִּתְאוֹם וְיִסְתַּכֵּל לְעֵין הַשֶּׁמֶשׁ יֶחְשְׁכוּ רְאִיּוֹתָיו, וְעַל כֵּן צָרִיךְ שֶׁיִּסְתַּכֵּל בָּאוֹר מְעַט מְעַט עַד שֶׁיִּהְיֶה רָגִיל בְּכָךְ. וּכְשֵׁם שֶׁיִּקְרֶה זֶה בְּאוֹר הַשֶּׁמֶשׁ, הוּא הַדִּין וְהוּא הַטַּעַם בְּעַצְמוֹ בְּאוֹר הַשֵּׂכֶל, כִּי הַדְּבָרִים הַשִּׂכְלִיִּים בְּדִמְיוֹן הַדְּבָרִים הַטִּבְעִיִּים, כִּי יִקְרֶה לַשֵּׂכֶל כְּמִקְרֶה הַחוּשִׁים, וְכֹחוֹת הַנֶּפֶשׁ הֲלֹא הֵם קְשׁוּרִים עִם כֹּחוֹת הַגּוּף?

Appendix 3
Hebrew Versions of the Texts

דַּע, שֶׁיֵּשׁ אוֹר, שֶׁהוּא לְמַעְלָה מִנַּפְשִׁין וְרוּחִין וְנִשְׁמָתִין, וְהוּא אוֹר אֵין־סוֹף, וְאַף־עַל־פִּי שֶׁאֵין הַשֵּׂכֶל מַשִּׂיג אוֹתוֹ, אַף־עַל־פִּי־כֵן רְדִיפָה דְּמַחֲשָׁבָה לְמִרְדַּף אֲבַתְרֵהּ, וְעַל יְדֵי הָרְדִיפָה, אָז הַשֵּׂכֶל מַשִּׂיג אוֹתוֹ בִּבְחִינַת מָטֵי וְלָא מָטֵי, כִּי בֶּאֱמֶת אִי אֶפְשָׁר לְהַשִּׂיג אוֹתוֹ, כִּי הוּא לְמַעְלָה מִנֶּפֶשׁ רוּחַ נְשָׁמָה.	Likutei Moharan, 24:1
וְצָרִיךְ כָּל אָדָם לְרַחֵם מְאֹד עַל בְּשַׂר הַגּוּף לְהַרְאוֹת לוֹ מִכָּל הֶאָרָה וּמִכָּל הַשָּׂגָה שֶׁהַנְּשָׁמָה מַשֶּׂגֶת שֶׁהַגּוּף גַּם כֵּן יֵדַע מִזֹּאת הַהַשָּׂגָה בִּבְחִינַת: "וּמִבְּשָׂרְךָ לֹא תִתְעַלָּם" (יְשַׁעְיָהוּ נח, ז) 'מִבְּשָׂרְךָ' דַּיְקָא שֶׁלֹּא תַּעְלִים עֵינֶיךָ מִלְּרַחֵם עַל בְּשָׂרְךָ הַיְנוּ בְּשַׂר גּוּפְךָ כִּי צְרִיכִין לְרַחֵם מְאֹד עַל הַגּוּף לִרְאוֹת לְזַכְּכוֹ כְּדֵי שֶׁיּוּכַל לְהוֹדִיעַ לוֹ מִכָּל הֶהָאָרוֹת וְהַהַשָּׂגוֹת שֶׁהַנְּשָׁמָה מַשֶּׂגֶת כִּי הַנְּשָׁמָה שֶׁל כָּל אָדָם הִיא רוֹאָה וּמַשֶּׂגֶת תָּמִיד דְּבָרִים עֶלְיוֹנִים מְאֹד אֲבָל הַגּוּף אֵינוֹ יוֹדֵעַ מֵהֶם עַל כֵּן צָרִיךְ כָּל אָדָם לְרַחֵם מְאֹד עַל בְּשַׂר הַגּוּף לִרְאוֹת לְזַכֵּךְ הַגּוּף עַד שֶׁתּוּכַל הַנְּשָׁמָה לְהוֹדִיעַ לוֹ מִכָּל מָה שֶׁהִיא רוֹאָה וּמַשֶּׂגֶת תָּמִיד.	Likutei Moharan, 22:5
וְהִנֵּה בֶּאֱמֶת, בִּשְׁעַת בִּטּוּל שֶׁנִּתְבַּטֵּל אֶל הַתַּכְלִית, שֶׁהוּא כֻּלּוֹ טוֹב, כֻּלּוֹ אֶחָד, אֲזַי בֶּאֱמֶת נִתְבַּטְּלִין הַיִּסּוּרִין. אַךְ אִי אֶפְשָׁר לִהְיוֹת תָּמִיד קָבוּעַ בִּבְחִינוֹת הַבִּטּוּל, כִּי אִם כֵּן יָצָא מִגֶּדֶר אֱנוֹשִׁי, וְעַל כֵּן, מֻכְרָח שֶׁיִּהְיֶה הַבִּטּוּל בִּבְחִינוֹת רָצוֹא וָשׁוֹב. עַל-כֵּן, כְּשֶׁחוֹזֵר הַשֵּׂכֶל מֵהַבִּטּוּל אֶל הַמּוֹחַ, שֶׁהוּא כְּלִי הַשֵּׂכֶל, אֲזַי אִי אֶפְשָׁר לְהַמֹּחִין, שֶׁהֵם הַכֵּלִים, לְקַבֵּל זֶה הַשֵּׂכֶל שֶׁל בְּחִינוֹת בִּטּוּל. כִּי הוּא בְּחִינוֹת אֵין סוֹף, שֶׁהוּא בְּחִינוֹת הַתַּכְלִית, שֶׁהוּא כֻּלּוֹ אֶחָד, כֻּלּוֹ טוֹב, וּמֵחֲמַת זֶה מַרְגִּישׁ הַמּוֹחַ הַצַּעַר שֶׁל הַיִּסּוּרִין... וְאַחַר כָּךְ, אַף עַל פִּי שֶׁשָּׁב מֵהַבִּטּוּל, אַף עַל פִּי כֵן מֵהָרְשִׁימוּ שֶׁנִּשְׁאָר מֵהַבִּטּוּל, עַל-יְדֵי זֶה נַעֲשֶׂה הִתְחַדְּשׁוּת הַתּוֹרָה. כִּי עַל-יְדֵי הַבִּטּוּל שֶׁנִּתְבַּטֵּל אֶל הַתַּכְלִית, וְהִשִּׂיג שֶׁכָּל הַיִּסּוּרִין הֵם טוֹבוֹת גְּדוֹלוֹת מְאֹד, עַל יְדֵי זֶה נִתְמַלֵּא שִׂמְחָה. וְהַשִּׂמְחָה הוּא כְּלִי אֶל חִדּוּשִׁין דְּאוֹרַיְתָא.	Likutei Moharan, 65:4
מִצְוָה גְּדוֹלָה לִהְיוֹת בְּשִׂמְחָה תָּמִיד, וּלְהִתְגַּבֵּר לְהַרְחִיק הָעַצְבוּת וְהַמָּרָה שְׁחֹרָה בְּכָל כֹּחוֹ... כִּי טֶבַע הָאָדָם לִמְשֹׁךְ עַצְמוֹ לְמָרָה שְׁחֹרָה וְעַצְבוּת מֵחֲמַת פִּגְעֵי וּמִקְרֵי הַזְּמַן, וְכָל אָדָם מָלֵא יִסּוּרִים, עַל־כֵּן צָרִיךְ לְהַכְרִיחַ אֶת עַצְמוֹ בְּכֹחַ גָּדוֹל לִהְיוֹת בְּשִׂמְחָה תָּמִיד וּלְשַׂמֵּחַ אֶת עַצְמוֹ בְּכָל אֲשֶׁר יוּכַל, וַאֲפִלּוּ בְּמִלֵּי דִּשְׁטוּתָא... אַף שֶׁגַּם לֵב נִשְׁבָּר הוּא טוֹב מְאֹד, עִם כָּל זֶה הוּא רַק בְּאֵיזוֹ שָׁעָה, וְרָאוּי לִקְבֹּעַ לוֹ אֵיזֶה שָׁעָה בַּיּוֹם לְשַׁבֵּר לִבּוֹ וּלְפָרֵשׁ שִׂיחָתוֹ לְפָנָיו יִתְבָּרַךְ... עַל־כֵּן צָרִיךְ שֶׁיִּהְיֶה בְּשִׂמְחָה תָּמִיד, רַק בְּשָׁעָה מְיֻחֶדֶת יִהְיֶה לוֹ לֵב נִשְׁבָּר.	Likutei Moharan, 2:24:1–2
הוּא יִתְבָּרַךְ נִמְצָא בְּבָתֵּי גַּוָּאֵי וּבוֹכֶה, וּמִי שֶׁדּוֹחֵק וּמִתְקָרֵב אֵלָיו בַּתּוֹרָה, אָז בּוֹכֶה הוּא שָׁם עִם הַקָּדוֹשׁ בָּרוּךְ הוּא וְגַם לוֹמֵד תּוֹרָה עִמּוֹ, וְזֶה הַחִלּוּק, הַבְּכִיּוֹת וְהַצַּעַר שֶׁהָאָדָם מִצְטַעֵר בְּעַצְמוֹ לְבַדּוֹ עַל צָרוֹתָיו יֵשׁ שֶׁנִּשְׁבַּר וְנוֹפֵל מֵהֶם עַד שֶׁאֵינוֹ יָכוֹל לַעֲשׂוֹת מְאוּמָה, וְהַבְּכִיּוֹת שֶׁבּוֹכֶה עִם הַקָּדוֹשׁ בָּרוּךְ הוּא יַחַד, מַחֲזִיקִים אוֹתוֹ, בּוֹכֶה וּמִתְחַזֵּק נִשְׁבָּר וּמִתְאַמֵּץ לִלְמֹד וְלַעֲבֹד, קָשֶׁה הוּא רַק לְהִתְרוֹמֵם פַּעַם הָרִאשׁוֹנָה וְהַשְּׁנִיָּה מִן הַצָּרוֹת, אֲבָל כְּשֶׁמִּתְאַמֵּץ וּמוֹשִׁיט אֶת רֹאשׁוֹ וְנוֹגֵעַ בַּתּוֹרָה וּבַעֲבוֹדָה, אָז נִכְנָס הוּא אֶל הַבָּתֵּי גַּוָּאֵי שֶׁשָּׁם הַקָּדוֹשׁ בָּרוּךְ הוּא, וְשָׁם בּוֹכֶה וּמְיַלֵּל עִמּוֹ כִּבְיָכוֹל יַחַד, אַף מִתְחַזֵּק לוֹמֵד תּוֹרָה וְעוֹבֵד עֲבוֹדָתוֹ יִתְבָּרַךְ.	Esh Kodesh, pp. 178–179

Appendix 3
Hebrew Versions of the Texts

Keter Shem Tov, 1:24:2	"אָמַר רֵישׁ לָקִישׁ פְּעָמִים שֶׁבִּטּוּלָהּ שֶׁל תּוֹרָה זֶהוּ יְסוּדָהּ" (מְנָחוֹת צט:). וְהוּא תְּמוּהַּ אֵיךְ אֶפְשָׁר שֶׁבִּטּוּלָהּ שֶׁל תּוֹרָה זֶהוּ יְסוּדָהּ? וּפֵרֵשׁ הַבַּעַל שֵׁם טוֹב, כִּי "וְהַחַיּוֹת רָצוֹא וָשׁוֹב" (יְחֶזְקֵאל א, יד), לְפִי שֶׁכָּל דָּבָר מִתְלַהֵב לָשׁוּב לְשָׁרְשׁוֹ וּלְכָךְ עַל יְדֵי אֲכִילָה וּשְׁתִיָּה וְעֵסֶק מַשָּׂא וּמַתָּן מִתְבַּטֵּל הָאָדָם מִלִּמּוּד תּוֹרָה וּבַעֲבוֹדַת הַשֵּׁם, אָז נָחָה הַנְּשָׁמָה מֵהִתְלַהֲבוּתָהּ וּמִתְחַזֶּקֶת לָשׁוּב לִדְבֵיקוּת יוֹתֵר עֶלְיוֹן. וּבָזֶה אָמַר האר"י, "פְּעָמִים שֶׁבִּטּוּלָהּ שֶׁל תּוֹרָה זֶה יְסוּדוֹ, בְּסוֹד 'וְהַחַיּוֹת' רָצוֹא וָשׁוֹב.'" וְהָבֵן!
Keter Shem Tov, 1:27:1	עִנְיַן מִלְּתָא דִּבְדִיחוּתָא קֹדֶם הַלִּמּוּד (שַׁבָּת ל:): כִּי "הַחַיּוֹת רָצוֹא וָשׁוֹב," (יְחֶזְקֵאל א, יד) וְהָאָדָם בְּסוֹד קַטְנוּת וְגַדְלוּת, וְעַל יְדֵי הַשִּׂמְחָה וּמִלְּתָא דִּבְדִיחוּתָא יוֹצֵא מִקַּטְנוּת לְגַדְלוּת לִלְמֹד וּלְדָבְקָה בּוֹ יִתְבָּרַךְ. וְזֶה שֶׁאָמְרוּ בְּהָנֵי תְּרֵי בַּדְחֵי שֶׁהָיוּ מְפַקְּחִין צַעַר הָאָדָם עַל יְדֵי מִלְּתָא דִּבְדִיחוּתָא וְאָז יוּכְלוּ לְקָרְבוֹ וּלְהַעֲלוֹתוֹ (תַּעֲנִית כב.). וְזֶה שֶׁכָּתוּב "וַיִּקַּח אֶת שְׁנֵי נְעָרָיו עִמּוֹ וְאֵת יִצְחָק בְּנוֹ" (בְּרֵאשִׁית כב, ג), כִּי עַל יְדֵי הַצְּחוֹק לְשֵׁם שָׁמַיִם יָכוֹל לְהַעֲלוֹת הַשָּׁנִים שֶׁל נַעֲרוּת גַּם כֵּן עִמּוֹ.
Keter Shem Tov, 1:39:3	וְיֵשׁ לְהָבִין, הָא הַשֵּׁם יִתְבָּרַךְ "מְלֹא כָל הָאָרֶץ כְּבוֹדוֹ,"(יְשַׁעְיָהוּ ו, ג) "לֵית אֲתַר פָּנוּי מִנֵּיהּ," (תִּקּוּנֵי הַזֹּהַר צא:) וּבְמָקוֹם שֶׁאָדָם—שָׁם כְּבוֹדוֹ יִתְבָּרַךְ מָצוּי. וְאִם כֵּן לָמָּה לִי שֶׁיְּקַבֵּל הַתְּפִלָּה עַל יְדֵי מַלְאָכִים שֶׁיֵּלְכוּ מֵהֵיכָל לְהֵיכָל. וְיֵשׁ לוֹמַר דְּהַקָּדוֹשׁ בָּרוּךְ הוּא עָשָׂה זֶה כְּדֵי שֶׁיֵּרָאֶה לוֹ לָאָדָם שֶׁהוּא רָחוֹק וְיִשְׁתַּדֵּל לְהִתְקָרֵב מְאֹד כְּמוֹ שֶׁאָמַר הַבַּעַל שֵׁם טוֹב זִכְרוֹנוֹ לִבְרָכָה (מָשָׁל שֶׁאָמַר קֹדֶם תְּקִיעַת שׁוֹפָר): שֶׁהָיָה מֶלֶךְ אֶחָד חָכָם גָּדוֹל וְעָשָׂה בַּאֲחִיזַת עֵינַיִם חוֹמוֹת וּמִגְדָּלִים וּשְׁעָרִים, וְצִוָּה שֶׁיֵּלְכוּ אֶצְלוֹ דֶּרֶךְ הַשְּׁעָרִים וְהַמִּגְדָּלִים. וְצִוָּה לְפַזֵּר בְּכָל שַׁעַר וְשַׁעַר אוֹצָרוֹת הַמֶּלֶךְ. וְיֵשׁ שֶׁהָלַךְ עַד שַׁעַר א' וְלָקַח מָמוֹן וְחָזַר. וְיֵשׁ וְכוּ'... עַד שֶׁבְּנוֹ יְדִידוֹ הִתְאַמֵּץ מְאֹד שֶׁיֵּלֵךְ דַּוְקָא אֶל אָבִיו הַמֶּלֶךְ—אָז רָאָה שֶׁאֵין שׁוּם מְחִצָּה מַפְסִיק בֵּינוֹ לְבֵין אָבִיו, כִּי הַכֹּל הָיָה אֲחִיזַת עֵינַיִם. וְהַנִּמְשָׁל מוּבָן דְּהַקָּדוֹשׁ בָּרוּךְ הוּא מִסְתַּתֵּר בְּכַמָּה לְבוּשִׁין וּמְחִיצוֹת, וּבְיָדוּעַ שֶׁהַשֵּׁם יִתְבָּרַךְ מְלֹא כָל הָאָרֶץ כְּבוֹדוֹ, וְכָל תְּנוּעָה וּמַחֲשָׁבָה הַכֹּל מִמֶּנּוּ יִתְבָּרַךְ, וְכֵן כָּל הַמַּלְאָכִים וְהַהֵיכָלוֹת הַכֹּל נִבְרָא וְנַעֲשָׂה כִּבְיָכוֹל מֵעַצְמוּתוֹ יִתְבָּרַךְ, כְּהָדֵין קַמְצָא דִּלְבוּשֵׁהּ מִינֵּיהּ וּבֵיהּ, וְאֵין שׁוּם מְחִצָּה מַבְדִּיל בֵּין הָאָדָם וּבֵינוֹ יִתְבָּרַךְ. בִּידִיעָה זֹאת וְעַל יְדֵי זֶה "יִתְפָּרְדוּ כָּל פּוֹעֲלֵי אָוֶן" (תְּהִלִּים צב, י).
Keter Shem Tov, 1:61:1	עִנְיַן "רָצוֹא וָשׁוֹב" (יְחֶזְקֵאל א, יד) אֲפִלּוּ בְּגַשְׁמִי, "וֶהֱוֵי מִתְחַמֵּם כְּנֶגֶד אוּרָן שֶׁל חֲכָמִים" (מִשְׁנָה אָבוֹת ב, י), רָצָה לוֹמַר שֶׁלֹּא לְחַמֵּם מֵרָחוֹק וְלֹא לְהִתְקָרֵב מְאֹד עַד גַּחֶלֶת הָאֵשׁ כִּי "וֶהֱזָּהֵר בְּגֶחָלִים שֶׁלֹּא תִּכָּוֶה" (מִשְׁנָה אָבוֹת ב, י)
Keter Shem Tov, 2:13	בִּגְמָרָא "הַצַּדִּיקִים דּוֹמִים לְאִילָן הַנָּטוּעַ בְּמָקוֹם טָהֳרָה" (קִדּוּשִׁין מ:). פֵּרוּשׁ, שֶׁכְּמוֹ שֶׁזּוֹרְעִין דָּבָר בָּאָרֶץ אָז מַמְשִׁיךְ כָּל הַכּוֹחוֹת שֶׁיֵּשׁ בָּאָרֶץ לְתוֹךְ הַזֶּרַע וּמוֹצִיא הַפֵּרוֹת, כָּךְ הַצַּדִּיק בָּעוֹלָם הַזֶּה מַמְשִׁיךְ הַנִּיצוֹצוֹת שֶׁמִּשֹׁרֶשׁ נִשְׁמָתוֹ בְּכָל דָּבָר שֶׁבָּעוֹלָם וּמַעֲלֶה אוֹתָן הַנִּצוֹצִין לַבּוֹרֵא יִתְבָּרֵךְ.

Appendix 3

Hebrew Versions of the Texts

Sefer Ba'al Shem Tov Kedoshim 21

"וְאָהַבְתָּ לְרֵעֲךָ כָּמוֹךָ וגוֹ'" (וַיִּקְרָא יט, יח). פֵּרוּשׁ הַפָּסוּק וְאָהַבְתָּ לְרֵעֲךָ, שֶׁכְּמוֹ שֶׁאַתָּה תִּתְנַהֵג
עִם רֵעֲךָ בְּאַהֲבָה וְאַחְדוּת, כָּמוֹךָ אֲנִי הַשֵּׁם, שֶׁאֲנִי הַשֵּׁם אֶהְיֶה כָּמוֹךָ, וְהוּא בְּסוֹד "הַשֵּׁם צִלְּךָ"
(תְּהִלִּים קכא, ה) שֶׁנִּתְבָּאֵר בְּדִבְרֵי מָרָן אֱלֹהִי הַבַּעַל שֵׁם טוֹב, שֶׁכְּמוֹ שֶׁאָדָם מִתְנַהֵג לְמַטָּה
עִם חֲבֵרוֹ וְרֵעוֹ, בְּאַהֲבָה וּבְמִדּוֹת טוֹבוֹת, וְכָךְ יִתְנַהֵג עִמּוֹ מֶלֶךְ עֶלְיוֹן, וּכְמוֹ הַצֵּל, שֶׁכָּל תְּנוּעָה
שֶׁאָדָם עוֹשֶׂה כָּךְ עוֹשֶׂה הַצֵּל כְּנֶגְדּוֹ, כֵּן הוּא יִתְבָּרֵךְ עִם הָאָדָם, וְזֶהוּ וְאָהַבְתָּ לְרֵעֲךָ—כִּי כָּמוֹךָ
אֲנִי הַשֵּׁם, לְהִתְנַהֵג גַּם עִמְּךָ בְּאַהֲבָה וְכָל טוּב.

Tzava'at HaRivash, 64

פְּעָמִים שֶׁנּוֹפֵל אָדָם מִמַּדְרֵגָה מֵחֲמַת עַצְמוֹ, שֶׁהַשֵּׁם יִתְבָּרַךְ יוֹדֵעַ שֶׁצָּרִיךְ לְכָךְ, וּפְעָמִים הָעוֹלָם
גּוֹרְמִים שֶׁיִּפֹּל אָדָם מִמַּדְרֵגָתוֹ, וְהַיְּרִידָה הוּא צֹרֶךְ עֲלִיָּה כְּדֵי לָבֹא לְמַדְרֵגָה גְּדוֹלָה, כְּמוֹ שֶׁנֶּאֱמַר
"הוּא יְנַהֲגֵנוּ עַל מוּת" (תְּהִלִּים מח, טו), וּכְתִיב "וַיֵּרֶד אַבְרָם מִצְרַיְמָה" (בְּרֵאשִׁית יב, י), "וַיַּעַל
אַבְרָם מִמִּצְרָיִם" (בְּרֵאשִׁית יג, א). אַבְרָם הוּא הַנְּשָׁמָה וּמִצְרַיִם הֵם הַקְּלִפּוֹת.

Bnei Yisaskhar, Adar, 6:8

"יְחַיּוּ דָגָן וְיִפְרְחוּ כַגָּפֶן וְגוֹ'" (הוֹשֵׁעַ יד, ח)

דְּהִנֵּה (בְּרָכוֹת לח:) כָּל הַפֵּרוֹת כְּמִשְׁתַּנִּין מִבְּרִיָּתָן גְּרִיעוּתָא הוּא גַּבַּיְהוּ וְאָבְדוּ בִּרְכָתָם הָרִאשׁוֹנָה
וּמְבָרְכִין עֲלֵיהֶם שֶׁהַכֹּל, מַה שֶּׁאֵין כֵּן דָּגָן וְיַיִן מִשְׁתַּנִּין לְמַעַלְיוּתָא וְקוֹבְעִים בְּרָכָה לְעַצְמָם לְבָרֵךְ
עֲלֵיהֶם הַמּוֹצִיא וּבוֹרֵא פְּרִי הַגָּפֶן.

כְּמוֹ כֵן הוּא הַבַּעַל תְּשׁוּבָה מֵאַהֲבָה אִשְׁתַּנֵּי לְמַעַלְיוּתָא שֶׁזְּדוֹנוֹת נַעֲשִׂין לוֹ כִּזְכֻיּוֹת וְקוֹבֵעַ בְּרָכָה
לְעַצְמוֹ בְּהַשִּׁנּוּי כְּמוֹ דָגָן וְיַיִן.

Kedushat Levi, Yitro 8

"וַיֹּאמֶר הַשֵּׁם אֶל מֹשֶׁה רֵד הָעֵד בָּעָם וְכוּ'", "וַיֹּאמֶר מֹשֶׁה אֶל הַשֵּׁם וְכוּ'", "וַיֹּאמֶר אֵלָיו הַשֵּׁם
לֶךְ רֵד וְכוּ'" (שְׁמוֹת יֵט, כא-כד).

וְהִנֵּה רַשִׁ"י זִכְרוֹנוֹ לִבְרָכָה מְפָרֵשׁ שֶׁמְּזָרְזִין וְכוּ'. וְהַנִּרְאֶה כָּךְ, דְּהִנֵּה מֹשֶׁה רַבֵּינוּ עָלָיו הַשָּׁלוֹם
הָיָה מַאֲמִין בְּדִבְרֵי הַבּוֹרֵא יִתְבָּרַךְ בֶּאֱמוּנָה גְּדוֹלָה וּשְׁלֵמָה, וְהָיָה מְקַיֵּם דִּבְרֵי הַבּוֹרֵא יִתְבָּרַךְ
תֵּיכֶף כְּשֶׁשָּׁמַע הַצִּוּוּי מִפִּי הַבּוֹרֵא יִתְבָּרַךְ בִּזְרִיזוּת גָּדוֹל. וְהִנֵּה מֹשֶׁה רַבֵּינוּ עָלָיו הַשָּׁלוֹם הָיָה
סָבוּר כְּמוֹ שֶׁהוּא מַאֲמִין לְדִבְרֵי הַבּוֹרֵא יִתְבָּרַךְ וְאֵינוֹ עוֹבֵר עַל דְּבָרָיו, כֵּן הָאֱמוּנָה וְהַהַנְהָגָה בְּלֵב
כָּל אִישׁ יִשְׂרָאֵל. וּבֶאֱמֶת אֵין אָנוּ בְּמַדְרֵיגָה גְּדוֹלָה כְּמֹשֶׁה רַבֵּינוּ עָלָיו הַשָּׁלוֹם אֲשֶׁר יְדָעוֹ הַשֵּׁם
"פָּנִים אֶל פָּנִים וְכוּ'" (דְּבָרִים לד, י), וְהָיָה רוֹאֶה תָּמִיד כָּל עֵת גְּדֻלַּת הַבּוֹרֵא יִתְבָּרַךְ שְׁמוֹ, וְהָיָה
לוֹ אֱמוּנָה חֲזָקָה לִשְׁמוֹר הַצִּוּוּי אֲשֶׁר יָצָא מִפִּי הַשֵּׁם וְשֶׁלֹּא לַעֲבֹר חַס וְשָׁלוֹם עַל רְצוֹנוֹ, כִּי הָיָה
תָּמִיד דָּבוּק בְּהַשֵּׁם וְהָיָה בְּמַדְרֵיגָה גְּדוֹלָה. וְזֶהוּ הָרֶמֶז בַּפָּסוּק, "וַיֹּאמֶר מֹשֶׁה אֶל הַשֵּׁם לֹא יוּכַל
הָעָם לַעֲלֹת" וְכוּ', "כִּי אַתָּה הַעֵדֹתָה" וְגוֹ': כְּלוֹמַר מֹשֶׁה אָמַר אֶל הַשֵּׁם, לָמָּה אָשׁוּב לוֹמַר עוֹד
לָהֶם כֵּיוָן שֶׁצִּוִּיתָ לָהֶם פַּעַם אֶחָד בְּוַדַּאי לֹא יַעַבְרוּ עַל דְּבָרֶיךָ, כִּי זֶה הָיָה זָר בְּעֵינֵי מֹשֶׁה שֶׁיִּהְיֶה
אָדָם בָּעוֹלָם שֶׁיַּעֲבֹר עַל צִוּוּי הַבּוֹרֵא יִתְבָּרַךְ. כִּי מֹשֶׁה הָיָה בְּמַדְרֵיגָה גְּדוֹלָה, וְהָיָה סָבוּר שֶׁאִי
אֶפְשָׁר לְאָדָם בָּעוֹלָם שֶׁיַּעֲבֹר עַל צִוּוּי הַבּוֹרֵא יִתְבָּרַךְ. וְזֶהוּ "וַיֹּאמֶר אֵלָיו ה' לֶךְ רֵד" וכו', הַשֵּׁם
יִתְבָּרַךְ אָמַר לְמֹשֶׁה, אַתָּה בְּמַדְרֵיגָה גְּדוֹלָה וְאַתָּה תָּמִיד דָּבוּק אֵלַי, לְכָךְ קָשֶׁה לְךָ אֵיךְ אֶפְשָׁר
לַעֲבֹר אָדָם עַל צִוּוּי שֶׁלִּי. "לֶךְ רֵד", כְּלוֹמַר רֵד מִמַּדְרֵגָתְךָ וְתִרְאֶה שֶׁבְּמַדְרֵגָה הַתַּחְתּוֹנָה יָכוֹל
אָדָם לַעֲבֹר עַל צִוּוּי שֶׁלִּי, וּלְכָךְ "לֶךְ" פַּעַם שֵׁנִית וְהָעֵד בָּם.

Appendix 3

Hebrew Versions of the Texts

Arvei Naḥal, Lekh Lekha 3

הָאָדָם אֲשֶׁר יֵשׁ בּוֹ שֶׁמֶץ מֵרַע וְעַל יְדֵי זֶה מַזְמִין לוֹ הַשֵּׁם יִתְבָּרַךְ שֶׁרוֹאֶה אוֹ שׁוֹמֵעַ בָּרַע וּמְתַקֵּן אֶצְלוֹ הַדָּבָר הַהוּא וְעַל יְדֵי זֶה מְתַקֵּן גַּם אֶת הָאִישׁ הָעוֹשֶׂה הָרַע בְּפוֹעַל. מַה שֶּׁאֵין כֵּן הָאִישׁ אֲשֶׁר נִתְפַּשֵּׁט מִכָּל גַּשְׁמִיּוּת עוֹלָם הַזֶּה אָז אֵין בּוֹ שֶׁמֶץ רַע וְאֵין לוֹ חִבּוּר כְּלָל עִם עוֹשֵׂי רַע אָז אֵינוֹ יָכוֹל לְתַקְּנָם. הוּא הַדָּבָר אֲשֶׁר אָמַרְנוּ שֶׁמִּצַּד אֶחָד יֵשׁ בּוֹ חִסָּרוֹן בַּצַּדִּיק אֲשֶׁר יָצָא מֵהַטֶּבַע לְגַמְרֵי, דְּהַיְנוּ שֶׁאֵין בְּכֹחוֹ לְהַחֲזִיר הָרְשָׁעִים לְמוּטָב, וְאָמְנָם הַצַּדִּיק הַהוּא אֲשֶׁר יָצָא מֵהַטֶּבַע וַדַּאי לֹא יַפְסִיד שֶׁלֹּא לִהְיוֹת בִּכְלָל מְזַכֶּה לְחַיָּבִים, וְלָכֵן צָרִיךְ לִהְיוֹת לוֹ יְרִידָה לְצֹרֶךְ עֲלִיָּה. וְהַיְנוּ, שֶׁצָּרִיךְ בְּכַוָּנָה לִפְרָקִים לֵרֵד מִמַּדְרֵיגָתוֹ וּלְהִתְעָרֵב בְּעִנְיְנֵי הָעוֹלָם הַזֶּה בִּכְדֵי שֶׁעַל יְדֵי זֶה יִהְיֶה לוֹ שַׁיָּכוּת אֵצֶל הָרְשָׁעִים וְיוּכַל לְהַעֲלוֹתָם. וְאִם אָמְנָם הַדָּבָר מְסֻכָּן לֵרֵד לִמְקוֹם הַתַּאֲווֹת, וְכִי אוֹמְרִים לְאָדָם חַטֵּא כְּדֵי שֶׁיִּזְכֶּה חֲבֵרְךָ? מִכָּל מָקוֹם כְּבָר הֻבְטַח מֵהַשֵּׁם יִתְבָּרַךְ כְּמַאֲמָרָם זִכְרוֹנָם לִבְרָכָה (יוֹמָא פז.) כָּל הַמְזַכֶּה אֶת הָרַבִּים אֵין חֵטְא בָּא עַל יָדוֹ.

Noam Elimelekh, Shemot 2

אִיתָא בַּזֹּהַר הַקָּדוֹשׁ דְּהַצַּדִּיק נִקְרָא "שַׁבָּת" (זֹהַר ב צד:), מֵחֲמַת שֶׁיֵּשׁ לוֹ בַּחוֹל נְשָׁמָה כִּשְׁאַר בְּנֵי אָדָם בְּשַׁבָּת, אַךְ מָה יֵשׁ בּוֹ תּוֹסָפוֹת מַעֲלָה בְּשַׁבָּת? יֵשׁ לוֹמַר דְּהַנְּשָׁמָה נִתְוַסְּפָה בִּקְדֻשָּׁה יְתֵרָה עַד שֶׁהוּא מְעֻנָּג לְהַבּוֹרֵא יִתְבָּרֵךְ... נוֹתְנִין לוֹ "נַחֲלָה בְּלִי מְצָרִים" (שַׁבָּת קיח.), דְּהַצַּדִּיק הַזֶּה הוּא תָּמִיד מְקֻשָּׁר וְדָבוּק בָּעוֹלָמוֹת הָעֶלְיוֹנִים אֲשֶׁר אֵין לָהֶם סוֹף וּמֵיצַר וּגְבוּל, דְּעוֹלָם הַזֶּה יֵשׁ לוֹ גְּבוּל, וּבְיַד הַצַּדִּיק הַזֶּה לְקַשֵּׁר כָּל הָעוֹלָמוֹת עַד אֵין סוֹף בָּרוּךְ הוּא... וְהִנֵּה יֵשׁ צַדִּיק שֶׁאֵינוֹ דָּבוּק תָּמִיד בְּעוֹלָמוֹת עֶלְיוֹנִים, מֵחֲמַת שֶׁצָּרִיךְ עֲדַיִן לְתַקֵּן אֶת מִדּוֹתָיו בְּיִרְאָה וַעֲנָוָה, וְצָרִיךְ לֵרֵד מִדְּבֵקוּתוֹ כְּדֵי לְתַקֵּן, אַךְ אַף עַל פִּי כֵן הוּא תָּמִיד בִּפְנִימִיּוּתוֹ שֶׁאֵינוֹ נִכְשַׁל חָלִילָה בְּשׁוּם חֵטְא בִּירִידוֹ לְמַטָּה מִמַּדְרֵגָתוֹ.

Zohar, 1:83a

"וַיַּעַל אַבְרָם וְגוֹ' הַנֶּגְבָּה" (בְּרֵאשִׁית יג, א)

אָמַר רַבִּי שִׁמְעוֹן: תָּא חֲזֵי, כֹּלָּא רָזָא דְּחָכְמְתָא אִיהוּ, וְקָא רָמַז הָכָא בְּחָכְמָתָא וְדַרְגִּין דִּלְתַתָּא דְּקָא נָחִית אַבְרָהָם לְעֻמְקַיָּא דִּלְהוֹן וְיָדַע לוֹן, וְלָא אִתְדַּבַּק בְּהוּ וְתָב לְקַיּוּמֵיהּ. וְלָא אִתְפְּתָא בְּהוּ כְּאָדָם, דְּכַד מְטָא לְהַהוּא דַּרְגָּא אִתְפְּתָא בְּנָחָשׁ וְגָרִים מוֹתָא לְעָלְמָא... אֲבָל בְּאַבְרָהָם מָה כְּתִיב? "וַיַּעַל אַבְרָם מִמִּצְרַיִם" (בְּרֵאשִׁית יג, א)—דְּסָלֵיק וְלָא נָחִית, וְתַב לְאַתְרֵיהּ לְדַרְגָּא עִלָּאָה דְּאִתְדַּבֵּק בֵּהּ בְּקַדְמִיתָא. וְעוֹבָדָא דָּא הֲוָה בְּגִין לְאַחֲזָאָה חָכְמָתָא, דְּאִתְקַיֵּם בְּקִיּוּמָא שְׁלִים כִּדְקָא חָזֵי לֵיהּ וְלָא אִתְפְּתָא, וְקָם בְּקִיּוּמָא וְתַב לְאַתְרֵיהּ... הַנֶּגְבָּה—אֲתַר דְּאִתְדַּבֵּק בֵּהּ בְּקַדְמִיתָא. תָּא חֲזֵי, רָזָא דְּמִלָּה אִי אַבְרָם לָא יֵיחוֹת לְמִצְרַיִם וְלָא יִצְטָרֵף תַּמָּן בְּקַדְמִיתָא, לָא יְהֵא חוּלָק עַדְבֵהּ בְּקוּדְשָׁא בְּרִיךְ הוּא.

Zohar, 1:180b

שְׁכִינְתָּא לָא שַׁרְיָא בְּאַתַר עֲצִיבוּ אֶלָּא בְּאַתַר דְּאִית בֵּהּ חֶדְוָה. אִי חֶדְוָה לֵית בֵּהּ, לָא שַׁרְיָא שְׁכִינְתָּא בְּהַהוּא אֲתַר. כְּמָה דְּאַתְּ אָמַר, "וְעַתָּה קְחוּ לִי מְנַגֵּן וְהָיָה כְּנַגֵּן הַמְנַגֵּן וַתְּהִי עָלָיו יַד יהוה" (מְלָכִים ב ג, טו), דְּהָא שְׁכִינְתָּא וַדַּאי לָא שָׁרְיָא בְּאַתַר עֲצִיבוּ. מְנָלָן? מִיַּעֲקֹב. דִּבְגִין דַּהֲוָה עֲצִיב עֲלֵהּ דְּיוֹסֵף אִסְתַּלְּקַת שְׁכִינְתָּא מִנֵּהּ, כֵּיוָן דְּאָתָא לֵיהּ חֶדְוָה דִּבְשׂוֹרָה דְּיוֹסֵף מִיָּד "וַתְּחִי רוּחַ יַעֲקֹב אֲבִיהֶם" (בְּרֵאשִׁית מה, כז).

Appendix 3

Hebrew Versions of the Texts

יֵשׁ כַּמָּה מַדְרֵגוֹת בֶּאֱמוּנָה. יֵשׁ אֱמוּנַת הַמֹּחַ, לְמַעְלָה מִמֶּנָּה הִיא אֱמוּנַת הַלֵּב, וּכְמוֹ שֶׁכָּתַב הַיְּסוֹד הָעֲבוֹדָה (מִכְתַּב כה) בְּשֵׁם הַצַּדִּיק רַבִּי לֵיבּ מִדְקָאר זֵכֶר צַדִּיק לִבְרָכָה (תַּלְמִיד הַמַּגִּיד מִמֶּזֶרִיטְשׁ זְכוּתוֹ יָגֵן עָלֵינוּ) כִּי מֵאֱמוּנַת הַמּוֹחַ לֶאֱמוּנַת הַלֵּב רָחוֹק יוֹתֵר מִמֶּרְחָק שָׁמַיִם מֵאָרֶץ. וְיֵשׁ עוֹד מַדְרֵגָה גְּבוֹהָה מֵהֶם, הִיא אֱמוּנַת הָאֵבָרִים, שֶׁאֱמוּנַת הַשֵּׁם חֲדוּרָה בְּכָל אֵבָרָיו כְּמַאֲמָר הַכָּתוּב ׳כָּל עַצְמוֹתַי תֹּאמַרְנָה ה' מִי כָמוֹךָ׳ (תְּהִלִּים לה, י), דְּהַיְנוּ שֶׁכָּל הָאֵבָרִים וַאֲפִלּוּ הָעֲצָמוֹת מַרְגִּישִׁים שֶׁאֵין עוֹד מִלְּבַדּוֹ, וּכְמוֹ שֶׁרוֹאִים דַּאֲפִילוּ אָדָם שֶׁאֱמוּנָתוֹ בְּהִירָה, אִם יֶאֱרַע שֶׁחַיָּה רָעָה מִתְנַפֶּלֶת עָלָיו הֲרֵיהוּ נִבְהָל מְאֹד, וְהַסִּבָּה לְכָךְ מִשּׁוּם שֶׁהָאֱמוּנָה אֵינָהּ חֲדוּרָה בְּאֵבָרָיו, אֲבָל זֶה שֶׁיֵּשׁ לוֹ אֱמוּנָה בְּהִירָה הַמְּשֻׁרֶשֶׁת עַד לָאֵבָרִים שׁוּב אֵינוֹ מִתְיָרֵא מִשּׁוּם דָּבָר.

Netivot Shalom, 2: 281

"וְאָכַלְתָּ וְשָׂבָעְתָּ וּבֵרַכְתָּ אֶת הַשֵּׁם אֱלֹהֶיךָ וְגוֹ'" (דְּבָרִים ח, י)

פֵּירוּשׁ עַל דֶּרֶךְ מָשָׁל: הַמַּעְיָן הַנּוֹבֵעַ כְּשֶׁשּׁוֹאֲבִים מִמֶּנּוּ תָּמִיד, אֲזַי מִתְגַּבֵּר וְנוֹבֵעַ תָּמִיד וּמִתְבָּרֵךְ. עַל דֶּרֶךְ שֶׁאָמְרוּ רַבּוֹתֵינוּ זִכְרוֹנָם לִבְרָכָה "נַהֲרָא מִכֵּיפֵהּ מִתְבָּרֵךְ (נְדָרִים מ.), וּכְשֶׁאֵין שׁוֹאֲבִים מִמֶּנּוּ אֲזַי חוֹזֵר הַמָּקוֹר לַאֲחוֹרָיו. הַנִּמְשָׁל, כְּשֶׁיִּשְׂרָאֵל רְאוּיִן לְקַבֵּל הַשְׁפָּעָתוֹ יִתְבָּרַךְ וְשׁוֹאֲבִים מִמֶּנּוּ יִתְבָּרַךְ הַשְׁפָּעָתָם, מִזֶּה מִתְבָּרֵךְ שְׁמוֹ יִתְבָּרַךְ, עַל דֶּרֶךְ שֶׁכָּתוּב "וּשְׁאַבְתֶּם מַיִם בְּשָׂשׂוֹן מִמַּעַיְנֵי הַיְשׁוּעָה" (יְשַׁעְיָהוּ יב, ג). רוֹצֶה לוֹמַר שֶׁצָּרִיךְ [הַמַּעְיָן, הַיְנוּ הַקָּדוֹשׁ בָּרוּךְ הוּא] לִתְשׁוּעָה, וְהַתְּשׁוּעָה הוּא מִמַּה שֶׁשּׁוֹאֲבִים מִמֶּנּוּ. נִמְצָא הָאֲכִילָה וְהַשְּׂבִיעָה הוּא גַּם כֵּן מִצְוָה מַעֲשִׂית. וְזוֹ 'וְאָכַלְתָּ וְשָׂבָעְתָּ' רוֹצֶה לוֹמַר מִצְוָה מַעֲשִׂית, 'וּבֵרַכְתָּ', מִצְוָה שֶׁבְּדִבּוּר.

Tzemaḥ HaShem LeZvi, Ekev 2

"וּמַדּוּעַ תִּתְנַשְּׂאוּ עַל קְהַל יהוה" (בַּמִּדְבָּר טז, ג)

הִנֵּה טַעֲנוּת קֹרַח הָיְתָה שֶׁאֵין שׁוּם הִתְנַשְּׂאוּת בֵּין יִשְׂרָאֵל לְאֶחָד עַל חֲבֵרוֹ כִּי בְּתוֹכָם הַשֵּׁם. הַיְנוּ שֶׁהַשֵּׁם יִתְבָּרַךְ שׁוֹכֵן בְּתוֹךְ כֻּלָּם שָׁוֶה בְּשָׁוֶה כְּמוֹ שֶׁמְּבֹאָר בַּמִּדְרָשׁ (תַּעֲנִית לא.) שֶׁלֶּעָתִיד יַעֲשֶׂה הַקָּדוֹשׁ בָּרוּךְ הוּא מָחוֹל לַצַּדִּיקִים, וּמָחוֹל הַיְנוּ בְּעִגּוּל שֶׁאֵין אֶחָד קָרוֹב יוֹתֵר מֵחֲבֵרוֹ. וְהָיָה טוֹעֵן שֶׁעַתָּה גַּם כֵּן הוּא כָּךְ, אַךְ עַל זֶה אָמַר שְׁלֹמֹה הַמֶּלֶךְ (מִשְׁלֵי כ, כו) "מְזָרֶה רְשָׁעִים מֶלֶךְ חָכָם וַיָּשֶׁב עֲלֵיהֶם אוֹפָן", הַיְנוּ שֶׁעַל יְדֵי הַנֵּזֶר וְהַכֶּתֶר שֶׁנִּתָּן לָהֶם דְּהַיְנוּ כֶּתֶר הַלְּוִיִּים וְנָתַן לָהֶם הַהִתְנַשְּׂאוּת, עַל זֶה "וַיָּשֶׁב עֲלֵיהֶם אֹפָן", דְּהַיְנוּ שֶׁהָיָה מֵשִׁיב לָהֶם מַדּוּעַ כְּשֶׁנָּתַתִּי לָכֶם הִתְנַשְּׂאוּת לֹא טְעַנְתֶּם שֶׁאֵין בְּיִשְׂרָאֵל שׁוּם הִתְנַשְּׂאוּת לְאֶחָד עַל חֲבֵרוֹ.

Mei HaShiloaḥ, Koraḥ 3

כִּי הִנֵּה בֶּאֱמֶת מִדָּתוֹ שֶׁל אַבְרָהָם אָבִינוּ עָלָיו הַשָּׁלוֹם הוּא מִדַּת הַחֶסֶד, עוֹלָם הָאַהֲבָה בִּמְקוֹמָהּ הוּא עוֹלָם בָּהִיר, לֵית מַחֲשָׁבָה תְּפִיסָה בֵּהּ כְּלָל מַהוּת עֶרְכָּהּ וְטִיבָהּ... אָמְנָם לִהְיוֹת שֶׁקִּשֵּׁט מְלֹא קוֹמָתוֹ לַעֲבֹד אֶת הַבּוֹרֵא בָּרוּךְ הוּא בְּאַהֲבָה רַבָּה, עַד שֶׁנַּעֲשָׂה כָּל גּוּפוֹ מֶרְכָּבָה לְמִדַּת הָאַהֲבָה, וְהִרְגִּיל אֱלֹהוּתוֹ וְהִתְפַּשְּׁטוּת מִדָּה זֹאת בְּפִי הַבְּרִיּוֹת, עַל דֶּרֶךְ מַאֲמָרָם זִכְרוֹנָם לִבְרָכָה "לְשֶׁעָבַר נִקְרָא אֱלֹהֵי הַשָּׁמַיִם, וְעַכְשָׁו הִרְגַּלְתִּי שִׁמְךָ בְּפִי הַבְּרִיּוֹת, וְנִקְרָא אֱלֹהֵי הָאָרֶץ" (בְּרֵאשִׁית רַבָּה נט, ז), לִהְיוֹת שֶׁהֶרְאָה לְכָל בָּאֵי עוֹלָם, שֶׁיֵּשׁ הִתְפַּשְּׁטוּת מִדַּת הַחֶסֶד אֲפִלּוּ בְּאַרְצִיּוּת.

Or HaMeir, Lekh Lekha 1

Appendix 3

Hebrew Versions of the Texts

Or HaMeir, Shavuot

וְאִם כֵּן לָמָּה הִלְבִּישׁ הַקָּדוֹשׁ בָּרוּךְ הוּא אוֹר בְּהִירוּת הַתּוֹרָה בְּסִפּוּרֵי מַעֲשִׂיּוֹת, עַד שֶׁנַּעֲשָׂה עַתָּה כַּאֲשֶׁר יְדַבֵּר אִישׁ אֶל רֵעֵהוּ? וּכְמוֹ שֶׁכָּתַבְתִּי לְעֵיל פֵּרוּשׁ הַפָּסוּק "וְדִבֶּר הַשֵּׁם אֶל מֹשֶׁה פָּנִים אֶל פָּנִים כַּאֲשֶׁר יְדַבֵּר אִישׁ אֶל רֵעֵהוּ" (שְׁמוֹת לג, יא), וְהַכַּוָּנָה עוֹצֶם בְּהִירוּת הַתּוֹרָה הִלְבִּישׁ הַקָּדוֹשׁ בָּרוּךְ הוּא "פָּנִים אֶל פָּנִים". וּבֶאֱמֶת יֵשׁ שִׁבְעִים פָּנִים לַתּוֹרָה. וְשָׁם בִּמְקוֹמָהּ הָיָה אוֹר בָּהִיר רַק שֵׁמוֹת קְדוֹשִׁים, וּכְלָלוּתָם אֵינָהּ רַק שֵׁם הַגָּדוֹל וְקָדוֹשׁ הוי"ה בָּרוּךְ הוּא. וְלָכֵן נִקְרָא "פִּקּוּדֵי הַשֵּׁם" (תְּהִלִּים יט, ט), שֶׁכְּלָלוּת וְסִפּוּרִים פְּקוּדָה וּגְנוּזָה בְּשֵׁם הוי"ה בָּרוּךְ הוּא, וְהִלְבִּישׁ אוֹתָהּ כָּל כָּךְ "פָּנִים אֶל פָּנִים" עַד שֶׁנִּרְאֶה עַתָּה סִפּוּרֵי מַעֲשִׂיּוֹת "כַּאֲשֶׁר יְדַבֵּר אִישׁ אֶל רֵעֵהוּ", וּבֶאֱמֶת פֶּתַח דְּבָרֶיהָ יָאִיר אוֹר בָּהִיר... כִּי הִנֵּה אָנוּ רוֹאִין לִפְעָמִים נוֹפֶלֶת לְאָדָם הַמַּשְׂכִּיל חָכְמָה נִפְלָאָה בִּפְנִימִיּוּת מַחֲשַׁבְתּוֹ בְּהַשָּׂגַת רוֹמְמוּת אֱלֹהוּת, וְכַאֲשֶׁר עָלָה בִּרְצוֹנוֹ לְגַלּוֹת זֹאת הַמַּחֲשָׁבָה לְזוּלָתוֹ, בְּוַדַּאי בִּלְתִּי אֶפְשָׁרִי לְגַלּוֹת פְּנִימִיּוּת מַחֲשַׁבְתּוֹ עִם הַחָכְמָה כַּאֲשֶׁר הִיא שָׁם בְּנְקֻדַּת הַלֵּב, כִּי לֹא יֵדְעוּ וְלֹא יָבִינוּ הַשּׁוֹמְעִים מֵרֹב דַּקּוּתָהּ. וַאֲזַי מֻכְרָח לְהַלְבִּישׁ פְּנִימִיּוּת דַּקּוּת מַחֲשַׁבְתּוֹ בְּאֵיזֶה פָּסוּק אוֹ מַאֲמָר מִדִּבְרֵיהֶם, בְּאֶמְצָעוּת אַרְבַּע בְּחִינוֹת פַּרְדֵּ"ס כְּפִי הַצֹּרֶךְ. וְהַשּׁוֹמְעִים אֵין הַשָּׂגָתָם חֲזָקָה לְהָבִין וּלְהַשְׂכִּיל עוֹמֶק מַחֲשַׁבְתּוֹ הַפְּקֻדָּה וּגְנוּזָה בִּפְשַׁט אוֹ רֶמֶז אוֹ דְּרוּשׁ אוֹ סוֹד, אֲזַי אֵינָם נוֹתְנִים עֵינֵיהֶם כִּי אִם עַל בְּחִינַת הַהַלְבָּשָׁה, לוֹמַר כַּמָּה זֶה נָאֶה דּוֹרֵשׁ וְנָאֶה אוֹמֵר! וְנִבְעָרִים מִדַּעַת לְהַשְׁגִּיחַ עַל פְּנִימִיּוּת חָכְמָה נִפְלָאָה וְעֵצָה לַעֲבוֹדַת הַבּוֹרֵא הַמְּלֻבָּשׁוֹת שָׁם בְּאַרְבַּע בְּחִינוֹת פַּרְדֵּ"ס. וְדוֹמֶה לָזֶה תּוֹרָתֵנוּ הַקְּדוֹשָׁה. פֶּתַח דְּבָרֶיהָ בִּמְקוֹמָהּ יָאִיר גָּבוֹהַּ וְרָמָה לְרוֹב דַּקּוּתָהּ, לֵית מַחֲשָׁבָה תְּפִיסָא כְּלָל, וְכַאֲשֶׁר בָּאָה אֶל בְּחִינַת הַדִּבְּרוֹת בְּמַעֲמַד הַקָּדוֹשׁ עַל הַר סִינַי, הֻכְרְחָה לְהִתְלַבֵּשׁ וּלְהִצְטַמְצֵם פָּנִים אֶל פָּנִים, חָכְמָה נִפְלָאָה וְסוֹדוֹת נוֹרָאִים וַעֲמֻקִּים נִתְלַבְּשׁוּ בִּפְשׁוּטֵי תּוֹרָה כְּמוֹ סִפּוּרֵי מַעֲשִׂיּוֹת...

Pardes Rimonim 22:2

וְאוֹתָם הָעִנְיָנִים שֶׁאָנוּ קוֹרְאִים בַּתּוֹרָה, כְּגוֹן יָד אוֹ רֶגֶל אֹזֶן עַיִן וְכָל כַּיּוֹצֵא בָּהֶם, מַהוּ? דַּע וְהַאֲמֵן כִּי כָּל אוֹתָם הָעִנְיָנִים אַף עַל פִּי שֶׁהֵם מוֹרִים וּמְעִידִים עַל גְּדֻלָּתוֹ וַאֲמִתָּתוֹ אֵין כָּל בְּרִיָּה יְכוֹלָה לָדַעַת וּלְהִתְבּוֹנֵן מַהוּת אוֹתוֹ הַדָּבָר הַנִּקְרָא יָד אוֹ רֶגֶל אוֹ עַיִן אוֹ אֹזֶן וְכַיּוֹצֵא. וְאִם אָנוּ עֲשׂוּיִים בְּצֶלֶם וּבִדְמוּת אַל יַעֲלֶה בְּדַעְתְּךָ כִּי עַיִן כְּצוּרַת עַיִן מַמָּשׁ אוֹ יָד כְּצוּרַת יָד מַמָּשׁ אוֹ רֶגֶל כְּצוּרַת רֶגֶל מַמָּשׁ. אֲבָל הֵם עִנְיָנִים פְּנִימִיִּים וּפְנִימִים לַפְּנִימִיִּים בָּאֲמִתּוּת מְצִיאוּת הַשֵּׁם אֲשֶׁר מֵהֶם הַמָּקוֹר וְהַשֶּׁפַע יוֹצֵא לַכֹּל הַנִּמְצָאִים (בִּגְזֵרַת הַשֵּׁם יִתְבָּרַךְ). אֲבָל אֵין מַהוּת יָד כְּמַהוּת יָד וְלֹא תַּבְנִית כְּתַבְנִית יָד כְּמוֹ שֶׁאָמַר הַכָּתוּב (יְשַׁעְיָהוּ מ, כה) וְאֶל מִי תְּדַמְּיוּנִי וְאֶשְׁוֶה. וְדַע וְהָבֵן שֶׁאֵין בֵּינוֹ וּבֵינֵינוּ דִּמְיוֹן מִצַּד הָעֶצֶם וְהַתַּבְנִית, אֶלָּא עַל כַּוָּנַת צוּרַת הָאֵבָרִים אֲשֶׁר בָּנוּ, שֶׁהֵן עֲשׂוּיִם בְּדִמְיוֹן סִימָנִים לְעִנְיָנִים פְּנִימִיִּים סְתוּמִים עֶלְיוֹנִים שֶׁאֵין הַדַּעַת יְכוֹלָה לְדַעְתָּם אֶלָּא כְּדִמְיוֹן זִכָּרוֹן. כְּמוֹ שֶׁכּוֹתֵב רְאוּבֵן בֶּן יַעֲקֹב שֶׁהֲרֵי אֵין אֵלּוּ הָאוֹתִיּוֹת וְזוֹ הַצּוּרָה עַצְמוּתוֹ שֶׁל רְאוּבֵן בֶּן יַעֲקֹב וְצוּרָתוֹ וְתַבְנִיתוֹ וּמַהוּתוֹ, אֶלָּא זִכָּרוֹן. שֶׁזֶּה רְאוּבֵן בֶּן יַעֲקֹב הַכָּתוּב הוּא סִימָן כְּנֶגֶד אוֹתוֹ עֶצֶם וְהַתַּבְנִית הַיָּדוּעַ הַנִּקְרָא רְאוּבֵן בֶּן יַעֲקֹב. וּלְפִי שֶׁהַשֵּׁם יִתְבָּרַךְ רָצָה לְזַכּוֹתֵנוּ בָּרָא בְּגוּף הָאָדָם כַּמָּה אֵבָרִים נִסְתָּרִים וְנִגְלִים בְּדִמְיוֹן סִימָן לְמַעֲשֶׂה מֶרְכָּבָה, וְאִלּוּ יִזְכֶּה הָאָדָם לְטַהֵר אֵבֶר מֵאֵבָרָיו יִהְיֶה אוֹתוֹ הָאֵבֶר כְּדִמְיוֹן כִּסֵּא לְאוֹתוֹ דָּבָר הָעֶלְיוֹן הַפְּנִימִי הַנִּקְרָא בְּשֵׁם זֶה אִם עַיִן עַיִן אִם יָד יָד. כֵּיצַד? כְּגוֹן שֶׁנִּשְׁמַר וְנִזְהַר בְּמַרְאֶה עֵינָיו שֶׁלֹּא יַבִּיט בַּעֲרָיוֹת וְלֹא בִּשְׁאָר דָּבָר שֶׁל גְּנַאי, אֶלָּא בְּכָל דָּבָר שֶׁהוּא קְדֻשַּׁת הַשֵּׁם וַעֲבוֹדָתוֹ אָז אוֹתוֹ עַיִן נַעֲשֵׂית כְּמוֹ כִּסֵּא לְאוֹתוֹ דָּבָר הַנִּקְרָא לְמַעְלָה עַיִן וְכֵן הַיָּד וְכֵן הָרֶגֶל וּשְׁאָר הַדְּבָרִים.

Pardes Rimonim, 3:1

וְעוֹד פֵּרוּשׁ אַחֵר מִפְּנֵי שֶׁהַחֲקִירָה בּוֹ אֵין לוֹ סוֹף. שֶׁאֵינָהּ כְּדֶרֶךְ שְׁאָר הַחֲקִירוֹת שֶׁיֵּשׁ לָהּ סוֹף וְהַסְכָּמָה אֶל מַסְקָנָא אֶחָת. אָמְנָם הַחֲקִירָה בֶּאֱלֹקוּת הִיא בְּאֵין סוֹף וְלָכֵן אֵין מִי שֶׁיֵּדַע בּוֹ מַהוּת כְּלָל אִם לֹא עַל יְדֵי סְפִירוֹת הַמְּגֻלּוֹת קְצָת מִגְּדֻלָּתוֹ אָמְנָם מִסְּפִירוֹתָיו וּלְמַעְלָה אֵין הַשָּׂגָה מִצַּד עֹמֶק הַמֻּשָּׂג וְלָכֵן תֵּאֲרוּהוּ בְּאֵין סוֹף.

Appendix 3

Hebrew Versions of the Texts

Tikkunei Zohar, 17a

פָּתַח אֵלִיָּהוּ וְאָמַר רִבּוֹן עָלְמִין דְּאַנְתְּ הוּא חָד וְלָא בְּחֻשְׁבָּן, אַנְתְּ הוּא עִלָּאָה עַל כָּל עִלָּאִין סְתִימָא עַל כָּל סְתִימִין, לֵית מַחֲשָׁבָה תְּפִיסָא בָּךְ כְּלָל; אַנְתְּ הוּא דְּאַפַּקְתְּ עֶשֶׂר תִּקּוּנִין וְקָרֵינָן לוֹן עֶשֶׂר סְפִירָן, לְאַנְהָגָא בְהוֹן עָלְמִין סְתִימִין דְּלָא אִתְגַּלְיָן וְעָלְמִין דְּאִתְגַּלְיָן, וּבְהוֹן אִתְכַּסִּיאַת מִבְּנֵי נָשָׁא. וְאַנְתְּ הוּא דְּקָשִׁיר לוֹן וּמְיַחֵד לוֹן. וּבְגִין דְּאַנְתְּ מִלְּגָאו כָּל מָאן דְּאַפְרִישׁ חַד מִן חַבְרֵיהּ מֵאִלֵּין עֶשֶׂר אִתְחַשִׁיב לֵיהּ כְּאִלּוּ אַפְרִישׁ בָּךְ.

Tanya
Sha'ar HaHaYiḥud, 9

כִּי עִנְיַן הַהַשָּׂגָה מִתְיַיחֵס וְנוֹפֵל עַל דְּבַר חָכְמָה וָשֵׂכֶל, לוֹמַר שֶׁאֶפְשָׁר לְהַשִּׂיגוֹ אוֹ אִי אֶפְשָׁר לְהַשִּׂיגוֹ מִפְּנֵי עוֹמֶק הַמּוּשָּׂג. אֲבָל הַקָּדוֹשׁ בָּרוּךְ הוּא שֶׁהוּא לְמַעְלָה מִן הַשֵּׂכֶל וְהַחָכְמָה, לֹא שַׁיָּיךְ כְּלָל לוֹמַר בּוֹ שֶׁאִי אֶפְשָׁר לְהַשִּׂיגוֹ מִפְּנֵי עוֹמֶק הַמּוּשָּׂג, כִּי אֵינוֹ בִּבְחִינַת הַשָּׂגָה כְּלָל. וְהָאוֹמֵר עָלָיו שֶׁאִי אֶפְשָׁר לְהַשִּׂיגוֹ, הוּא כְּאוֹמֵר עַל אֵיזוֹ חָכְמָה רָמָה וַעֲמוּקָה, שֶׁאִי אֶפְשָׁר לְמַשְׁשָׁהּ בְּיָדַיִם מִפְּנֵי עוֹמֶק הַמּוּשָּׂג, שֶׁכָּל הַשּׁוֹמֵעַ יִצְחַק לוֹ, לְפִי שֶׁחוּשׁ הַמִּישׁוּשׁ אֵינוֹ מִתְיַיחֵס וְנוֹפֵל אֶלָּא עַל עֲשִׂיָּה גַשְׁמִית הַנִּתְפֶּסֶת בְּיָדַיִם. וְכָכָה מַמָּשׁ, נֶחְשֶׁבֶת לְגַבֵּי הַקָּדוֹשׁ בָּרוּךְ הוּא מַדְרֵגַת הַשֵּׂכֶל וְהַהַשָּׂגָה כַּעֲשִׂיָּה גַשְׁמִית מַמָּשׁ.

Meor Einayim, Ki Tisa 1

"אַךְ אֶת שַׁבְּתֹתַי תִּשְׁמֹרוּ" (שְׁמוֹת לא, יג)

נוֹדַע הָאָמוּר בַּזֹּהַר "מַהוּ שַׁבָּת, שְׁמָא דְקוּדְשָׁא בְּרִיךְ הוּא דְאִיהוּ שָׁלֵם מִכָּל סִטְרוֹי" (זֹהַר חֵלֶק ב פַּח:), וְכֵיוָן שֶׁהוּא שָׁלֵם בְּכָל מִינֵי שְׁלֵמוּת בְּוַדַּאי לֹא תֶּחְסַר כֹּל בָּהּ. וְהִנֵּה הָעוֹשֶׂה מְלָאכָה הוּא מִפְּנֵי שֶׁצָּרִיךְ לְאוֹתוֹ דָּבָר, וְזוּלָתָהּ הָיָה חָסֵר וּמַשְׁלִים חֶסְרוֹנָהּ עַל יָדָהּ. אָמְנָם שַׁבָּת, דְּאִיהוּ שָׁלֵם מִכָּל סִטְרוֹי וְאֵינוֹ חָסֵר כְּלוּם, אֵין צָרִיךְ לִמְלָאכָה לְהַשְׁלִים אֵיזֶה חִסָּרוֹן. וְלָכֵן אָמְרוּ רַבּוֹתֵינוּ זִכְרוֹנָם לִבְרָכָה "שֶׁיְּהֵא בְעֵינֶיךָ כְּאִלּוּ כָּל מְלַאכְתְּךָ עֲשׂוּיָה, וְאֵין מַחְסוֹר דָּבָר" (מְכִילְתָא, יִתְרוֹ). שֶׁהֲרֵי בְּשַׁבָּת אֱלֹהוּתוֹ יִתְבָּרַךְ מִתְפַּשֵּׁט וּמִתְגַּלֶּה בִּבְנֵי יִשְׂרָאֵל, וְאִיהוּ שָׁלֵם בְּכָל סִטְרוֹי בְּכָל מִינֵי שְׁלֵמוּת. וְאִם מוֹרֶה הֶפֶךְ חַס וְשָׁלוֹם, מַרְאֶה שֶׁאֵינוֹ מֵהֶם וְאֵין בּוֹ הַשְׁרָאָתוֹ כִּבְיָכוֹל. וְאָמְנָם לֹא לְבַד מְלֶאכֶת הֶדְיוֹט אָסוּר בְּשַׁבָּת, אַךְ אֲפִלּוּ מְלֶאכֶת הַמִּשְׁכָּן, רָצָה לוֹמַר מִשְׁכָּן נִקְרָא עַל שֵׁם "וְשָׁכַנְתִּי בְּתוֹךְ בְּנֵי יִשְׂרָאֵל" (שְׁמוֹת כט, מה), שֶׁהַקָּדוֹשׁ בָּרוּךְ הוּא שֹׁכֵן בְּתוֹךְ בְּנֵי יִשְׂרָאֵל, וְהָאָדָם צָרִיךְ לִהְיוֹת מִשְׁכָּן אֵלָיו. וְאִם לֹא טָהוֹר הוּא מֵחֶלְאַת עֲוֹנֹתָיו וּמְעַכֵּב הַשְׁרָאַת שְׁכִינָתוֹ בָּרוּךְ הוּא בְּשַׁבָּת, יָסִיר מִלִּבּוֹ גַּם דָּבָר זֶה שֶׁלֹּא יֵעָצֵב עַל זֶה, רַק יִשְׁמֹר שַׁבָּת כְּהִלְכָתוֹ וְיִשְׂמַח בְּהַשֵּׁם יִתְבָּרַךְ שֶׁלְּפָנָיו הוּא רַעֲוָא דְּרַעֲוִין וְשִׂמְחָה. וְנִמְצָא אֲפִלּוּ מְלֶאכֶת הַמִּשְׁכָּן, שֶׁיַּעֲשֶׂה דָּבָר הַצָּרִיךְ אֵלָיו שֶׁיִּהְיֶה מִשְׁכָּן לְהַשֵּׁם, גַּם זֶה מְמַעֵט בַּשַּׁבָּת.

Meor Einayim, Shemot 3:2

הַתּוֹרָה אַף שֶׁלֹּא נִתְּנָה קוֹדֶם הַמַּבּוּל מִכָּל מָקוֹם הָיְתָה גַּם בְּזֶה הָעוֹלָם כִּי כֹּחַ הַפּוֹעֵל בַּנִּפְעָל. רַק שֶׁלֹּא נִתְּנָה בִּלְבוּשִׁין כְּמוֹ אַחַר מַתַּן תּוֹרָה שֶׁנִּתְלַבְּשָׁה בִּלְבוּשִׁין כְּמוֹ זֶה הָעוֹלָם. וְהָיוּ יְחִידֵי סְגֻלָּה שֶׁהָיוּ מְקַיְּמִים הַתּוֹרָה כְּמוֹ שֶׁהִיא בִּמְקוֹם מֵחֲמַת שֶׁהָיוּ מַשִּׂיגִים אוֹתָהּ בְּמֹחִין גְּדוֹלִים שֶׁהָיָה לָהֶם עַד שֶׁהָיוּ מַשִּׂיגִים אֶת פְּנִימִיּוּתָהּ הָאֲמִתִּי כְּמוֹ שֶׁהָיְתָה מִקֹּדֶם שֶׁנִּתְּנָה כְּמוֹ מְתוּשֶׁלַח וַחֲנוֹךְ וְאָדָם הָרִאשׁוֹן שֶׁהָיוּ לוֹמְדֵי תּוֹרָה כַּנּוֹדָע.

Appendix 3

Hebrew Versions of the Texts

Meor Einayim, Ve'Etḥanan 4

נוֹדָע מָה שֶׁשָּׁנוּ חֲכָמִים בַּמִּשְׁנָה "בְּכָל לְבָבְךָ—בִּשְׁנֵי יְצָרֶיךָ, בְּיֵצֶר טוֹב וּבְיֵצֶר הָרָע," (מִשְׁנָה בְּרָכוֹת ט, ה). לְהָבִין זֶה אַהֲבָתוֹ יִתְבָּרַךְ בְּיֵצֶר הָרַע אֵיךְ הוּא? דְּנוֹדָע כִּי הַבּוֹרֵא בָּרוּךְ הוּא בָּרָא הָעוֹלָם בִּבְחִינַת אוֹר וְחֹשֶׁךְ, כִּי כָּל יוֹם הוּא כָּלוּל מֵחֹשֶׁךְ וְאוֹר. כִּי בַּתְּחִלָּה הוּא הַלַּיְלָה וְאַחַר כָּךְ בָּא אוֹר הַיּוֹם וְנִכְלָלִין שְׁנֵיהֶם, אַף שֶׁהֵם שְׁנֵי הֲפָכִים מִכָּל מָקוֹם נִכְלָלִין וְנִקְרָאִים הַלַּיְלָה וְהַיּוֹם שְׁנֵיהֶם יוֹם אֶחָד שָׁלֵם... וּלְכָךְ בָּאָדָם גַּם כֵּן בְּחִינַת הַחַשְׁכוּת הוּא קוֹדֶם אֶצְלוֹ, קֹדֶם שֶׁיָּבוֹא לוֹ אוֹר הַשֵּׂכֶל הוּא בְּקַטְנוּת וַחֲשֵׁכוּת שֶׁהוּא מָקוֹם דִּינִים. וְכָל זֶה הֶטְבֵּעַ בָּאָדָם טוֹב וָרַע כְּדֵי שֶׁיִּהְיֶה לוֹ בְּחִירָה... וְצָרִיךְ כָּל אֶחָד לְהַכְנִיעַ הָרַע אֶל הַטּוֹב וְכָלְלָן יַחַד שֶׁיִּהְיוּ נִקְרָאִים שְׁנֵיהֶם בְּחִינַת יוֹם, אַף הַחַשְׁכוּת שֶׁיִּהְיֶה מִקֹּדֶם וְלַיְלָה כַּיּוֹם יָאִיר לוֹ.

Ohev Yisrael, BeShalaḥ 7:8

יֵשׁ לוֹמַר דְּהִנֵּה תַּכְלִית הַהִתְנַהֲגוּת עֲבוֹדַת הָאָדָם הוּא מִתְּחִלָּה צָרִיךְ לְשַׁעְבֵּד כָּל חֶלְקֵי הַגּוּף וְהַנֶּפֶשׁ וְכָל הַתַּאֲווֹת וְהַחִיצוֹנִיּוּת שֶׁלּוֹ אֶל הַשֵּׂכֶל שֶׁהוּא בְּמוֹחַ הָרֹאשׁ. וְהַשֵּׂכֶל יִמְשֹׁל עַל הַכֹּל. וּמֵאָז יַעֲשֶׂה כָּל דָּבָר וְדָבָר בְּדֵעָה וְהַשְׂכֵּל. עַל פִּי דַּרְכֵי נֹעַם וְחָכְמוֹת הַתּוֹרָה לִמְנֹעַ מִמַּה שֶּׁאָסוּר לַעֲשׂוֹת וְלַעֲשׂוֹת כַּמְצֻוֶּה. וּלְהִתְיַשֵּׁב הֵיטֵב בְּהַמֻּתָּר לַעֲשׂוֹת. וּבְהֶרְגֵּלוֹ בָּזֶה בַּעֲשִׂיָּתוֹ כַּנִּמְצָא לְעֵיל. וְכָל כּוֹחוֹת הַגּוּף וְהַנֶּפֶשׁ יִתְבַּטְּלוּ נֶגֶד הַשֵּׂכֶל וְחָכְמוֹת הַתּוֹרָה. עַד שֶׁיִּהְיוּ כָּל כּוֹחוֹת הַגּוּף וְהַנֶּפֶשׁ כִּסֵּא וּמֶרְכָּבָה לְהַשֵּׂכֶל וְחָכְמָה שֶׁל הַתּוֹרָה. וְאָז יִהְיוּ כָּל הַתַּאֲווֹת רָעוֹת וּבִפְרָט הָעֲבֵרוֹת נִבְזִים וְנִמְאָסִים בְּעֵינָיו כְּאִלּוּ הָיָה זֶה נִטְבַּע בְּטִבְעוֹ מֵעֵת הִוָּלְדוֹ וְשֶׁלֹּא יִהְיֶה בְּאֶפְשָׁרִי לִנְטוֹת אַחַר הָרַע חַס וְשָׁלוֹם כְּלָל בְּשׁוּם פַּעַם בָּעוֹלָם. וְאָז יְהֵא צָרִיךְ לֵילֵךְ לְמַדְרֵגָה גְּדוֹלָה מִמֶּנָּה. וְהוּא שֶׁיִּהְיוּ כָּל מַחְשְׁבוֹתָיו וְכַוָּנוֹתָיו בַּתּוֹרָה וּבַמִּצְוֹת וּבַתְּפִלָּה רַק לְקַיֵּם מִצְוַת בּוֹרְאוֹ יִתְבָּרַךְ לְבַד. הַיְנוּ לֹא לְבַד מֵחֲמַת־־ שֶׁהַשֵּׂכֶל וְהַחָכְמָה מְחַיֵּב לָזֶה לִשְׂנֹא אֶת הָרַע וְלִבְחֹר בַּטּוֹב. רַק לִהְיוֹת הַכַּוָּנָה לַעֲשׂוֹת רְצוֹנוֹ שֶׁל הַבּוֹרֵא יִתְבָּרַךְ וְיִתְעַלֶּה. וְזֶהוּ כַּוָּנַת מַאֲמַר חֲכָמֵינוּ זִכְרוֹנָם לִבְרָכָה "אַל תֹּאמַר קָצָה נַפְשִׁי בִּבְשַׂר חֲזִיר, רַק אֶפְשִׁי וּמָה אֶעֱשֶׂה שֶׁאָבִי שֶׁבַּשָּׁמַיִם גָּזַר עָלַי" (סִפְרָא עַל וַיִּקְרָא כ, כו). וְכַאֲשֶׁר יַעֲשֶׂה כָּל עֲשִׂיּוֹתָיו בְּדֶרֶךְ זֶה אָז נַעֲשָׂה שִׂכְלוֹ, שֶׁהוּא הַנְּשָׁמָה, מֶרְכָּבָה וְכִסֵּא לַבְּחִינָה שֶׁלְּמַעְלָה מִמֶּנָּה, הַיְנוּ בְּחִינַת חי"ה.

וְכֵן צָרִיךְ לֵילֵךְ מִמַּדְרֵיגָה לְמַדְרֵגָה עַד שֶׁיִּתְעַלּוּ כָּל כּוֹחוֹת הַנֶּפֶשׁ וְהַנְּשָׁמָה לִבְחִינַת בִּטּוּל מְצִיאוּת לְגַמְרֵי נֶגֶד כְּבוֹד הַשֵּׁם יִתְבָּרַךְ, וְהוּא בְּחִינַת אַיִן. וְכֵן הָיָה כִּבְיָכוֹל כַּאֲשֶׁר עָלָה בְּמַחְשָׁבָה לְפָנָיו יִתְבָּרַךְ שְׁמוֹ לִבְרֹא אֶת הָעוֹלָם.

Sefat Emet, 2:91

בְּפָּסוּק "וְכָל הָעָם רֹאִים אֶת הַקּוֹלֹת וְכוּ'" (שְׁמוֹת כ, טו). פֵּרוּשׁ, כְּמוֹ שֶׁכָּתוּב "אָנֹכִי הַשֵּׁם אֱלֹקֶיךָ" (שְׁמוֹת כ, ב), שֶׁרָאוּ בְּנֵי יִשְׂרָאֵל כָּל אֶחָד אֶת שֹׁרֶשׁ חַיּוּתוֹ, וְרָאוּ עַיִן בְּעַיִן חֵלֶק נִשְׁמַת הַשֵּׁם מִמַּעַל שֶׁיֵּשׁ לְכָל אֶחָד. וְלֹא הָיוּ צְרִיכִין לְהַאֲמִין אֶת הַדִּבְּרוֹת—רַק רָאוּ אֶת הַקּוֹלוֹת שֶׁכָּךְ הוּא כַּאֲשֶׁר הַשֵּׁם דּוֹבֵר.

Appendix 3

Hebrew Versions of the Texts

וְהַזּוֹכֶה לְסוֹד הַהִתְדַּבְּקוּת יִזְכֶּה לְסוֹד הַהִשְׁתַּוּוּת, וְאִם יִזְכֶּה לְסוֹד הַהִשְׁתַּוּוּת יִזְכֶּה לְסוֹד הַהִתְבּוֹדְדוּת, וְאַחַר שֶׁיִּזְכֶּה לְסוֹד הַהִתְבּוֹדְדוּת הֲרֵי זֶה יִזְכֶּה לְרוּחַ הַקֹּדֶשׁ, וּמִזֶּה לִנְבוּאָה עַד שֶׁיִּתְנַבֵּא וְיֹאמַר עֲתִידוֹת. וְסוֹד הַהִשְׁתַּוּוּת אָמַר לִי ר' אַבְנֵר כִּי בָּא אִישׁ חָכָם לְאֶחָד מֵהַמִּתְבּוֹדְדִים וּבִקֵּשׁ מִמֶּנּוּ שֶׁיְּקַבְּלוּהוּ לִהְיוֹת מֵהַמִּתְבּוֹדְדִים. אָמַר לוֹ הַמִּתְבּוֹדֵד: בְּנִי, בָּרוּר לַשֵּׁם כִּי כַּוָּנָתְךָ טוֹבָה הִיא אָמְנָם הוֹדִיעֵנִי הִשְׁתַּוֵּיתָה אִם לֹא? אָמַר לוֹ: רַבִּי, בָּאֵר דְּבָרֶיךָ. אָמַר לוֹ: אִם שְׁנֵי בְּנֵי אָדָם, הָאֶחָד מֵהֶם מְכַבְּדֶךָ וְהָאֶחָד מְבַזֶּה אוֹתְךָ הֵם שָׁוִים בְּעֵינֶיךָ אִם לָאו? אָמַר לוֹ: לֹא אֲדֹנִי כִּי אֲנִי מַרְגִּישׁ הֲנָאָה וְנַחַת רוּחַ מֵהַמְּכַבֵּד וְצַעַר מֵהַמְּבַזֶּה אֲבָל אֵינִי נוֹקֵם וְנוֹטֵר. אָמַר לוֹ: בְּנִי, לֵךְ לְשָׁלוֹם כִּי כָּל זְמַן שֶׁלֹּא נִשְׁתַּוֵּיתָה, שֶׁלֹּא תַּרְגִּישׁ נַפְשְׁךָ בְּבִזָּיוֹן הָעוֹשֶׂה לָךְ, אֵינְךָ מְזֻמָּן לִהְיוֹת מַחֲשַׁבְתְּךָ קְשׁוּרָה בָּעֶלְיוֹן שֶׁתָּבֹא וְתִתְבּוֹדֵד, אָמְנָם לֵךְ וְתַכְנִיעַ עוֹד לְבָבְךָ הַכְנָעָה אֲמִתִּית עַד שֶׁתִּשְׁתַּוֶּה, וְאָז תּוּכַל לְהִתְבּוֹדֵד. וְטַעַם הַהִשְׁתַּוּוּת הוּא דִּבּוּק הַמַּחְשָׁבָה בַּשֵּׁם יִתְבָּרֵךְ כִּי דִּבּוּק וְחִבּוּר הַמַּחְשָׁבָה בַּשֵּׁם אַף עַל פִּי שֶׁעוֹשִׂין לוֹ אֵינוֹ מַרְגִּישׁ. וְאֶל "מְעוֹנְנִים וְקוֹסְמִים" (דְּבָרִים יח, יד) לֹא יִשְׁמָע.

Meirat Einayim, pp. 281–282

צָרִיךְ הָאָדָם לַחְשֹׁב אֶת עַצְמוֹ כְּאַיִן וְיִשְׁכַּח אֶת עַצְמוֹ מִכֹּל וָכֹל וִיבַקֵּשׁ הַכֹּל בְּכָל תְּפִלָּתוֹ עַל הַשְּׁכִינָה, וַאֲזַי יָכוֹל לָבֹא לְמַעְלָה מִזְּמַן—דְּהַיְנוּ לְעוֹלָם הַמַּחֲשָׁבָה—שֶׁשָּׁם הַכֹּל שָׁוֶה, חַיִּים וּמָוֶת יָם וְיַבָּשָׁה... שֶׁהָיוּ צְרִיכִין לְהַפְקִיר אֶת עַצְמָם וְלִשְׁכֹּחַ בְּצָרָתָן כְּדֵי שֶׁיָּבוֹאוּ לְעוֹלָם הַמַּחֲשָׁבָה, וְשָׁם הַכֹּל שָׁוֶה. מַה שֶּׁאֵין כֵּן כְּשֶׁהוּא דָּבוּק בְּגַשְׁמִיּוּת עוֹלָם הַזֶּה הוּא דָּבוּק בְּהִתְחַלְּקוּת טוֹב וָרַע, דְּהַיְנוּ ז' יְמֵי הַבִּנְיָן, וְאֵיךְ יָבֹא לְמַעְלָה מִזְּמַנִּיּוּת שֶׁשָּׁם אַחְדוּת גָּמוּר? וְכֵן כְּשֶׁחוֹשֵׁב אֶת עַצְמוֹ לְיֵשׁ וּמְבַקֵּשׁ צְרָכָיו, אָז אֵין הַקָּדוֹשׁ בָּרוּךְ הוּא יָכוֹל לְהִתְלַבֵּשׁ בּוֹ שֶׁהוּא יִתְבָּרַךְ אֵין סוֹף וְאֵין כְּלִי יָכוֹל לְסָבְלוֹ, מַה שֶּׁאֵין כֵּן כְּשֶׁחוֹשֵׁב אֶת עַצְמוֹ לְאַיִן.

Maggid D'varav L'Ya'akov 68:6

"וַיְדַבֵּר יהוה אֶל-מֹשֶׁה, אַחֲרֵי מוֹת, שְׁנֵי בְּנֵי אַהֲרֹן—בְּקָרְבָתָם לִפְנֵי-יְהוָה, וַיָּמֻתוּ." (וַיִּקְרָא טז, א)

אוֹ יֹאמַר עַל זֶה הַדֶּרֶךְ "אַחֲרֵי מוֹת וְגוֹ'" דִּבֵּר הַשֵּׁם לְמֹשֶׁה דֶּרֶךְ מִיתָתָן שֶׁהָיְתָה עַל זֶה הַדֶּרֶךְ "בְּקָרְבָתָם לִפְנֵי הַשֵּׁם", פֵּרוּשׁ, שֶׁנִּתְקָרְבוּ לִפְנֵי אוֹר הָעֶלְיוֹן בְּחִבַּת הַקֹּדֶשׁ וּבָזֶה מֵתוּ, וְהוּא סוֹד הַנְּשִׁיקָה שֶׁבָּהּ מֵתִים הַצַּדִּיקִים, וְהִנֵּה הֵם שָׁוִים לְמִיתַת כָּל הַצַּדִּיקִים, אֶלָּא שֶׁהַהֶפְרֵשׁ הוּא שֶׁהַצַּדִּיקִים הַנְּשִׁיקָה מִתְקָרֶבֶת לָהֶם וְאִלּוּ הֵם נִתְקָרְבוּ לָהּ, וְהוּא אוֹמְרוֹ "בְּקָרְבָתָם לִפְנֵי הַשֵּׁם"... רָמַז הַכָּתוּב הַפְלָאַת חִבַּת הַצַּדִּיקִים, שֶׁהַגַּם שֶׁהָיוּ מַרְגִּישִׁים בְּמִיתָתָם, לֹא נִמְנְעוּ מִקָּרוֹב לִדְבֵקוּת נְעִימוּת עֲרֵבוּת יְדִידוּת חֲבִיבוּת חֲשִׁיקוּת מְתִיקוּת עַד כְּלוֹת נַפְשׁוֹתָם מֵהֶם, וְהָבֵן, וּבְחִינָה זוֹ אֵין מַכִּיר אֵיכוּתָהּ, וְהִיא מְשֻׁלֶּלֶת הַהַכָּרָה.

Or HaḤayim, Leviticus 16:1

Appendix 3
Hebrew Versions of the Texts

Shmoneh Kevatzim, 4:6

כָּל אָדָם צָרִיךְ לָדַעַת, שֶׁקָּרוּי הוּא לַעֲבֹד עַל פִּי אֹפֶן הַהַכָּרָה וְהַהַרְגָּשָׁה הַמְיֻחָד שֶׁלּוֹ, עַל פִּי שֹׁרֶשׁ נִשְׁמָתוֹ, וּבָעוֹלָם זֶה, הַכּוֹלֵל עוֹלָמִים אֵין סְפִירוֹת, יִמְצָא אֶת אוֹצַר חַיָּיו. אַל יְבַלְבְּלוּהוּ תּוֹכְנִים שׁוֹטְפִים אֶל תּוֹכוֹ מֵעָלְמוֹת זָרִים, שֶׁאֵינוֹ קוֹלְטָם כַּהֹגֶן, שֶׁאֵינוֹ מֻכְשָׁר לְאָגְדָם יָפֶה בִּצְרוֹר הַחַיִּים שֶׁלּוֹ. אֵלֶּה הָעוֹלָמוֹת יִמְצְאוּ תִּקּוּנָם בִּמְקוֹמָם, אֵצֶל הַמְסֻגָּלִים לְבִנְיָנָם וְשִׁכְלוּלָם. אֲבָל הוּא צָרִיךְ לְרַכֵּז אֶת חַיָּיו בְּעוֹלָמוֹתָיו הוּא, בְּעוֹלָמוֹת הַפְּנִימִיִּים שֶׁלּוֹ, שֶׁהֵם לוֹ מְלוּאִים כֹּל וּמַקִּיפִים אֶת כָּל. חַיָּב אָדָם לוֹמַר בִּשְׁבִילִי נִבְרָא הָעוֹלָם, גְּדוֹלָה עַנְוְתָנִית זוֹ מְאַשֶּׁרֶת הִיא אֶת הָאָדָם, וּמְבִיאָתוֹ לִשְׁלֵמוּת הָעֶלְיוֹנָה,הָעוֹמֶדֶת וּמְחַכָּה לוֹ, וּבִהְיוֹתוֹ צוֹעֵד בְּדֶרֶךְ חַיִּים בְּטוּחָה זוֹ, בִּמְסִלּוּלוֹ הַמְיֻחָד, בְּאֹרַח צַדִּיקִים הַמְיֻחָד שֶׁלּוֹ, יְמַלֵּא גְּבוּרַת חַיִּים וַעֲלִיזוּת רוּחָנִית, וְאוֹר הַשֵּׁם עָלָיו יִגָּלֶה, מֵהָאוֹת הַמְיֻחָד שֶׁלּוֹ בַּתּוֹרָה, יֵצֵא לוֹ עֻזּוֹ וְאוֹרוֹ.

Naphshi Takshiv Shiro,
MeOlam Raḥok

וּמֵעוֹלָם רָחוֹק, מָלֵא נְגוֹהוֹת
שִׁמְשׁוֹת שָׁם רְחָבוֹת כַּיָּם
וְכוֹכָבִים, כְּאוֹר שִׁמְשֵׁנוּ
עַל פְּנֵי רָקִיעַ אֶבֶן סַפִּיר, שָׁם.

בְּשׂוֹרוֹת לִי יַגִּיעוּ,
כִּטְלָלִים מְלֵאִים צוּף פַּנַּג
נִהֲלוּנִי לְעֵדֶן נֶעֱלָם
שָׁם חֶבְיוֹן הָעֹנֶג

וְכָל פָּנִים שָׁם עַלִּיזִים
וְכָל פֶּה יָשִׁיר שִׁירֵי תְּהִלָּה
וְנִשְׂגָּבוֹת יָחוּשׁ כָּל לֵב
וְכָל רַגְלַיִם מְפַזְּזוֹת בְּגִילָה.

עָבָר וְעָתִיד כְּסֵפֶר נִגְלָל,
וְאֵין סָתוּם, וְהַכֹּל יָדוּעַ,
וְכָל נֶפֶשׁ מְלֵאָה אַהֲבָה לַכֹּל,
וְחוּשִׁים לַאֲלָפִים, וְאוֹר זָרוּעַ.

בְּכָל עֲבָרִים שׁוֹטְפִים כִּנְחָלִים,
וְטֹהַר, וָהוֹד, וּגְבוּרָה וָאוֹר,
וְחַיִּים רַעֲנַנִּים, וְחֹפֶשׁ וּדְרוֹר,
מְמַלְּאִים בְּכָל הִגָּיוֹן וּמִפְעָלִים.

וּבְאֵין מוֹרֶה וּמַדְרִיךְ, שׁוֹפֵט וָשַׂר,
הַכֹּל טוֹב, הַכֹּל בָּהִיר,
וְאֵין עִוּוּת, וְאֵין עִקּוּם, הַכֹּל יָשָׁר,
וְלַיְלָה כַּיּוֹם יָאִיר.

לְעוֹלָם זֶה נַפְשִׁי שׁוֹאֶפֶת,
וּבְחַיִּים כָּאֵלֶּה רוּחִי מְרַחֶפֶת

יֵשׁ שֶׁהוּא שַׁר שִׁירַת נַפְשׁוֹ, וּבְנַפְשׁוֹ הוּא מוֹצֵא אֶת הַכֹּל, אֶת מְלֹא הַסִּפּוּק הָרוּחָנִי בִּמְלוֹאוֹ.

וְיֵשׁ שֶׁהוּא שַׁר שִׁירַת הָאֻמָּה, יוֹצֵא הוּא מִתּוֹךְ הַמַּעְגָּל שֶׁל נַפְשׁוֹ הַפְּרָטִית, שֶׁאֵינוֹ מוֹצֵא אוֹתָהּ מְרוּחֶבֶת כָּרָאוּי וְלֹא מְיֻשֶּׁבֶת יִשּׁוּב אִידֵאָלִי, שׁוֹאֵף לִמְרוֹמֵי עֹז, וְהוּא מִתְדַּבֵּק בְּאַהֲבָה עֲדִינָה עִם כְּלָלוּתָהּ שֶׁל כְּנֶסֶת יִשְׂרָאֵל, וְעִמָּהּ הוּא שַׁר אֶת שִׁירֶיהָ, מֵצֵר בְּצָרוֹתֶיהָ, וּמִשְׁתַּעְשֵׁעַ בְּתִקְווֹתֶיהָ, הוֹגֶה דֵּעוֹת עֶלְיוֹנוֹת וּטְהוֹרוֹת עַל עָבְרָהּ וְעַל עֲתִידָהּ, וְחוֹקֵר בְּאַהֲבָה וּבְחָכְמַת לֵב אֶת תֹּכֶן רוּחָהּ הַפְּנִימִי.

וְיֵשׁ אֲשֶׁר עוֹד תִּתְרַחֵב נַפְשׁוֹ עַד שֶׁיּוֹצֵא וּמִתְפַּשֵּׁט מֵעַל גְּבוּל יִשְׂרָאֵל, לָשִׁיר אֶת שִׁירַת הָאָדָם, רוּחוֹ הוֹלֵךְ וּמִתְרַחֵב בִּגְאוֹן כְּלָלוּת הָאָדָם וְהוֹד צַלְמוֹ, שׁוֹאֵף אֶל תְּעוּדָתוֹ הַכְּלָלִית וּמְצַפֶּה לְהִשְׁתַּלְמוּתוֹ הָעֶלְיוֹנָה, וּמִמְּקוֹר חַיִּים זֶה הוּא שׁוֹאֵב אֶת כְּלָלוּת הֶגְיוֹנוֹתָיו וּמֶחְקָרָיו, שְׁאִיפוֹתָיו וְחֶזְיוֹנוֹתָיו.

Shmoneh Kevatzim, 7:112

וְיֵשׁ אֲשֶׁר עוֹד מִזֶּה לְמַעְלָה בָּרֹחַב יִתְנַשָּׂא, עַד שֶׁמִּתְאַחֵד עִם כָּל הַיְקוּם כֻּלּוֹ, עִם כָּל הַבְּרִיּוֹת, וְעִם כָּל הָעוֹלָמִים, וְעִם כֻּלָּם אוֹמֵר שִׁירָה, זֶה הוּא הָעוֹסֵק בְּפֶרֶק שִׁירָה בְּכָל יוֹם שֶׁמֻּבְטָח לוֹ שֶׁהוּא בֶּן הָעוֹלָם הַבָּא.

וְיֵשׁ אֲשֶׁר עוֹלֶה עִם כָּל הַשִּׁירִים הַלָּלוּ בְּיַחַד בַּאֲגֻדָּה אַחַת, וְכֻלָּם נוֹתְנִים אֶת קוֹלוֹתֵיהֶם, כֻּלָּם יַחַד מַנְעִימִים אֶת זְמִרֵיהֶם, וְזֶה לְתוֹךְ זֶה נוֹתֵן לְשַׁד וְחַיִּים, קוֹל שָׂשׂוֹן וְקוֹל שִׂמְחָה, קוֹל צָהֳלָה וְקוֹל רִנָּה, קוֹל חֶדְוָה וְקוֹל קְדֻשָּׁה. שִׁירַת הַנֶּפֶשׁ, שִׁירַת הָאֻמָּה, שִׁירַת הָאָדָם, שִׁירַת הָעוֹלָם, כֻּלָּן יַחַד מִתְמַזְּגוֹת בְּקִרְבּוֹ בְּכָל עֵת וּבְכָל שָׁעָה.

וְהַתְּמִימוּת הַזֹּאת בִּמְלוֹאָהּ עוֹלָה הִיא לִהְיוֹת שִׁירַת קוֹדֶשׁ, שִׁירַת אֵל, שִׁירַת יִשְׂרָאֵל, בְּעֹצֶם עֻזָּהּ וְתִפְאַרְתָּהּ, בְּעֹצֶם אֲמִתָּהּ וּגְדֻלָּהּ, יִשְׂרָאֵל שִׁיר אֵל, שִׁיר פָּשׁוּט, שִׁיר כָּפוּל, שִׁיר מְשֻׁלָּשׁ, שִׁיר מְרֻבָּע. שִׁיר הַשִּׁירִים אֲשֶׁר לִשְׁלֹמֹה, לַמֶּלֶךְ שֶׁהַשָּׁלוֹם שֶׁלּוֹ.

Glossary

All terms from Hebrew unless otherwise indicated.

aequanimitas	Equanimity in Latin, a feeling of evenness and neutrality towards all experience.
al mut	Often translated as "eternally" in Biblical Hebrew though its exact meaning is unknown; "beyond death" in the Ba'al Shem Tov's usage.
askara	Croup, inflammation of the upper airways in children that is usually non-fatal; alternatively may be another more fatal form of illness which affects the upper airways in adults and children.
avar	The past.
aveirah	Transgression or misdeed; sometimes known as a "sin," an *aveirah* is a missed opportunity that can be transformed and undone through self-reflection, apologizing, and changing one's behavior for the better.
ayin	Nothing, often associated with the highest *Sephirah* of *Keter*—the sacred nothingness which was the first element of existence;
ba'al teshuvah	Master of Return or Repentance; someone who has left a community of Jewish practice and then later returned to it.
breishit	In the beginning; the first word of the Hebrew Bible.
chakras	Energy centers that correspond to different parts of the body as described in Hindu tradition.
devekut	Cleaving; attachment; direct contact with the Divine; mystical connection; spiritual state.
dinim	Judgments; negativity that arises when the *Sephirah* of *Gevurah* becomes misaligned.
El	Name of God often incorporated into proper names like "Yisrael" and "Eliyahu."
Elohim	Name of God associated with strictness or judgment; name signifying the *Sephirot* of *Bina*, *Gevurah*, or *Shekhinah*; some contemporary scholars associate this name with one of the authors of the Torah.
emunah	Trust, faith in God's guidance of the world and our lives.
Eretz Yisrael	The land of Israel.
Esh Kodesh	Holy fire; the revised title of the last book of the Piaseczner Rebbe
etzem	Bone, essence.
gadlut	Expanded consciousness which comes in moments of deep connection to the Infinite.
gadol	Large, big.
Gematria	A Hebrew numerological system for finding meaning and synchronicity in a number, letter, or word.
Gevurah	The *Sephirah* of power, judgment, and boundaries (see appendix 1 for more detail).
gilgul	Reincarnation; a view of the afterlife most fully articulated in Lurianic Kabbalah.
ḥakhamim	Sages, wise ones.
halakhah	Jewish law.
Ḥasidim	Hasidic Jews, community of particular Hasidic Jews such as the Ger *Ḥasidim*
Ḥasidut	Hasidic thought, the highly experiential mystical perspective through which Hasidic practitioners understand Jewish texts.
ḥaya	Layer of the soul associated with the foundational reality of all existence.

Glossary

All terms from Hebrew unless otherwise indicated.

ḥayot	Angels with four faces mentioned in the first chapter of Ezekiel; each has the face of a human, lion, ox, and eagle.
Ḥesed	The *Sephirah* of lovingkindness (see appendix 1 for more detail)
hitbodedut	Solo heartfelt prayer in one's own words as taught by Rebbe Naḥman of Bratslav; lit. self-seclusion; meditation more broadly
Ḥokhmah	The *Sephirah* of wisdom; the first Somethingness of all existence; our essential nature (see appendix 1 for more detail).
ḥul	Circle.
itaruta delitata	Awakening from below in Aramaic kabbalistic terminology; when human action affects a reaction from the spiritual world.
kamokha	As yourself; like you.
katan	Small; a child.
katnut	Contracted, limited, or everyday consciousness; a state of disconnection from Divinity.
kelipot	Husks or shells; a kabbalistic metaphor for the demonic realm and evil.
Keter	The highest *Sephirah* associated with Nothingness; lit. crown (see appendix 1 for more detail).
kohanim	Jewish Priests who originally officiated at the ancient temple or tabernacle.
kol	Voice, sound, or thunder.
lemala meta'am veda'at	Beyond reason and knowledge.
mezareh	Sift.
Ma'aseh HaMerkavah	lit. The Realm of the Chariot; the Divine chambers in early Jewish mysticism; the *Sephirot* in Kabbalah
maḥol	Dance.
meitzar	Narrow place.
merkavah	lit. Chariot; the spiritual realm in early Jewish mysticism.
Merkavah Mysticism	Chariot Mysticism of spiritual ascents first documented in early Rabbinic Judaism.
meshiv	Answers.
midrash	Rabbinic interpretation of the Hebrew Bible.
midrashim	Plural form of *midrash*.
milui	lit. Filling out; an interpretive method in which each letter that makes up a word is spelled out.
minyanim	Groups of people who pray together.
Mitzrayim	Egypt.
mitzvah	Commandment from the Torah; good deed.
mitzvot	Plural of *mitzvah*.
ne'arav	His youths.
nephesh	First level of the soul, associated with physicality.
neshamah	Third level of the soul, associated with the mind; breath.

Glossary

All terms from Hebrew unless otherwise indicated.

nigunim	Wordless melodies dung as meditations; lit. melodies.
pekudei	Keepings, precepts.
rakia	Expanse, Heaven, or sky.
reshimu	The trace of Divinity left in the world after the Infinite withdrew itself in order to leave space for the physical world; the trace of the Divine left in us after a spiritual experience.
ruaḥ	Second level of soul, associated with the emotions.
Shabbat	Jewish day of rest and spiritual refreshment.
Sephirot	The ten emanations of God; the ten qualities through which the Infinite manifests in our world (see appendix 1 for more detail).
shaktipat	Sanskrit word for the transmission of spiritual energy through eye contact or touch from teacher to student in Kundalini yoga.
shanim ne'arut	Years of youth.
shefa	The flow of blessings from the Creator which nourishes the world.
Shekhinah	Divine Presence; the lowest *sephirah* associated with receptivity (see appendix 1 for more detail)
Shir El	Song of God.
shnei	Two.
Sitra Aḥra	The Other Side, the realm of negativity from which evil arises in Kabbalah.
sofit	The altered form of certain Hebrew letters when they appear at the end of a word; lit. final.
sukkah	Temporary dwelling constructed for the fall festival of *Sukkot.*
Sukkot	Fall festival linked with the last harvest in Israel.
tefilin	Phylacteries, two leather boxes with sacred scrolls inside wrapped around the arm and head (usually during morning prayers).
teshuvah	Repentance or return, the process of repairing and transforming past misdeeds or negative internal traits.
tikkun	Repairing the world in Lurianic Kabbalah; repairing or healing the inner world in Hasidic thought.
tikkun olam	see tikkun
totzaot	Issues.
Tree of Life	English synonym for the *Sephirot* in Kabbalah.
tzadik	Righteous person; mystic leader in Hasidic thought.
tzadikim	Plural of *tzadik.*
tzḥok	Laughter.
Tzfat	Also Safed, Sefat, Tsefat, a city in the north of Israel.
upekkh	Onlooking in Pali.
upekkha	Equanimity in Pali.
veya'al	Went up, both geographically and spiritually.

Glossary

All terms from Hebrew unless otherwise indicated.

vayashev	He placed.
via negativa	The negative path in Latin, a spiritual mode that intentionally engages with hardship and suffering.
via positiva	The positive path in Latin, a spiritual mode that directly cultivates good feelings.
yeridah letzorekh aliyah	lit. Descending for the sake of ascending, a spiritual mode of facing negativity directly in order to be transformed.
yesh	Something; Somethingness; the tangible spiritual world; the physical world; the opposite of Nothingness.
YHWH	The unpronounceable name of God; the central Divine name sometimes written "*YHVH*." The third Hebrew letter, depending on dialect, is pronounced either *waw* or *vav*.
Yitzḥak	Isaac.
zar	Crown.

Endnotes

1 Translated by Moshe Idel

2 Leonard Cohen, though not an "official" Jewish theologian or Rabbi, is beloved in the Jewish world. Besides being a practicing Jew, he was also ordained as a Zen Buddhist Monk.

3 Translated by Nehemia Polen

4 Besides being a renowned Hindu mystic, Swami Muktananda engaged in highly questionable sexual practices with students that were mostly kept secret until his death.

5 Translated by Avraham Greenbaum

6 Translated by Daniel Matt

7 Translated by Arthur Green

8 Translated by Arthur Green

9 Translated by Arthur Green

10 Translation by Adin Steinsaltz. The words in bold are the literal script of the Talmud and the regular font denotes the explanatory commentary in this terse text.

11 See Likutei Moharan 64 by Rebbe Naḥman of Bratslav for a beautiful and bittersweet reflection on this paradox.

12 Translated by Matthew Ponak based on a translation by Itzchak Marmorstein

13 Translated by Matthew Ponak based on translations by Itzchak Marmorstein and Ben-Zion Bokser

Works Cited

Primary Sources

Abraham Isaac Kook. *Naphshi Takshiv Shiro.* HaMakhon Lehaker Mishnat HaRa'aya, Ramat Gan, 1997.

Abraham Isaac Kook. *Shmoneh Kevatzim.*

Abraham Joshua Heschel of Apt. *Ohev Yisrael.* Zhitomir, 1863.

Abraham, Abulafia. *Sefer HaYashar.*

Baḥya ben Asher. *Commentary on the Torah.* Naples, 1492.

David Shlomo Eibshitz. *Arvei Naḥal.* Warsaw, 1905.

Dov Ber of Mezeritch. *Maggid D'varav L'Ya'akov.* New York, 2003.

Elimelekh Weisblum. *Noam Elimelekh.* Lvov, 1788.

Hayim ibn Atar. *Or HaHayim.* Venice, 1742.

Isaac of Acco. *Me'irat Eynayim.* Jerusalem, 1992.

Isaiah Horowitz. *Shnei Luḥot HaBrit.* Amsterdam, 1698.

Israel ben Eliezer. *Keter Shem Tov.* Zholkva, 1794.

Israel ben Eliezer. *Sefer Ba'al Shem Tov.* Lodz, 1938.

Israel ben Eliezer. *Tzava'at HaRivash.* Warsaw, 1934.

Kalonymous Kalman Epstein. *Maor VeShemesh.* Warsaw, 1859.

Kalonymus Kalman Shapira. *Esh Kodesh.* Jerusalem, 1960.

Levi Yitzḥak of Berditchev. *Kedushat Levi.* Slavuta, 1798.

Menaḥem Naḥum Twersky. *Meor Einayim.* Warsaw, 1889.

Mordekhai Yoseph Leiner. *Mei HaShiloaḥ.* Lvov, 1849.

Moshe Cordovero. *Pardes Rimonim.* Yarid, Jerusalem, 2000.

Naḥman of Bratslav. *Likutei Moharan.* A.Y. Halter, Warsaw, 1916.

Shalom Noaḥ Berezovsky. *Netivot Shalom.* Jerusalem, 1982.

Shneur Zalman of Liadi. *Tanya.* New York, 1796.

Tikkunei Zohar. Mantua, 1558.

Zvi Hirsch of Nadvorna. *Tzemah HaShem LeTsevi.* Berditchev, 1818.

Ze'ev Wolf of Zhitormir. *Or HaMe'ir.* Jerusalem, 1999.

Zohar. Cremona, 1558.

Zvi Elimelekh Spira. *Bnei Yisaskhar.* HaMesorah, Bnei Brak, 1982.

Works Cited

Secondary Sources

Almaas, A. H. *Runaway Realization: Living a Life of Ceaseless Discovery.* (Boulder, Colorado: Shambhala Publications, 2014).

Alter, Judah Aryeh Leib, Arthur Green, and Shai Gluskin. *The Language of Truth: the Torah Commentary of the Sefat Emet, Rabbi Yehudah Leib Alter of Ger.* (Philadelphia: Jewish Publication Society, 1998).

Brown, Karen McCarthy. *Mama Lola: A Vodou Priestess in Brooklyn.* (Berkeley ; Los Angeles ; London: University of California Press, 2018).

Buddhaghosa, and Ñāṇamoli. *The Path of Purification. Visuddhimagga.* (Kandy, Sri Lanka: Buddhist Publication Society, 2010).

Bokser, Ben Zion. *Abraham Isaac Kook—The Lights of Penitence, Lights of Holiness, The Moral Principles, Essays, Letters, and Poems. The Classics of Western Spirituality I.* (New York: Paulist Press, 2012),

Cohen, Leonard, "Anthem," 1992, track #5 on The Future, Columbia Records.

Fox, Matthew. *Creation Spirituality: Liberating Gifts for the Peoples of the Earth.* (New York: HarperCollins, 1991).

Gendlin, Eugene. *Focusing.* (New York, New York: Bantam, 1982).

Green, Arthur. *Devotion and Commandment: The Faith of Abraham in the Hasidic Imagination.* (Bristol, Connecticut: ISD LLC, 2015).

Green, Arthur. *Radical Judaism Rethinking God and Tradition.* (Cumberland: Yale University Press, 2014).

Green, Arthur. *Speaking Torah. Spiritual Teachings from around the Maggids Table. Volume 2, Numbers, Deuteronomy, the Holiday Cycle.* (Woodstock, VT: Jewish Lights Publishing, 2013).

Grof, Stanislav, and Christina Grof. *Spiritual Emergency: When Personal Transformation Becomes a Crisis.* (New York, New York: Jeremy P. Tarcher/ Putnam, 1989).

Hays, Gregory, trans. *Meditations: Marcus Aurelius.* (London, England: Penguin Books, 2014).

Idel, Moshe. *The Mystical Experience in Abraham Abulafia.* (Albany: State University of New York Press, 1987).

Ingber, David. *Kol Nidrei Vort.* (Romemu, New York, November 8, 2019).

Ish-Shalom, Zvi. *The Kedumah Experience: The Primordial Torah.* (Boulder, Colorado: Albion-Andalus, Incorporated, 2017).

Khan, Inayat. *The Way of Illumination.* (Delhi, India: Motilal Banarsidass, 1988).

Kason, Yvonne. *Farther Shores: Exploring How near-Death, Kundalini and Mystical Experiences Transform Ordinary Lives.* (New York, New York: iUniverse, 2008).

Lertzman, David. *Telephone call.* (Calgary, Alberta, fall 2007).

Works Cited

Secondary Sources

Matt, Daniel Chanan. *Zohar: the Book of Enlightenment.* (London: SPCK, 1983).

McGinn, Bernard. *The Essential Writings of Christian Mysticism.* (New York, New York: The Modern Library, 2006).

Monbourquette, Jean. *How to Befriend Your Shadow: Welcoming Your Unloved Side.* (Quezon City, Philippines: Claretian Publications, 2009).

Mussen, Paul. (ed.), *Handbook of Child Psychology, Vol. 1. 4th ed.* (New York, New York: Wiley, 1983).

Nahman, Yaakov Schlomo Ephraim. "The Turkey Prince." (trans. Rabbi Avraham Greenbaum) *The Essential Rabbi Nahman*, Azamra.org

Olson, Carl. *Hindu Primary Sources: a Sectarian Reader.* (New Brunswick, N.J: Rutgers University Press, 2007).

Polen, Nehemia. "Sealing the Book with Tears: Divine Weeping on Mount Nebo and in the Warsaw Ghetto." In *Holy Tears: Weeping in the Religious Imagination edited by Kimberley Christine Patton and John Stratton Hawley.* (Princeton, New Jersey: Princeton University Press, 2005).

Ramakrishna. "Approaching Ramakrishna." in *Commemoration of the 175th Birth Anniversary of Sri Ramakrishna.* (Kolkata: Advaita Ashrama, 2011).

Raz, Simcha, Levin, Edward (trans.) *The sayings of Menachem Mendel of Kotsk.* (Northvale, N.J.:Jason Aronson Inc. 1995).

Roberts, Bernadette. *The Experience of No-Self: A Contemplative Journey.* (SUNY Press, 1993).

Saraswati, Swami Satyananda. *Kundalini Tantra (2nd ed.).* (Munger, Bihar, India: Bihar School of Yoga, 1984).

Scholem, Gershom. *Major Trends in Jewish Mysticism.* (New York, New York: SchockenBooks, 1995).

Scholem, Gershom. *The Messianic Idea in Judaism.* (New York, New York: Schocken Books, 1974).

Sofer, D. "Rav Yosef Yoizel Horowitz ZT'L The Alter of Novardok." Internet Archive Wayback Machine. Tzemach Dovid, February 4, 2012. https://web.archive.org/web/20120204040448/http://www.tzemachdovid.org/Musar/navordok1.html.

Somé, Malidoma Patrice. *Of Water and the Spirit: Ritual, Magic, and Initiation in the Life of an African Shaman.* (New York, New York: Penguin, 1995).

Suzuki, Daisetz Teitaro. *Essays in Zen Buddhism, First Series.* (New York, New York: Grove Press, 1926).

Steel, Piers. *The Procrastination Equation: The Science of Getting Things Done.* (Sydney, Australia: Murdoch Books, 2011).

Steinsaltz, Adin. *Talmud Bavli, Berakhot, ed.* (Jerusalem, Israel: Koren Publishers, 1967).

Wilber, Ken. *Integral Spirituality: a Startling New Role for Religion in the Modern and Postmodern World.* (Boston, MA: Integral Books, 2007).

Yocom, Guy. "My Shot: Gary Player." in Golf Digest, August 12, 2010.

Index

Aaron
  death of sons, 51
  Koraḥ, story of, 33
  sapphire, vision of, 53
Abraham
  in Egypt, 22
  Ḥesed and, 29–30, 34
  holy laughter and, 17
  sacred contemplation by, 6
Abraham Joshua Heschel, of Apt, Rebbe, 46–47
Abulafia, Rabbi Abraham, 3, 8, 12, 58
Abundance, 32
Adam
  as ancestor of all humanity, 52
  created in God's image, 38
  neshamah of, 12
  snake, encounter with, 29
Aequanimitas, 50, 73
Afterlife. *See* Death and afterlife
Alignment with soul's purpose, 52, 56
Almaas, A. H., 11
Al mut, 22, 73
Alter, Yehudah Aryeh Leib, Rebbe, 48
Alter Rebbe, 40
Angels
  at burning bush, 9–10
  ḥayot, 74
  "living creatures," 16–17
  Metatron, 8, 58
  prayer and, 18
  strength of consciousness needed to perceive, 9–10
Anger, 45
The Apter Rav, 28, 46–47
The Ari, 16
Arjuna, 39
Arvei Naḥal, 26–27, 65
Asceticism, 1, 50–51
Askara, 73
Astral travel, 29
Astrology, 49
Attachment, 50
Attaining but not attaining, 11
Attar, Rabbi Ḥayim ben Moshe, 51
Avar, 54, 73
Aveirah, 54, 73
Avihu, 51
Ayin, 50, 73

Ba'al mel'akhah, ix
Ba'al Shem Tov
  benefits of balance and bodily health, 12
  on *devekut*, 16
  on facing difficulties, 22
  Hasidism, founding of, 59
  on joy and humor, 17
  on love for others, 21
  Maggid and, 50
  parables, 18–19
  on prayer, 18–19
  Rabbi Ḥayim ben Moshe ibn Attar and, 51
  Rebbe Naḥman of Bratslav and, 11
  as teacher of the Chernobyler, 41
  texts by, 16–22
  tzadikim, nature of, 20
Ba'al teshuvah, 23, 73
The Babylonian Talmud, 51
Bahir, 58
Bahya ben Asher ben Hlava, Rabbi, 9–10
The Berdichever, 24–25
Berezovsky, Rebbe Sholom Noah, 31
Besht. *See* Ba'al Shem Tov
Bhagavad Gita, 39
Bina, 31, 57
Blessings, on food, 23, 32
Bliss, 40
Bly, Robert, 29
Bnei Yisaskhar, 23, 64
The body. *See also* Embodiment
  benefits of life balance and bodily health, 12
  bones, 31
  brain as vessel of consciousness, 13
  as bridge between conscious and unconscious, 12
  burning bush and, 9–10
  emotional awareness and, 12
  equanimity and, 50
  faith manifested in, 31
  fingers, Hebrew letters and, 7
  health and awareness, xi, 12
  heart, 14, 44, 53
  holy purposes, using for, 36–37
  limbs, 31
  mysticism grounded in, 50
  receiving divine energy through, 40
  self-discipline, 46–47
  Sephirot and, 37
  spiritual qualities, correlation with body parts, 36–37
Bones, 31
Brain as vessel of consciousness, 13
Breishit, 4, 39, 73
Broken heart, 14
Brown, Karen McCarthy: Mama Lola: *A Vodou Priestess in Brooklyn*, 34
Buddhism
  enlightenment, 13
  equanimity, 50
  non-conceptual realization, 38
  parable from, 6
  spiritual bypassing, 26
  spiritual emergency, 9
  Tibetan, on working with the body, 12
  Zen and spiritual journey, 11
Bunim, Simḥa, 52
Burning bush, 9–10

Caterpillar and cocoon, 19
Chabad Hasidic Dynasty, 40
Chakras, 37, 73
Channeling, 34
Chariot. *See Merkavah*
The Chernobyler, 41–45
Christian mysticism, 11, 17, 22, 41
Cohen, Leonard, 14

Index

Commentary
  how to read, 5
  types of, 2–3
Community
  feeding each other, 53
  honoring others, 21
  importance of, xi
  magical moments in, 48
  pathways to societal change, 33
  song of, 55–56
Comprehension, 40
Consciousness
  body and, 12
  nothingness and, 13
  stages of consciousness, 18
  strengthening, 9
Contemplation, 6. *See also* Meditation
Cordovero, Rabbi Moshe, 36–38
Creation
  Creation Spirituality, 41
  purpose of, 52
  Sephirot's relation to days if, 50
  of the world, 43
Croup, 51

Da'at, 31, 57
Dance, 33
Darkness
  "Dark Night of the Soul" (Saint John of the Cross), 22
  incorporating with light, 44–45
Day, cycle of, 44
Death and afterlife
  Adam and, 22
  afterlife, Jewish views of, 54
  al mut, 22, 73
  descent for sake of ascent, 22
  Keter consciousness and, 50
  Kiss of death, 51
Deep Reality, 39
Descent for sake of ascent, 22, 24–27, 76
Devekut
  defined, 73
  Kiss of Death and, 51
  meditation and, 49
  Moses and, 24–25
  Scholem on, 8
  Torah study as path to, 15–16
  tzadikim and, 6, 28
Diamond Approach, 11
Dinim, 44, 73
Discernment, 31, 46. *See also Tipheret*
Distractions, minimizing, 46
Divination practices, 49
Divinity
  definition of divine, 2
  Divine Body, 18
  divine fire, 51
  Divine Light, 53–54
  Divine Presence. *See Shekhinah*
  Divine Throne, 16–17, 19, 53, 58
  saturation with, 53–54

Donovan, 11
Dov Baer, of Mezeritch (The Maggid). *See* Maggid of Mezeritch

Early Rabbinic era, 58
Eckhart, Meister, 17
Eden, 53–54
Ego formation, 44
Egypt (*Mitzrayim*)
  Abraham in, 22
  Luria's life in, 59
  Mitzrayim, defined, 74
  Sea of Reeds, 50
  as symbol for struggle/suffering, 29–30
Eibeschitz, Rebbe David Solomon, 26–27
Eichenstein, Zevi Hirsch, 32
Eightfold Noble Path, 13
Ein Sof, 18, 38
El, 73
Elijah, 39, 58
Elimelekh, of Lizhensk, 6, 28, 46
Elisha, 30, 58
Elohim, 8, 10, 73
Elohi Rabbi Yitzhak, 16
Embodiment. *See also* The body
  body, compassion for, 12
  defined, xii
  grounding, 10
  intense spiritual experiences and, 16
  introduction to, 1
  ways God is found in body, 7
Emotional catharsis
  equanimity and, 50
  hitbodedut, 22
  unhappiness, coming out of, 14–15
Emptiness, xii, 13, 50
Emunah, 31, 73
Enjoyment. *See* Joy
Enlightenment
  body awareness and, 12
  in Buddhism, 13
  journey towards, 56
  place of, 54
  stages of consciousness on path to, 18
  types of, 8
  unceasing, 28
Epstein, Rebbe Kalonymus Kalman, 6
Equality, 33
Equanimity
  aequanimitas, 50, 73
  bodily pain and pleasure, 50
  devekut and, 47
  healing and, 20
  neutrality, 49
  upekkha, 50, 75
Eretz Yisrael
  The Ari in, 16
  defined, 73
  meaning, 41
  Rabbi Ḥayim ben Moshe ibn Attar in, 51
  Rabbi Isaac ben Samuel of Acco in, 49

Index

Rabbi Isaiah ben Avraham HaLevi Horowitz in, 7
Rabbi Moshe Cordovero in, 36
"Rabbi," origin of term, 3
Rebbe David Solomon Eibeschitz in, 26
as sacred community, 48
song of (*Shir El*), 55–56
Tzfat, 16, 36, 75
veya'al, 29
Esh Kodesh, 15, 62, 73
Etzem, 31, 73
Evil, 26, 44–45, 50
Exile, 28
Expansiveness, 17
Ezekiel, 53

Faith, 31, 48
Fear, 31
Fingers, Hebrew letters and, 7
Firestone, Rabbi Tirzah, xi
First Nation peoples, 38, 43
Focusing, 12
Food
banquet in heaven and hell, 53
bounty, enjoying, 32
food blessings, hierarchy of, 23
Sabbath meals, 41
Four Noble Truths, 13
Fox, Matthew, 41

Gadlut, 17, 73
Gadol, 17, 73
Gemara, 58
Gematria
defined, 73
of *YHVH*, 7
Gendlin, Eugene, 12
Gerrer Rebbe, 48
Gevurah
days of week, association with, 50
defined, 73
dinim, 44, 73
left hand, association with, 37
names and associations, 57
Gikatilla, Joseph, 9
Gilgul, 53–54, 73
Giving and receiving, 32
Global spirituality, 2
God. *See also* God, names of
bringing pleasure to, 28
ecstatic love of, 51
experiencing voice of, 48
face to face with, 25, 35
garment of, 50
God of Earth, 34
Maimonides view of, 39
in monotheism, 39
physical characteristics of, 36–37
as source of equanimity, 49
God, names of
Ein Sof, 18, 38
El, 73
Elohim, 8, 10, 73
the Infinite, 38–40, 50
I will be as I will be, 38
King, 56
The Sacred Mystery, 38
YHWH. *See YHWH*
Good and evil, 26, 44–45, 50
Green, Avraham Yitshak (Arthur), ix, xiii, 3–4
Devotion and Commandment: The Faith of Abraham in the Hasidic Imagination, 6, 28
interpretation of Israelites, 41
Radical Judaism, 48
Grof, Stanislov, 19
Grof, Stanislov and Christina: *Spiritual Emergency: When Personal Transformation Becomes a Crisis*, 9
Grounded spirituality. *See* Embodiment
Grounding, 10
Growth through hardship, 23

Habits, overcoming, 38, 46
Haitian Vodou, 34
Hakhamim, 19, 73
Halakhah, 7, 73
Happiness, 14
Harmony, 33
Hasidism
Ba'al Shem Tov as founder, 16
Chabad Hasidic Dynasty, 40
early, 6, 17, 40–41, 48
founding of, 11, 16
Ger Hasidic lineage, 48
Ḥasidim, defined, 73
history of, 59
Neo-Hasidism, 59
Slonomir Ḥasidim, 31
Ḥasidut, 73
Hatred, 45
Ḥaya, 11, 47, 73
Ḥayot, 74
Heart, 14, 44, 53
Heaven, 53–54
Hebrew College, xii–xiii
Hebrew letters
ayin, 73
beit, 4
fingers and, 7
gematria, 7, 73
milui, 7, 74
root souls, letters in Torah and, 52–53
YHVH. *See YHWH*
Hell, 53
Henotheism, 39
Ḥesed
Abraham, revelation through, 29
days of week associated with, 50
defined, 74
Moses and, 34
names and associations, 57
right hand, association with, 37
Hierarchy, 33

Index

Hinduism
  enlightenment, 13, 24
  gods in, 39
Hitbodedut, 14, 22, 49, 74. *See also* Meditation
Hod, 50, 57
Ḥokhmah
  defined, 74
  Eden as symbol for, 53
  ḥaya, association with, 47
  insight, spark of, 31
  names and associations, 57
  Shabbat lunch, association with, 41
Holiness, 55–56
Holocaust, 15, 31
Holy fire, *Esh Kodesh*, 73
Holy of Holies, 51
Horowitz, Rabbi Isaiah ben Avraham HaLevi, 7
Ḥul, 33, 74
Humanity, song of, 55
Humor, 14, 17
Hurwitz, Rabbi Yosef Yoizel, of Novogrudok, 49
Husks/shells, 22, 33

Idel, Moshe, 8
Impurity, 42
The Infinite, 38–40, 50
Ingber, Rabbi David, 38
Initiation rites, 29, 43
Inner alignment, 42
Inner divinity, 48
Insight, 31
Integration of nothingness, 13
Intuition/Intuitive Mind, 4, 16, 18–19
Isaac, 17
Isaac, Jacob, "The Seer" of Lublin, 6
Isaac ben Samuel, of Acco, Rabbi, 48
Isaac Luria, 59
Isaac the Blind, 58
Isaiah, 18
Ishbitzer Rebbe, 33
Ish-Shalom, Rabbi Zvi, 4, 34
  The Kedumah Experience, 47
Islam, 8, 29, 43
Israel. *See Eretz Yisrael*
Israel ben Eliezer, Rabbi. *See* Ba'al Shem Tov
Itaruta delitata, 21, 74
I will be as I will be, 38

Jacob, 30
Jeremiah, 55–56
Jesters, 17
Jewish law, 7, 73
Jewish mysticism. *See also* Mysticism
  for all people, 2
  mystical union in, 8
  timeline of, 58–59
Jewish Renewal, 59
John of the Cross, Saint, 22
Joseph, 30
Joy
  enjoying God's bounty, 32
  expansion through, 17
  mitzvah of joyfulness, 14
  purpose, living in alignment with, 52–53
  Seven Blessings, 55
  Shabbat consciousness and enjoyment, 28, 42
  sharing, 24
  spiritual connection through, 30
  tzadikim and, 54
  as vessel for receiving new Torah insights, 13
Judgments, 44
Jung, Carl, 29–30

Kabbalah
  Ecstatic Kabbalah, 58
  Elohim and *Shekhinah*, 10
  history of, 39, 58
  introduction to, 1
  Lurianic, 54, 59
  Prophetic, 8
Kahn, Hazrat Inayat: *The Way of Illumination*, 43
Kamokha, 21, 74
Karma, 21
Kason, Yvonne, 19
Katan, 17, 74
Katnut, 17, 74
Kedumah, 4, 37
The Kedumah Experience (Rabbi Zvi Ish-Shalom), 4, 34, 47
Kedushat Levi, 24–25, 64
Kelipot, 22, 74
Keter
  ayin and, 73
  defined, 74
  I will be as I will be, association with, 38
  names and associations, 57
  nothingness and, 13
  Shabbat, association with, 41, 50
Keter Shem Tov, 16–20, 63
Kindness, 21
Knowledge, 31, 40
Kohanim, 51, 74
Kol, 74
Kolot, 48
Kook, Rav Abraham Isaac, 33, 52–55
  The Moral Principles, 53
Koraḥ, 33
Krishna, 39
Kundalini yoga
  shaktipat, 19, 75
  spiritual emergency and, 9–10

Laughter, 17, 24, 40, 49, 75
Leadership. *See Tzadik/tzadikim*
Leiner, Rebbe Mordekhai Yoseph of Izbica, 33
Lemala meta'am veda'at, 38, 74
Lertzman, David, 27
Letters. *See* Hebrew letters
Levi Yitzḥak ben Meir, of Berdichev, Rebbe, 24–25
Liberation, 13, 37, 54
Lieb of Dokar, 31
Life's purpose, 52

Index

Light
  darkness, incorporating, 44–45
  divine and World to Come, 53–54
  Infinite Light, 11
  sunshine, 10
Likutei Moharan, 11–14, 62
Limitations, personal, 28
Love
  Abraham as symbol of, 30
  ba'al teshuvah and, 23
  ethical life, role in, 53–54
  of God, 44, 51
  healing and, 20–21
  of humanity, 55
  lovingkindness, 34
  pleasure and, 32
  suffering and, 26
  transcendent, 40
Lurianic Kabbalah, 59
Luzzato, Moshe Ḥayim, 53

Ma'aseh HaMerkavah, 74. *See also Sephirot*
Maggid D'varav L'Ya'akov, 50, 70
Maggid of Kozienice, 15
Maggid of Mezeritch
  Hasidic movement, importance in, 59
  students of, 24, 28, 31, 33, 40–41
  writings by, 50
Maḥol, 33, 74
Maimonides, Moses, 16–22, 36–37, 39
Malkhut, 41, 57
Maor VeShemesh, 6, 28, 61
Marcus Aurelius, Emperor of Rome, 50
Meditation. *See also Hitbodedut*
  contemplation as main spiritual practice, 6
  nigunim as, 31, 48, 75
  song as, 55–56
  as source of bliss, 40
  in spiritual development, 49
  task of Kabbalist and, 22
Mei HaShiloaḥ, 33, 66
Meirat Einayim, 48, 70
Meister Eckhart, 41
Menaḥem Naḥum ben Zvi, of Chernobyl, Rebbe, 41–45
Mendel, Menahem, 32
Mental illness, 9–10, 19
Meor Einayim, 41–45, 68–69
Merkavah
  Abraham, chariot for *Ḥesed*, 34
  biblical characters as chariots for *Sephirot*, 29
  Merkavah Mysticism, 58, 74
  Metatron and, 8
  nephesh as, 46–47
  realm of Chariot, 37
Meshiv, 33, 74
Metaphor, 35–37
Metatron, 8, 58
Mezareh, 33, 74
Midrash/midrashim, 74
Midrash Rabeinu Bahya, 9–10, 61
Milui, 7, 74
Minyanim, 74
Misalignment, 26
Mishnah, 58
Mistakes, learning from, 27
Mitzrayim. See Egypt (*Mitzrayim*)
Mitzvah/Mitzvot, 14, 74
Monbourquette, John, 29–30
Moses
  blessing after meal, 32
  at burning bush, 9–10, 38
  death of Aaron's sons, 51
  God speaking to, 35–36
  Koraḥ's rebellion, 33
  on Mt. Sinai, 24–25
  as prophet, 58
  sapphire, vision of, 53
  on soothsayers and diviners, 49
Moses de Leon, 49
Mount Sinai, 24–25, 36, 48
Mourning, 30
Muktananda, Swami, 19
Music
  four spiritual ways person can sing, 55–56
  nigunim, 75
  prophecy and, 30
  techno music for ecstatic dance, 14
Mysticism. *See also* Kabbalah
  Abraham as mystic, 6
  defined, 1
  difficulty of teaching, 35
  humor as, 17
  Jewish mysticism for all people, 2
  levels of progression, 49
  making spiritual progress, 47
  mystical experiences as sources of knowledge, 40
  mystical pleasure, 53
  mystical teachings of sages, 19
  mystical union, 8
  mystics, types of, 24
  physical world, connection to, 50
  seeing good in others as mystical practice, 20
  spiritual state vs. spiritual stage, 42
  timeline of Jewish, 58–59
  Torah in nature, 43
  Torah study as mystical practice, 17

Nadav, 51
Naḥmanides, 49
Naḥman of Bratslav, Rebbe, 11–14, 25, 39, 53, 74
Naphshi Takshiv Shiro, 53–54, 71
Naropa University, xi–xii
Native American, 38, 43
Nature
  grounding, 10
  sacred manuscript of, 43
  spending time in, 20, 22
  tzadik going beyond, 26, 51
Ne'arav, 17, 74
Near-death experiences, 22
Negativity, 26, 45
Neo-Hasidism, 59

Index

Nephesh, 11, 46–47, 54, 74
Neshamah, 11–12, 46–47, 54, 74
Netivot Shalom, 31, 66
Netzaḥ, 57
Nigunim, 31, 48, 75
Noah, 43
Noam Elimelekh, 28, 65
Nonconceptuality, 40
Non-duality, 8, 13, 33
Nothingness, xii, 13, 50
Numerological systems/numerology
  forty-two, significance of, 4
  Gematria, 7, 73

Ohev Yisrael, 46–47, 69
Olam Haba, 28, 33, 53, 55–56
Olamot, 52
Optical illusions, 18–19
Or HaḤayim, 51, 70
Or HaMeir, 34–36, 66, 67
Other Side, 29–30

Palestine, 52
Parables, 6, 18–19, 25
Pardes Rimonim, 36–38, 67
Peacemaking, 17
Pekudei, 75
Perek Shirah, 55
Pharoah, 29–30
Physicality. *See* The body
Piaget, Jean, 44
Piaseczner Rebbe, 15
Plato, 10
Player, Gary, 30
Pleasure, 53–54
Post-Jewish mystical trend, 59
Practices
  bliss, finding, 53
  connecting with nature, 20
  death and afterlife, 51
  directing feelings toward God, 22
  grounding, 10
  intense spiritual experiences, 16
  joy, finding, 17
  life's purpose, finding your, 52
  self-compassion, 12
  storytelling and metaphor, 35
  striving and resting, 42
  wisdom, finding new sources of, 43
Prayer
  hitbodedut, 14, 22, 49, 74
  as source of bliss, 40
  spiritual growth through, 50
  stages of, 18–19
  tefilin, 75
Presence
  Divine Presence. *See Shekhinah*
  God's, 42, 47, 51, 53–54

Prophecy
  during period of Tanakh, 58
  power of, 10, 30
  Prophetic Kabbalah, 8

Questions for reflection
  balancing joy and sorrow, 14
  becoming God, closeness to God, 8
  death and afterlife, 51
  finding alignment and bliss, 53
  life's purpose, 52
  passion, what practices set your soul on fire, 16
  physicality, for holy purposes, 37
  spiritual practices, letting go of, 6
  striving and resting, 42
  weeping with God, 15
  wisdom and divinity, sources of, 43
  your four songs, 55

Rabeinu Baḥya, 9–10
Rakia, 53, 75
Ramakrishna Paramahansa, Sri, 24
Ram Dass: *Polishing the Mirror*, 6
Rashi, 16, 21, 24–25
Rav/Rebbe/Rabbi meanings, 3
Reality
  dimensions of, 52
  ultimate, 39
Receiving and giving, 32
Redemption, 32
Reflection, questions for. *See* Questions for reflection
Reincarnation, 53–54, 73
Repentance, 23, 54, 73, 75
Reshimu, 13, 75
Rest, importance of, 16
Returning to God, 23
Roberts, Bernadette, 11
Ruaḥ, 11, 54, 75
Running and returning, 13, 16–17, 19

Sacred Mind, 4
Sacred time, 41
Sadness, 14–15, 30
Sages, 19
Sapphires, 53
Sarah, 29–30
Schachter-Shalomi, Reb Zalman, xii, 59
Schneur Zalman, of Lyady, Rebbe, 40
Scholem, Gershom, 8
Sea of Reeds, 50
Seer of Lublin, 15
Sefat Emet, 47, 48, 69
Sefer Ba'al Shem Tov, 21, 64
Sefer HaYashar, 8, 61
Self, song of, 55
Self-discipline, 18, 31, 46–47
Self-improvement, 42
Selflessness, 50
Sephirot. See also individual *Sephirot*
  Adam's misapprehension of, 29
  characters in Bible as representatives of, 29

Index

defined, 75
Divine Body, 18
Ein Sof and, 18
human body, correlation to, 36–37
as intermediary, 8
introduction to, 1
as layers between world and Infinite, 58
levels of soul and, 11
names and associations of, 57
reality beyond, 38
seven days of creation and, 50
Shabbat and, 41–42
unity of, 39
Seven Blessings, 55
Sexual energy/sexuality, 29, 42, 44–45, 57
Shabbat
balance, for seeking, 2
defined, 75
Sephirot associated with, 50
Shabbat Consciousness, 28, 41–42
tzadikim and, 28
Shadow, 21, 29, 44–45
Shaktipat, 19, 75
Shanim ne'arut, 17, 75
Shapira, Rabbi Kalonymos Kalmish, 15
Shattered vessels, 22
Shefa, 36–37, 75
Shekhinah
capacity to perceive, 9–10
defined, 75
dwelling in place of joy, 30
Elimelekh of Lizhensk's identification with, 28
Elohim and, 10
as *Malkhut*, 57
needs of, 50
separation from Tree of Life, 29
Shabbat meals and, 41
Shelah Ha-Kadosh (Holy Shelah), 7
Shells/husks, 22
Shir El, 56, 75
Shiva, 39
Shmoneh Kevatzim, 52, 55, 71–72
Shnei, 17, 75
Shnei Luhhot HaBrit, 7
Sitra Aḥra, 22, 29, 75
Slonimer Rebbe, 31
Sofit, 75
Solomon, 55–56
Somatics. *See* Embodiment
Some, Malidoma: *Of Water and the Spirit*, 29, 43
Song
nigunim, 75
Shir El, 56, 75
Song of Songs, 55–56
spiritual, four levels of, 55–56
Soul
at death, 51
ḥaya, 11, 47, 73
nephesh, 11, 46–47, 54, 74
neshamah, 12, 47, 54, 74
ruaḥ, 11, 54, 75
self-discipline of, 46–47
Sephirot, correlation to levels of soul, 11
soul roots, letters in Torah and, 52
three levels of, 11, 54
of *tzadik*, 28
Sparks, 20
Spiritual Emergency Network, 9–10
Spiritual groundedness. *See* Embodiment
Spiritual growth
aim of, 46–47
caring for others, 54
core spiritual essence, 52
darkness and light, incorporating, 44–45
inner divinity, finding, 48
inner work and, 30
mystical experiences as source of, 40
overcoming past habits and tendencies, 38
seeing God "face to face," 25, 35–36
song, four levels of, 55–56
spiritual bypassing, 26
spiritual emergency, 9–10
spiritual state vs. spiritual stage, 42
stages of, 22, 46–47, 49
through prayer, 50
Spiritual practices
body, using for sanctified purposes, 37
ignoring Torah as, 16
as obstacles, 6
spiritual integration, 19
Steel, Piers: *The Procrastination Equation*, 46
Stoicism, 50
Storytelling, 35–36
Suffering, transformation of, 23, 26–27
Sufism, 8, 43
Sukkah/Sukkot, 6, 75
Sunlight, 10
Surrender, 47
Synchronicity, xi, 2, 49
Synesthesia, 48

Tabernacle, 42, 51
Talmud
Adam, humanity's descent from, 52
ba'al teshuvah, 23
death, 51
elevating others, holy work of, 27
enjoyment of God's bounty, 32
God weeping, 15
humor, 17
on Metatron, 8
Shabbat, additional soul on, 28
tzadikim, 20
World to Come, 33
Tanakh, 58
Tanya, Sha'ar HaYiḥud, 40, 68
Tarot, 49
Tefilin, 6, 75
Teitelbaum, Moses: *Yismaḥ Moshe*, 51
Ten Commandments, 36, 48
Teshuvah, 23, 75
Texts, choice of, 4

Index

Tibetan Buddhism, 12
Tikkunei Zohar, 39, 68
Tikkun olam/tikkun, 20, 59, 75
Time
  day, cycle of, 44
  week, cycle of, 41–42
Tipheret, 50, 57
Tolle, Eckhart: *The Power of Now*, 34
Torah
  first word of (*Breishit*), 4, 39, 73
  letters and root souls, 52
  Torah Kedumah (Primordial Torah), 43
  true nature of, 35–36
Torah study
  devekut and, 15
  with intuitive mind, 4
  as mystical practice, 17
  neglecting for sake of actualizing its principles, 16
  as source of bliss, 40
Totzaot, 75
Trace of divinity/*reshimu*, 13
Transcendence, 13
Transformation
  Abraham's encounter with demonic realm, 30
  descent for sake of ascent, 22, 24–25
  growth through hardship, 23
  self-discipline and, 46–47
Translations, ix
Transpersonal psychology, 2
Tree of Life. *See Sephirot*
Trees, 20
Trust, 31
Tzadik/tzadikim
  death of, 51
  defined, 75
  devekut, level of, 6
  Elimelekh of Lizhensk's articulation of, 28
  embracing our inner *tzadik*, 38
  finding joy, 54
  in parables, 18–19
  tree analogy, 20
  who re-enter the world, 26–27
Tzava'at HaRivash, 22, 64
Tzel, 21
Tzemaḥ HaShem LeZvi, 32, 66
Tzfat, 75
Tzḥok, 75. *See also* Laughter

Ultimate Reality, 39
Understanding, levels of, 38
Ungroundedness, 1, 9–10
Union with Divine, 11, 22
Upekkh, 50, 75
Upekkha, 50, 75

Vayashev, 33, 76
Veya'al, 29, 75
Via negativa/Via positiva, 17, 41–42, 76
Vision quests, 43
Vodou, 34
Voice of God, 48

Warsaw Ghetto, 15
Water/wellsprings, 32
Weddings, 55
Week, cycle of, 41–42, 50
Weeping, 15
Welwood, John, 26
Wilber, Ken, 18, 42
Wisdom, 29–30, 53
World
  Godliness in fabric of, 43
  perfected, 53–54
  self-removal from, 26–27
  song of, 55
  World of Consciousness, 50
  worlds in inner dimension, 52
  World to Come, 28, 33, 53, 55–56

Yeridah letzorekh aliyah, 22, 24–27, 76
Yesh, 50, 76
Yeshiva, xi
Yesod, 41, 50, 57
YHWH
  darkness and light, 45
  defined, 76
  four songs and, 56
  gematria of, 7
  Metatron and, 8
  precepts or statutes of, 35
  relationship between our actions and God's, 21
  voice of, 48
Yitzḥak, 17, 76

Zar, 76
Ze'ev Wolf, of Zhitomir, 34–36
Zen Buddhism, 11
Zionist movement, 52
Zohar
  first publication of, 49
  Hebrew version of text, 65
  history of, 58
  Rabeinu Baḥya and, 9
  texts from, 29–30
  Tikkunei Zohar, 56
  on true nature of Torah, 35
Zvi Elimelekh, of Dinov, Rabbi, 23, 64
Zvi Hirsh, of Nadvorna, Rebbe, 32

About the Author

Rabbi Matthew Ponak is a teacher of Jewish mysticism, a spiritual counselor, and the cofounder of the Mekorah Institute—an online spiritual center for embodied practice. Ordained with honors as a rabbi at the neo-Hasidic Rabbinical School of Hebrew College, he also holds a Master's degree in Contemplative Religions from Naropa University. Matthew lives in Victoria, British Columbia and is certified as a Focusing Professional to guide others to deeper self-knowledge and healing through their bodies. To learn more about Matthew and his upcoming courses and speaking engagements, please visit **matthewponak.com**

www.ingramcontent.com/pod-product-compliance
Lightning Source LLC
Chambersburg PA
CBHW060408010526
44107CB00005B/623
* 9 7 8 1 9 5 3 2 2 0 2 3 3 *